The
Jewish
Home
Advisor

ALSO BY ALFRED J. KOLATCH

A Child's First Book of Jewish Holidays
Classic Bible Stories for Jewish Children
The Complete Dictionary of English and
    Hebrew First Names
The Concise Family Seder
El Libro Judio del Por Que
The Family Seder
Great Jewish Quotations
The Jewish Book of Why
The Jewish Child's First Book of Why
Jewish Information Quiz Book
The Jewish Mourner's Book of Why
The Jonathan David Dictionary
    of First Names
Let's Celebrate Our Jewish Holidays!
The New Name Dictionary
Our Religion: The Torah
The Second Jewish Book of Why
These Are the Names
This Is the Torah
Today's Best Baby Names
Who's Who in the Talmud

The Jewish Home Advisor

Alfred J. Kolatch

 Jonathan David Publishers, Inc.
Middle Village, New York 11379

THE JEWISH HOME ADVISOR

Copyright © 1990, 1998
by
Alfred J. Kolatch

Jonathan David Publishers, Inc.
68-22 Eliot Avenue
Middle Village, New York 11379
www.JonathanDavidOnline.com

6 8 10 9 7 5

Library of Congress Cataloging in Publication Data
Kolatch, Alfred J.,
The Jewish home advisor / Alfred J. Kolatch
     p. cm.
Includes bibliographical references
ISBN 0-82466-0344-3
1. Judaism—Customs and Practices.   I. Title
BM700.K5924   1990
296.7'4—dc20   CIP

Layout by Arlene Goldberg
Illustrations by Terry Guglielmino

Printed in the United States of America

For
JONATHAN AND DAVID

בֵּן חָכָם יְשַׂמַּח־אָב

*A wise son
brings joy to his father.*
PROVERBS 10:11

Contents

Blast • Breaking the Fast • Break-the-fast Meal • Chopped
Herring Recipe

12. The Fall Holidays II: Sukkot, Shemini Atzeret, Simchat Torah 272

SUKKOT: HISTORICAL BACKGROUND 273
A Pilgrim Festival • Sukkot in the Bible • Sukkot in Israel •
Sukkot in the Diaspora • The Yom Kippur/Sukkot Link •
Sukkot in Jerusalem

THE SUKKA STRUCTURE 274
The Sukka • Tabernacles • Sukka Construction • Sukka
Covering • Mezuza on a Sukka • Sukka Blessing • Candle-
lighting and Kiddush for Sukkot

SUKKOT SYMBOLS 276
The Four Species • The Etrog • Etrog Most Important • How
an Etrog Grows • Positioning the Etrog • Broken Pittom •
The Pittom-less Etrog • Biting the Pittom • Storing the Etrog
• Etrog Jam • The Lulav • The Myrtles • The Willows • How
to Assemble a Lulav Bouquet

BLESSING AND PARADING THE FOUR SPECIES 280
Blessing the Etrog and Lulav • Waving the Lulav • Lulav-
waving Procedure • Lulav Tradition • Procession With the
Four Species

HOSHANA RABBA 281
Last Day of Sukkot • Synagogue Procession • Beating Wil-
lows • Hoshana Rabba in Sephardic Practice • Kreplach for
Hoshana Rabba

SHEMINI ATZERET 283
The Holiday After Sukkot • Yizkor on Shemini Atzeret •
Candlelighting and Kiddush for Shemini Atzeret

SIMCHAT TORAH 284
Simchat Torah • Parade of the Torot • Aliyot for Everyone •
Simchat Torah in Israel • Candlelighting and Kiddush for
Simchat Torah • Revelry on Simchat Torah • Chatan Torah
and Chatan Bereshit

13. Chanuka, Purim, and Other Minor Holidays ... 286

CHANUKA HISTORY 287
The Story of Chanuka • Source of the Chanuka Story • The
Miracle of the Oil • Chanuka Date • The Word "Maccabee"

In Appreciation

Colleagues and friends of the various Jewish denominations have been good enough to read and comment on the contents of this volume in the course of its two years of preparation. I am grateful to them all for giving so generously of their time and energy.

My brother, Rabbi Arthur J. Kolatch, and his wife, Helen, of San Francisco, California, have been of singular help. Arthur's insightful comments, particularly those relating to practices of the Reform movement, have been invaluable. I am grateful to Helen not only for her meaningful suggestions but for contributing a delicious honey cake recipe.

Rabbi Ephraim Bennett and his wife, Helen, of Netanya, Israel, have reviewed the manuscript with great care and have made many important observations. Rabbi Bennett's careful checking of the sources and verifying of the information presented is deeply appreciated.

Rabbi Erwin Zimet, of blessed memory, read the early chapters of the manuscript and offered many cogent comments.

Special thanks are due my son David, who worked closely with me on a daily basis for almost a year and was immensely helpful in refining and reworking much of the material to make it sharper and more understandable for the layman.

To my son Jonathan I am indebted for his diligent review of the entire manuscript. His keen insights contributed greatly to its improvement.

To my wife, Thelma, my gratitude for always being available for consultation, particularly about apsects of the book that relate to the home.

To Marvin Sekler, vice-president of Jonathan David Publishers, my sincere appreciation for sharing with me his insights into the informational needs of the Jewish community.

And to Florence Weissman and Fiorella Torre, my secretaries, my thanks for helping with some of the research and for tirelessly typing the many drafts of the manuscript.

CALENDAR OF HOLIDAYS

	1997	1998	1999	2000	2001
Rosh Hashana	Th Oct 2	M Sep 21	Sa Sep 11	Sa Sep 30	Tu Sep 18
Fast of Gedaliah	Su Oct 5	W Sep 23	M Sep 13	M Oct 2	Th Sep 20
Yom Kippur	Sa Oct 11	W Sep 30	M Sep 20	M Oct 9	Th Sep 27
Sukkot	Th Oct 16	M Oct 5	Sa Sep 25	Sa Oct 14	Tu Oct 2
Shemini Atzeret	Th Oct 23	M Oct 12	Sa Oct 2	Sa Oct 21	Tu Oct 9
Simchat Torah	F Oct 24	Tu Oct 13	Su Oct 3	Su Oct 22	W Oct 10
Chanuka	W Dec 24	M Dec 14	Sa Dec 4	F Dec 22	M Dec 10
Tu Bi-shevat	Th Jan 23	W Feb 11	M Feb 1	Sa Jan 22	Th Feb 8
Fast of Esther	Th Mar 20	W Mar 11	M Mar 1	M Mar 20	Th Mar 8
Purim	Su Mar 23	Th Mar 12	Tu Mar 2	Tu Mar 21	F Mar 9
Passover (day 1)	Tu Apr 22	Sa Apr 11	Th Apr 1	Th Apr 20	Su Apr 8
Passover (day 7)	M Apr 28	F Apr 17	W Apr 7	W Apr 26	Sa Apr 14
Yom Ha-sho'ah	Su May 4	Th Apr 23	Tu Apr 13	Tu May 2	F Apr 20
Yom Ha-atzma'ut	M May 12	Th Apr 30	W May 10	W May 10	Sa Apr 28
Lag B'omer	Su May 25	Th May 14	Tu May 4	Tu May 23	F May 11
Shavuot	W Jun 11	Su May 31	F May 21	F Jun 9	M May 28
Fast of Tammuz	Tu Jul 22	Su Jul 12	Th Jul 1	Th Jul 20	Su Jul 8
Tisha B'Av	Tu Aug 12	Su Aug 2	Th Jul 22	Th Aug 10	Su Jul 29

NOTE: Holiday observances begin at sundown on the night
before the dates given above.

1997-2007

2002	2003	2004	2005	2006	2007
Sa Sep 7	Sa Sep 27	Th Sep 16	Tu Oct 4	Sa Sep 23	Th Sep 12
M Sep 9	M Sep 29	Su Sep 19	Th Oct 6	M Sep 25	Su Sep 16
M Sep 16	M Oct 6	Sa Sep 25	Th Oct 13	M Oct 2	Sa Sep 22
Sa Sep 21	Sa Oct 11	Th Sep 30	Tu Oct 18	Sa Oct 7	Th Sep 27
Sa Sep 28	Sa Oct 18	Th Oct 7	Tu Oct 25	Sa Oct 14	Th Oct 4
Su Sep 29	Su Oct 19	F Oct 8	W Oct 26	Su Oct 15	F Oct 5
Sa Nov 30	Sa Dec 20	W Dec 8	M Dec 26	Sa Dec 16	W Dec 5
M Jan 28	Sa Feb 7	Sa Feb 7	Tu Jan 25	M Feb 13	Sa Feb 3
M Feb 25	M Mar 17	Th Mar 4	Th Mar 24	M Mar 13	Th Mar 1
Tu Feb 26	Tu Mar 18	Su Mar 7	F Mar 25	Tu Mar 14	Su Mar 4
Th Mar 28	Th Apr 17	Tu Apr 6	Su Apr 24	Th Apr 13	Tu Apr 3
W Apr 3	W Apr 23	M Apr 12	Sa Apr 30	W Apr 19	M Apr 9
Tu Apr 9	M Apr 29	Su Apr 18	F May 6	Tu Apr 25	Su Apr 15
W Apr 17	W May 7	M Apr 26	Sa May 13	W May 3	M Apr 23
Tu Apr 30	Tu May 20	Su May 9	F May 27	Tu May 16	Su May 6
F May 17	F Jun 6	W May 26	M Jun 13	F Jun 2	W May 23
Th Jun 27	Th Jul 17	Tu Jul 6	Su Jul 24	Th Jul 13	Tu Jul 3
Th Jul 18	Th Aug 7	Tu Jul 27	Su Aug 14	Th Aug 3	Tu Jul 24

Minor fast days falling on Saturday are celebrated on Sunday.
When Yom Ha-atzma'ut falls on a Friday or Saturday, it is celebrated
on Thursday, the third of Iyyar.

JEWISH HOLIDAYS

Tishri 1	Rosh Hashana (first day)
Tishri 2	Rosh Hashana (second day)
Tishri 3	Fast of Gedaliah
Tishri 10	Yom Kippur
Tishri 15	Sukkot (first day)
Tishri 16	Sukkot (second day)
Tishri 17	Chol Ha-moed Sukkot (first Intermediate Day)
Tishri 18	Chol Ha-moed Sukkot (second Intermediate Day)
Tishri 19	Chol Ha-moed Sukkot (third Intermediate Day)
Tishri 20	Chol Ha-moed Sukkot (fourth Intermediate Day)
Tishri 21	Hoshana Rabba (seventh day of Sukkot)
Tishri 22	Shemini Atzeret
Tishri 23	Simchat Torah
Kislev 25	Chanuka (first day)
Tevet 2	Chanuka (last day)
Tevet 10	Asara B'Tevet
Shevat 15	Tu Bi-shevat
Adar 13	Fast of Esther
Adar 14	Purim

MONTH-BY-MONTH

Adar 15	Shushan Purim
Nissan 14	Fast of the Firstborn
Nissan 15	Passover (first day)
Nissan 16	Passover (second day)
Nissan 17	Chol Ha-moed Passover (first Intermediate Day)
Nissan 18	Chol Ha-moed Passover (second Intermediate Day)
Nissan 19	Chol Ha-moed Passover (third Intermediate Day)
Nissan 20	Chol Ha-moed Passover (fourth Intermediate Day)
Nissan 21	Passover (seventh day)
Nissan 22	Passover (last day)
Nissan 27	Yom Ha-sho'ah (Holocaust Day)
Iyyar 4	Yom Ha-zikaron (Israel Memorial Day)
Iyyar 5	Yom Ha-atzma'ut* (Israel Independence Day)
Iyyar 18	Lag B'Omer
Iyyar 28	Yom Yerushala'yim
Sivan 6	Shavuot (first day)
Sivan 7	Shavuot (second day)
Tammuz 17	Fast of Tammuz
Av 9	Tisha B'Av

* Celebrated on Thursday if Iyyar 5 falls on a Friday or Saturday.

General Introduction

The Jewish Home Advisor offers practical information and guidance relating to all aspects of Jewish life. It is designed to serve as a handbook for those who are experienced in carrying out the rituals of Judaism as well as for those whose familiarity with Jewish religious practice is limited.

The laws of Judaism are often quite detailed and the customs and practices many and varied. So as to make the subject matter less overwhelming and intimidating, it is put forward here in compact units and in easy-to-understand language. To make the information readily accessible, summaries of procedures are sometimes presented, even at the risk of occasional repetition.

The first half of *The Jewish Home Advisor* is devoted to a discussion of Jewish practices that relate to home and family; the second half concerns itself with synagogue practices and holiday celebrations. Whereas some of my earlier books—*The Jewish Book of Why, The Second Jewish Book of Why,* and *This Is the Torah*—treat these subject areas by focusing on the reasons behind particular laws and observances, the material is presented here almost exclusively from a how-to point of view.

* * *

The Jewish community is by no means monolithic. We do not all observe even the basic rituals in precisely the same way or with the same degree of intensity. Strong differences in interpretation and practice exist between the Orthodox, Conservative, Reform, and Reconstructionist denominations, and there are also variations in ideology and practice within each of the groups. But perhaps the greatest differences exist between Ashkenazic and Sephardic Jews. In this volume the varied observances of each of the groups are presented straight-forwardly and without bias.

*   *   *

While it is hoped that the information set forth in *The Jewish Home Advisor* will be adequate to the needs of the average Jew, by its very nature the book cannot be all-inclusive. Those desiring to deepen their knowledge of specific subjects will find the books recommended in Appendix III to be particularly useful.

ALFRED J. KOLATCH

January 2, 1990
Wassaic, New York

1

The Formative Years
FROM BIRTH TO BAR/BAT MITZVA

Introduction

For the first month after the birth of a newborn, the Jewish home is rife with activity. It is within this four-week span that some of the basic affirmations of a family's, and hence a child's, Jewishness are made.

The outstanding religious ceremony held during the first weeks of a girl's life is her formal naming. Traditionally, the naming is held in the synagogue on the first Sabbath after the child's birth, but recently many innovative home ceremonies have been introduced. Alternative practices are presented in this chapter.

For the male child, the activity of the first month includes the circumcision *(Brit)*, held on the eighth day after birth, and, for a firstborn son in most Jewish families, a redemption ceremony *(Pidyon Ha-ben)*, held on the thirty-first day after birth.

A child's formal Jewish education, which sometimes begins as early as age four or five (for those attending parochial schools), reaches its peak with the advent of the teen years. At age thirteen Jewish boys celebrate their Bar Mitzva, and at age twelve girls who are members of non-Orthodox congregations celebrate their Bat Mitzva as part of the Sabbath synagogue service. Conservative and Reform congregations also

1

hold a Confirmation service for boys and girls who have pursued their Jewish studies for an additional two or three years.

The Jewish customs and ceremonies that involve the child and his family during his or her formative years help create a positive religious environment in the home.

A BABY IS BORN

Welcome to the Male Child

Among Jews in ancient times, as among other religious and societal groups, the birth of a boy was celebrated with much greater enthusiasm than the birth of a girl. Two celebrations were held in connection with the arrival of a male child. The first, called the *Ben Zachar* (literally, "Male Child"), was so named based on the words in the Book of Jeremiah (20:15), ". . . A male child is born unto thee." The second celebration, the *Shalom Zachar* (literally, "Peace [Welcome] to the Male Child"), was so called based on the talmudic quotation, "As soon as a male comes into the world, peace comes into the world."

The *Ben Zachar* custom is not generally followed today, but the *Shalom Zachar* has retained some degree of popularity.

Ben Zachar

Among Jews of Eastern Europe, particularly in Germany of the fifteenth and subsequent centuries, it was customary for relatives, friends, and members of the local congregation to visit the home of new parents on the Friday night after the birth of a boy. The guests were served wine, cake, fruit, cider, beer, cooked beans and peas. The cantor of the congregation led the guests in song, and often the rabbi delivered a brief discourse.

Shalom Zachar

On the day following the Friday night *Ben Zachar* celebration, after Sabbath morning services, relatives and friends would assemble once again in the home of the new parents. They were served wine, liquor, cake, and other refreshments after the appropriate *Kiddush* blessings were recited.

In our days, those who celebrate a *Shalom Zachar* do so on Friday night in place of the earlier *Ben Zachar* ceremony. Sephardim hold the *Shalom Zachar* celebration on the night before the circumcision.

Welcome to the Female Child

In an effort to match the attention that traditionally has been lavished upon the newborn male child, Jewish feminists have in recent years created a score of new ceremonies to welcome the female child. Most have used the term *brit,* "covenant," as part of the title (*Brit Bat,* "Covenant of the Daughter"; *Brit Shalom,* "Covenant of Peace"; *Brit Kedusha,* "Covenant of Holiness"; etc.), and some have incorporated the word *simcha,* meaning "joy," or *shalom,* meaning "welcome," into the title (such as *Shalom Bat* and *Simchat Ha-bat*). *Shalom Bat,* "Welcome to the Daughter," and *Shalom Nekeva,* "Welcome to the Female" (to match *Shalom Zachar*), are names preferred by many who feel that the word *brit* should be reserved exclusively for the male *Brit Mila,* "Covenant of Circumcision."

The ceremony of welcome is generally held on a Friday night after the child is one month old, the age at which Jewish law considers the newborn to be viable. A definitive ceremony has not been established, so each family arranges its own. (See page 4 for a suggested ceremony.)

SUGGESTED "SHALOM BAT" CEREMONY

[If the Welcome to the Female Child ceremony is conducted
at any time other than the Sabbath, several tall lighted candles
are held aloft by relatives or friends as the child is carried
into the room and the leader begins the ceremony. The child
is placed on a high pillow set upon a table or is brought
into the room in a cradle.]

Leader:

We are assembled this day in festive mood to greet a new
daughter in Israel. We give thanks for the gift of new life that
has been granted us. We rejoice in her presence and pray
that she will be a source of blessing and joy to her family and
to the entire household of Israel.

בְּרוּכָה הַבָּאָה!

Berucha ha-ba'a!

Blessed is she who has come to grace our midst!

Participants:

בְּרוּכָה הַבָּאָה בָּשֵׁם יְיָ.

Berucha ha-ba'a b'shem Adonai.

Blessed is she who has come by the grace of God.

Participants continue:

We welcome her into our hearts and delight in her presence.
As a daughter of Israel, may she add strength and beauty to
our lives and be a source of strength to all her fellow Jews.

Leader:

We welcome our new daughter of Zion with the same love
and joy with which the daughters of Zion welcomed those whom
they adored in the early days of our history. As it is written:

צְאֶינָה וּרְאֶינָה בְּנוֹת צִיּוֹן בַּמֶּלֶךְ שְׁלֹמֹה, בָּעֲטָרָה
שֶׁעִטְּרָה-לּוֹ אִמּוֹ בְּיוֹם חֲתֻנָּתוֹ וּבְיוֹם שִׂמְחַת לִבּוֹ.

Tzena u-re'ena benot Tziyon ba-melech Shlomo, ba-

atara she-itra lo imo be-yom chatunato u-ve-yom simchat libo.

Go forth, O daughters of Zion, and gaze upon King Solomon, gaze upon the crown with which his mother adorned him on the day of his betrothal, on the day his heart rejoiced.

Participants:

The role of women is significant in our lives, and we pray that the newborn daughter of Israel whom we welcome this day will fill her role with distinction.

[The mother picks up the child.]

Mother:

You are so pure and beautiful and undefiled. Your face shines like the moon; it radiates beauty like the sun.

[Kisses the child.]

We welcome you into our family.

[Father takes the child from the mother.]

Father:

How peacefully you rest. How comforting is your presence in our midst. You are a fountain of joy for our family, and we pray you will be so for all Israel. We welcome you into our midst.

[Leader takes the child from the father.]

Leader:

Father and mother of this child, I ask you: How shall we name this baby?

Mother and father (in unison):

We desire that _____ [child's English name] be named in Hebrew _____ *bat* _____ [father's Hebrew name] and _____ [mother's Hebrew name].

Leader:

Henceforth this child shall be known as _____ [child's Hebrew name] *bat* _____ [father's Hebrew name] and _____ [mother's Hebrew name].

[The Hebrew *Mi She-berach* prayer for the naming of a child may be pronounced at this point, or it may be reserved for a naming that will take place in the Synagogue on Sabbath morning.]

מִי שֶׁבֵּרַךְ אֲבוֹתֵינוּ אַבְרָהָם, יִצְחָק, וְיַעֲקֹב,
וְאִמּוֹתֵינוּ שָׂרָה, רִבְקָה, רָחֵל, וְלֵאָה, הוּא יְבָרֵךְ
אֶת ‗‗‗‗‗ בֶּן ‗‗‗‗‗ וְאֶת אִשְׁתּוֹ
הַיּוֹלֶדֶת ‗‗‗‗‗ בַּת ‗‗‗‗‗ וְאֶת בִּתָּם
הַנּוֹלְדָה לָהֶם בְּמַזָּל טוֹב, וְיִקָּרֵא שְׁמָה
בְּיִשְׂרָאֵל ‗‗‗‗‗
בַּת ‗‗‗‗‗ וְ ‗‗‗‗‗. יִזְכּוּ הוֹרֶיהָ לְגַדְּלָהּ
לְתוֹרָה, וּלְחֻפָּה, וּלְמַעֲשִׂים טוֹבִים. וְנֹאמַר אָמֵן.

Mi she-berach avotenu, Avraham, Yitzchak, ve-Yaakov, ve-imotenu, Sara, Rivka, Rachel, ve-Leah, Hu ye-varech et _____ ben _____ ve'et ishto ha-yoledet _____ bat _____ ve'et bitam ha-nolda lahem be-mazal tov, ve-yikareh shma be-Yisrael _____ bat _____. Yizku horeha le-gadla l'Tora, u-le-chupa, u-le-ma'asim tovim. Ve-nomar, Amen.

May He who blessed our patriarchs Abraham, Isaac, and Jacob and our matriarchs Sarah, Rebecca, Rachel, and Leah bless _____ [full English name of child], who this day has been named _____ [girl's Hebrew name] *bat* _____ and _____ [Hebrew names of the father and mother]. Restore the mother speedily to full strength and vigor and provide the parents with the will and resources to nurture their newborn so that she will grow healthy in body and mind and soul. May she bring joy to her parents, to her kinfolk, to the whole community of Israel, and to all mankind. And let us say, Amen.

Participants:
  Amen.

  [The leader hands the baby to the father and then fills a
  cup with wine. Those holding candles gather around the
  father.]

Leader:

בָּרוּךְ אַתָּה יְיָ, אֱלֹהֵינוּ מֶלֶךְ הָעוֹלָם, בּוֹרֵא פְּרִי
הַגָּפֶן.

*Baruch ata Adonai, Elohenu melech ha-olam, boray
peri ha-gafen.*

Praised be Thou, O Lord our God, King of the universe,
who created the fruit of the vine.

Open your lips, dear child, and taste of the wine that we
have just sanctified.

  [Leader immerses a cotton swab in the wine and touches
  it to the lips of the child.]

Leader:

Now, let us all join in pronouncing the *She-hecheyanu* prayer
of thanksgiving.

בָּרוּךְ אַתָּה יְיָ, אֱלֹהֵינוּ מֶלֶךְ הָעוֹלָם, שֶׁהֶחֱיָנוּ,
וְקִיְמָנוּ, וְהִגִּיעָנוּ לַזְּמַן הַזֶּה.

*Baruch ata Adonai, Elohenu melech ha-olam, she-he-
cheyanu, ve-kiyemanu, ve-higiyanu la-zeman ha-zeh.*

Praised be Thou, O Lord our God, King of the universe,
who has given us life, and sustained us, and permitted
us to reach and enjoy this moment.

  [Leader raises his hands over the child's head.]

Leader:

יְשִׂימֵךְ אֱלֹהִים כְּשָׂרָה, רִבְקָה, רָחֵל, וְלֵאָה.

Yesimech Elohim k'Sara, Rivka, Rachel, ve-Leah.

May the Lord bless thee as he blessed our matriarchs Sarah, Rebecca, Rachel, and Leah.

May your life be rich in good deeds and acts of kindness, and may you be a source of blessing to your family, to Israel, and to all mankind.

[If participants are familiar with songs such as *Siman Tov, Hevenu Shalom Alechem, Eliyahu Ha-navi, Hinay Ma Tov,* and *Hava Nagila,* it is appropriate to sing one or more at this point and then to serve refreshments. See the Appendix for words and music to these and other songs.]

THE BRIT

Circumcision—A Religious Rite

As a health precaution, several days after birth most male children born in the United States are circumcised. Jewish children are circumcised as a religious obligation on the eighth day after birth. The rite of circumcision is mandated in the Bible (Genesis 17:11) to serve as a perpetual reminder of the Covenant between Abraham and God: "And you shall be circumcised in the flesh of your foreskin; and that will serve as a sign of the Covenant between you and me."

Sign of the Covenant

The word *Brit,* by which the circumcision ceremony is called, literally means "covenant." Circumcision is the sign or symbol of the Covenant. (One of the oldest Jewish fraternal organizations is B'nai B'rith, meaning "sons of the Covenant.")

Day of Circumcision

Circumcisions are held on the eighth day after birth even if that day is a Sabbath, a festival, or Yom Kippur. The Rabbis of the Talmud were of the opinion that circumcision outweighs all other commandments and should not be delayed unless there are pressing health reasons.

Early Circumcisions

All Jewish denominations are opposed to holding circumcisions before the eighth day.

Minyan at a Brit

It is preferable to have a quorum of ten *(minyan)* present at a *Brit,* but this is not mandatory because none of the prayers recited require a *minyan.*

Time of Day

Traditionally, the *Brit* is scheduled to be performed during daylight hours, as early in the day as possible. In Israel today it is almost always tied in with a noontime luncheon.

The Mohel

The person who performs circumcisions is called a *mohel.* According to rabbinic law, it is the father's duty to circumcise his son, but the father delegates the task to the *mohel,* an experienced professional who, though not usually a medical doctor, is a specialist in this procedure. The *mohel* must be a learned and pious Jew.

A Woman as Mohel

Although women are not forbidden by law to perform circumcisions, rabbinic authorities have felt that since the obligation to circumcise a son is incumbent upon the father, the father's surrogate should be male. (Abraham was the first *mohel* in history; Tzipporah, wife of Moses, was the second.)

Mohel vs. Medical Doctor

If a *mohel* is not available, any Jewish doctor may perform a circumcision. However, in selecting a physician, one would be well advised to choose one who is familiar with the ritual, is able to recite the Hebrew prayers, and is respectful of Jewish tradition. If the doctor is unable to read the Hebrew prayers, one should be sure that someone else is present who is able to do so.

Non-Orthodox Mohalim

Since 1984 the Reform Movement has been licensing medical doctors—including obstetricians, pediatricians, and urologists—to be *mohalim* (plural of *mohel*) after concluding a course of Jewish study. These doctors must be members of a Reform congregation and be sponsored by a rabbi. In 1989 the Conservative Movement decided to embark upon a similar program. The Orthodox do not have a licensing program for doctors who wish to serve as *mohalim*.

Non-Jewish Circumcisers

Moses Maimonides, in his twelfth-century code of Jewish law, ruled that an idol worshipper (*akum* in Hebrew) may not perform a circumcision, and only somebody who is a member of the Jewish faith and is subject to its laws may do so. In subsequent centuries it was generally agreed that Gentiles are not in the category of idol worshippers and, in actual practice, where a Jewish doctor is unavailable, a Gentile doctor may perform a circumcision in the presence of a rabbi or knowledgeable Jew who is able to recite the Hebrew prayers and name the baby.

This is a view subscribed to by the Conservative and Reform rabbinical groups but not by all segments of the Orthodox community.

How to Find a Mohel

If there is no rabbi in your city to whom you can turn for advice, contact one of the rabbinic or synagogue organizations listed in the Appendix.

Kvater and Kvaterin

Two persons given honors at all circumcisions are the *kvater* and *kvaterin*, Polish-Yiddish for "godfather" and "godmother."

During the circumcision, the *kvaterin* takes the child from the mother and hands it to the *kvater*, who in turn hands it to the *sandek*.

The Sandek

During the circumcision ceremony, the *sandek* holds the child on a pillow which rests on his lap (or the child is placed on a table and held by the *sandek*). Like the *kvater*, he is also considered a godfather. *Sandek* is Greek for "godfather."

Elijah's Chair

According to tradition, one of the missions of the prophet Elijah is to protect every infant from danger. To symbolize Elijah's protective presence at the *Brit*, a chair reserved for the prophet is often placed next to the seat of the *sandek*.

Death Before Eighth Day

The sixteenth-century *Code of Jewish Law* specifies that if a child lives for less than eight days, he is to be circumcised and named at the grave site before burial. Earlier, in the eleventh century, the outstanding scholar Rashi indicated his disapproval of such a practice, and the twelfth-century authority Moses Maimonides makes no mention of it in his code. Conservative and Reform Jews have expressed opposition to this practice. Orthodox Jews honor the practice.

Born "Circumcised"

If a boy is born with the foreskin of the penis absent, the *mohel* simply draws a drop of blood from the glans, and that blood droplet represents the sign of the *Brit*. This procedure, known as *Hatafat Dam Brit*, is followed by the recital of the regular *Brit* blessing (page 13).

Son of a Mixed Marriage

A son born to a couple in which the mother is Gentile and the father is Jewish may have a ritual circumcision on the eighth day if the father requests it. Although the circumcision does not make the child Jewish, since the mother is not Jewish, the action is considered the first step in a conversion which the boy has the right to accept or reject upon reaching maturity at age 13. If at maturity the boy decides that he wants to be Jewish, according to Jewish law he need only undergo immersion in a *mikva* (see page 33) to fulfill the requirements for conversion. Reform Judaism does not require immersion; when the boy becomes a Bar Mitzva, he is considered to be a full Jew.

The Se'udat Mitzva

A festive meal *(se'uda)* held in the home or synagogue to celebrate the fulfillment of a religious obligation *(mitzva)* is called a *Se'udat Mitzva,* meaning "*Mitzva* Meal." At the conclusion of the circumcision ceremony—as well as following a *Pidyon Ha-ben,* a Bar Mitzva or Bat Mitzva, a wedding, and other significant occasions—a meal of this kind is generally served.

Summary of
WHAT TO EXPECT AT A CIRCUMCISION CEREMONY

---

1. A *minyan* is assembled if possible. Included in the *minyan* are those who will be main participants in the circumcision ceremony: the *mohel,* the father, the godfather *(sandek).*
2. The mother and baby remain in a separate room together with the godmother *(kvaterin).*
3. The father designates a man (the *kvater,* usually the husband of the *kvaterin*) to enter the mother's room and bring the baby in for the *Brit.* The *kvaterin* takes the baby from the mother and hands it to the *kvater.*
4. When the *kvater* arrives with the baby, everyone except the *sandek* rises and remains standing throughout the brief ceremony.
5. The *mohel* takes the baby from the *kvater* and sings out *Baruch ha-ba,* meaning "Blessed is he who has arrived."

6. The *mohel* places the child for a moment on the Chair of Elijah and recites the appropriate blessings. If a doctor who is unfamiliar with the blessings is to perform the circumcision, a knowledgeable layman should recite them.

7. The *mohel* then hands the child to the father, who in turn hands it to the *sandek*. The *sandek* holds the child firmly in his lap while the circumcision is performed. Occasionally, especially when a doctor performs the circumcision, the child is placed on a table, with the *sandek* holding him securely.

8. Immediately before the foreskin is removed, the father recites the *Brit* blessing below. If the father of the child is not present at the *Brit,* the blessing is recited by the *sandek*.

בָּרוּךְ אַתָּה יְיָ, אֱלֹהֵינוּ מֶלֶךְ הָעוֹלָם, אֲשֶׁר קִדְּשָׁנוּ בְּמִצְוֹתָיו, וְצִוָּנוּ לְהַכְנִיסוֹ בִּבְרִיתוֹ שֶׁל אַבְרָהָם אָבִינוּ.

Baruch ata Adonai, Elohenu melech ha-olam, asher kideshanu be-mitzvotav ve-tzivanu lehachniso bi-verito shel Avraham avinu.

Blessed art Thou, O Lord our God, King of the universe, who has sanctified us with His commandments and commanded us to bring him into the Covenant of Abraham, our father.

9. After the operation is complete, the *mohel* recites a blessing over a cup of wine, at which time the Hebrew name selected for the baby is pronounced for the first time. (See page 14 for information on naming.)

10. After the naming of the child, the *mohel* dips a piece of cotton or gauze into the wine and lets the baby suck on it while the *mohel* pronounces the concluding blessings of the ceremony.

11. Refreshments or a festive meal *(Se'udat Mitzva)* are now served and the assembly joins in singing some of the songs found in the Appendix.

NAMING PRACTICES

Naming of Boys

Boys are named during the *Brit* ceremony.

Naming of Girls

Traditionally, girls are named in the synagogue on the first Sabbath after birth. The father is awarded an *aliya,* and after the Torah has been read, a *Mi She-berach* prayer is recited for the welfare of the mother, at which time the girl is named.

In more recent years the naming is also done as part of the *Shalom Bat* ceremony (see pages 4 through 8).

Conservative Naming Practice

In many Conservative synagogues today, the mother and father bring the newborn daughter to a Sabbath morning service within a month or two after birth. The parents are sometimes called to the Torah to recite the Torah blessings while the mother holds the baby. After the Torah portion has been read, the baby is named.

Reform Naming Ceremony

Reform Judaism urges parents to arrange a Covenant *(Brit)* service for girls either at home or in the synagogue. At the service, called "Covenant of Life," girls are named. It is recommended that the ceremony be held on the eighth day after birth or, if not feasible, at any time thereafter.

Hebrew Name Usage

Every Jew must be familiar with his or her Hebrew name. The Hebrew name is used in calling a person up to the Torah, in a Jewish marriage contract *(ketuba),* in a Jewish *get* (divorce decree), in tombstone inscriptions, and in the recitation of particular prayers.

It is advisable to list the Hebrew names of all family members in a record book or family Bible.

Use of the Patronymic

Traditionally, when a person is referred to in a Jewish religious ritual, the individual's father's name (patronymic) is mentioned. The first (and middle) name of the individual is followed by the word *ben* (son of) or *bat* (daughter of) and then the patronymic (the father's first and middle name). Thus, a male name might appear as Reuven *ben* Ya'akov Yosef, and a female name might appear as Dina *bat* Ya'akov Yosef.

Use of the Matronymic

Although it is traditional to use the patronymic form in Jewish ritual, an exception is made when a prayer for the recovery of a sick person is recited. In this case, the mother's name (matronymic) is used. In recent times, the name of the mother is used along with that of the father for other occasions as well, such as the naming of a child.

Naming an Adopted Child

In naming an adopted child, the patronymic of the adoptive father or the natural father may be used. The decision rests with the adoptive parents.

Naming After Living Relatives

In the twelfth century, Rabbi Yehuda He-chasid, the prominent German mystic, ruled that one should not name children after living relatives. Ashkenazim, for the most part, abide by this rule; Sephardim generally do not.

Sephardic Naming Formula

In the naming of babies, many Sephardim, who believe it proper to name after living relatives, follow this formula:

- The first male child is named for the paternal grandfather.
- The second male child is named for the maternal grandfather.
- The first female child is named for the paternal grandmother.
- The second female child is named for the maternal grandmother.

Judeo-Spanish Naming Practice

Among Jews in Turkey, Greece, and other Balkan countries, a firstborn boy is always named Bechor, meaning "oldest" or "firstborn," and a girl is called Bechora, the feminine form of Bechor. Generally, however, girls are given a Spanish name, such as Rose or Fortuna, but no Hebrew name. This is true of Syrian women as well, who until recently were given only Arabic first names at birth.

POPULAR HEBREW NAMES

The following are the most commonly used Hebrew names:

Masculine

Aryeh (אַרְיֵה), meaning "lion."
Avraham (אַבְרָהָם), meaning "father of a mighty nation."
Baruch (בָּרוּךְ), meaning "blessed."
Cha'yim (חַיִּים), meaning "life."
David (דָּוִד), meaning "beloved, friend."
Daniel (דָּנִיֵּאל), meaning "God is my judge."
Meir (מֵאִיר), meaning "shine, brighten."
Melech (מֶלֶךְ), meaning "king."
Menachem (מְנַחֵם), meaning "comforter."
Michael (מִיכָאֵל), meaning "Who is like God?."
Moshe (מֹשֶׁה), meaning "drawn from [the water]."
Nachum (נָחוּם), meaning "comfort."
Pinchas (פִּנְחָס), meaning "dark-complexioned."
Shlomo (שְׁלֹמֹה), meaning "peace."
Shmuel (שְׁמוּאֵל), meaning "His name is God."
Simcha (שִׂמְחָה), meaning "joy."
Tzevi (צְבִי), meaning "deer."
Yaakov (יַעֲקֹב), meaning "supplanted, held back."
Yehonatan (יְהוֹנָתָן), meaning "gift of God."
Yisrael (יִשְׂרָאֵל), meaning "prince of God."
Yitzchak (יִצְחָק), meaning "he will laugh."
Yosef (יוֹסֵף), meaning "[God will] increase."
Ze'ev (זְאֵב), meaning "wolf."

Feminine

Beracha (בְּרָכָה), meaning "blessing."

Chana (חַנָה), meaning "gracious."

Chaya (חַיָה), meaning "living, alive."

Devora (דְבוֹרָה), meaning "bee."

Dina (דִינָה), meaning "judgment."

Ester (אֶסְתֵּר), meaning "star."

Hadassa (הֲדַסָה), meaning "myrtle."

Leah (לֵאָה), meaning "to be weary."

Malka (מַלְכָּה), meaning "queen."

Miryam (מִרְיָם), meaning "sea of bitterness, sorrowful."

Naomi (נָעֳמִי), meaning "pleasant, sweet."

Penina (פְּנִינָה), meaning "pearl."

Rachel (רָחֵל), meaning "ewe."

Rivka (רִבְקָה), meaning "to bind."

Rut (רוּת), meaning "friendship."

Sara (שָׂרָה), meaning "noble, princess."

Shulamit (שׁוּלַמִּית), meaning "peace, peaceful."

Tamar (תָּמָר), meaning "palm tree."

Tzipora (צִפּוֹרָה), meaning "bird."

Tzivya (צִבְיָה), meaning "gazelle."

Yehudit (יְהוּדִית), meaning "praise."

JEWISH LINEAGE

Determining Lineage

In Jewish religious life there are three classes of Jews. These originated in biblical times and are still in effect today. The first and most notable class is the Priests, called *Kohanim* in Hebrew (singular, *Kohen*). Their position of primacy was specified in Deuteronomy 31:9, where the Bible says, "And Moses wrote down the Law and handed it to the Priests . . ." The second class is the Levites, called *Leviim* in Hebrew (singular, *Levi*), who were assistants to the Temple Priests. The remaining Jews are Israelites, *Yisre'elim* (singular, *Yisrael*).

A person's lineage is transmitted through the father. The son or daughter of a *Kohen* is a *Kohen;* the son or daughter of a *Levi* is a *Levi;* the son or daughter of a *Yisrael* is a *Yisrael.*

Reform Judaism does not accept the concept of lineage. That is, it does not distinguish between a *Kohen, Levi,* and *Yisrael.*

Ancestry of Adopted Children

An adopted Jewish child follows the lineage of his natural (biological) father. If the natural father is a *Kohen,* he/she is a *Kohen;* if the natural father is a *Levi,* the child is a *Levi;* if the natural father is a *Yisrael,* the child is a *Yisrael.* If the natural father is not Jewish, but the mother is Jewish, the child is assumed to be a *Yisrael.*

PIDYON HA-BEN

Pidyon Ha-ben Ceremony

Pidyon Ha-ben means "Redemption of the Firstborn Son." The Bible (Exodus 13:1-3) ordains that "the first issue of every womb [meaning firstborn son of a mother]" belongs to God. To free the child from the obligation of dedicating his life totally to the service of God, the firstborn is redeemed by having the father pay a Priest *(Kohen),* God's representative, five shekalim, which is traditionally considered to be roughly the equivalent of five silver dollars.

Pidyon Ha-ben Date

The Redemption of the Firstborn Son ceremony is conducted in the home on the thirty-first day after birth. The day of birth is counted as the first day. If the thirty-first day falls on a Sabbath or holiday, the ceremony is postponed until the next day, although some authorities suggest that it be held in the evening, immediately after the Sabbath or holiday is over. A Pidyon Ha-ben may be held on the Intermediate Days of Passover and Sukkot.

Firstborn of a Second Marriage

If a man with children remarries and his wife gives birth to a boy who is her firstborn, the husband is obligated to redeem the child in a Pidyon Ha-ben ceremony despite the fact that the child is not his firstborn.

Pidyon Ha-ben for a Kohen and Levi

Since Priests and Levites were obligated to serve in the Temple and could not be exempted from this service, the Pidyon Ha-ben ceremony does not apply to them. If the mother or father of the firstborn is the child of a Kohen or Levi, the Pidyon Ha-ben is not conducted.

Reform View

Reform Judaism does not accept the validity of a hereditary priesthood and therefore does not approve of the Pidyon Ha-ben ceremony.

Caesarean Section

A Pidyon Ha-ben is not required for children delivered by Caesarean section. It only applies to children who have exited the womb naturally (Exodus 13:1).

Second Child of Mother

The second child of a woman who at an earlier date had delivered a child by Caesarean section does not have to be redeemed since, although he is the first child to open the mother's womb, he is not considered to be the firstborn.

Miscarriage and Pidyon Ha-ben

A *Pidyon Ha-ben* is not required for a boy born to a woman who in an earlier pregnancy had miscarried forty days after conception or later. By the forty-first day the fetus is said to have begun to take on human form, and when it exits the womb as a miscarriage the discharge is sufficiently identifiable as an entity that "opens the womb." Hence, it falls into the category of firstborn—albeit a nonviable firstborn—and the next child born to the mother need not be redeemed.

Abortions and Pidyon Ha-ben

The same rules that apply to miscarriage apply to abortion. If the abortion takes place on the forty-first day of pregnancy or thereafter, when the fetus has already begun to take on human characteristics, the fetus is considered to be a firstborn to that mother and a *Pidyon Ha-ben* is not required for her next child.

Pidyon Ha-ben for an Adopted Child

If the firstborn of a Jewish woman was given out for adoption, and it is known that the natural father of the child is not a *Kohen* or a *Levi*, the adoptive father is obligated to make all the arrangements for a *Pidyon Ha-ben*, in the same manner as he would if he were the natural father.

Pidyon Ha-ben for Noncircumcised

A *Pidyon Ha-ben* must be performed for a child on the thirty-first day of his life even if his *Brit* had been postponed because of ill health.

Sephardic Customs

At a *Pidyon Ha-ben* ceremony of Sephardim from Syria, Morocco, and the Balkan area, mothers dress in their finest clothing, often in their wedding gowns, for the occasion. Many hang amulets on the walls and doors of the room in which the baby is kept, and also around the neck of the child. Amulets usually contain the names of angels such as Gabriel and Michael who are believed to guarantee protection from evil spirits.

Summary of
PIDYON HA-BEN PROCEDURE

1. Arrangements are made for a *Kohen* to be present in the home on the day the firstborn son will be thirty-one days old.
2. Whenever possible, a *minyan* is assembled and seated around a table graced by a covered *challa* and a goblet filled with wine.
3. The mother brings in the baby on a pillow and hands him to her husband, who either holds the child in one arm or places him on the table.
4. The father addresses the *Kohen* in these ancient Aramaic words:

זֶה בְּנִי בְכוֹרִי, הוּא פֶּטֶר רֶחֶם לְאִמּוֹ, וְהַקָּדוֹשׁ
בָּרוּךְ הוּא צִוָּה לִפְדּוֹתוֹ, שֶׁנֶּאֱמַר: וּפְדוּיָו מִבֶּן
חֹדֶשׁ תִּפְדֶּה בְּעֶרְכְּךָ כֶּסֶף חֲמֵשֶׁת שְׁקָלִים בְּשֶׁקֶל
הַקֹּדֶשׁ, עֶשְׂרִים גֵּרָה הוּא. וְנֶאֱמַר: קַדֶּשׁ־לִי כָּל
בְּכוֹר, פֶּטֶר כָּל רֶחֶם בִּבְנֵי יִשְׂרָאֵל, בָּאָדָם וּבַבְּהֵמָה
לִי הוּא.

Zeh b'ni bechori, hu peter rechem l'imo, ve-ha-Kadosh Baruch Hu tziva lifdoto, she-ne-emar: u-feduyav mi-ben chodesh tifdeh b'erkecha kesef chameshet shekalim b'shekel ha-kodesh, esrim gera hu. V'ne-emar: kadesh li kol bechor, peter kol rechem bi-venay Yisrael, ba-adam u-va-behema, li hu.

This, my firstborn son, is the firstborn of his mother. The Holy One, blessed be He, has commanded that he be redeemed, as it is written [in the Torah]: "The redemption price for each firstborn son of the age of one month shall be fixed at five sacred silver *shekels,* the equal of twenty *gerahs.*" And it is written: "Consecrate every firstborn unto Me, whatever is firstborn in Israel, of man or beast, since it belongs to Me."

5. The *Kohen* then asks the father:

מַאי בָּעִית טְפֵי? לִתֵּן לִי בִּנְךָ בְּכוֹרְךָ שֶׁהוּא פֶּטֶר רֶחֶם לְאִמּוֹ, אוֹ בָּעִית לִפְדוֹתוֹ בְּעַד חָמֵשׁ סְלָעִים, כִּדְמְחַיַּבְתְּ מִדְּאוֹרַיְתָא?

Mai ba'it tefay? Liten li bincha bechorcha she-hu peter rechem le-imo, o ba'it lifedoto be-ad chamesh sela'im, k'dimechu'yavt mi-de-oraita?

What would you prefer? To give this child to me and to have me dedicate him to the service of God, or would you prefer to redeem him as demanded by the Torah?

6. The father responds, holding up five silver coins:

חָפֵץ אֲנִי לִפְדּוֹת אֶת בְּנִי, וְהֵילָךְ דְּמֵי פִּדְיוֹנוֹ כִּדְמְחַיַּבְתִּי מִדְּאוֹרַיְתָא.

Chafetz ani lifdot et b'ni, ve-helach d'may fidyono, ke-di-mechu'yavti mi-de-oraita.

I wish to redeem my son, and here is the fee the Torah calls upon me to pay.

7. After handing the *Kohen* the five coins, the father recites:

בָּרוּךְ אַתָּה יְיָ, אֱלֹהֵינוּ מֶלֶךְ הָעוֹלָם, אֲשֶׁר קִדְּשָׁנוּ בְּמִצְוֹתָיו, וְצִוָּנוּ עַל פִּדְיוֹן הַבֵּן.

Baruch ata Adonai, Elohenu melech ha-olam, asher kideshanu be-mitzvotav ve-tzivanu al pidyon ha-ben.

Praised be Thou, O Lord our God, King of the universe, who has commanded us regarding the redemption of the firstborn son.

8. The father continues with the recitation of the *She-heche-yanu:*

בָּרוּךְ אַתָּה יְיָ, אֱלֹהֵינוּ מֶלֶךְ הָעוֹלָם, שֶׁהֶחֱיָנוּ,
וְקִיְּמָנוּ, וְהִגִּיעָנוּ לַזְּמַן הַזֶּה.

Baruch ata Adonai, Elohenu melech ha-olam, she-hecheyanu, ve-kiyemanu, ve-higiyanu la-zeman ha-zeh.

Praised art Thou, O Lord our God, King of the universe, who has kept us alive, and sustained us, and permitted us to enjoy this day.

9. Holding the redemption money over the child's head, the *Kohen* says:

זֶה תַּחַת זֶה, זֶה חִלּוּף זֶה, זֶה מָחוּל עַל זֶה; וְיִכָּנֵס
זֶה הַבֵּן לְחַיִּים, לַתּוֹרָה, וּלְיִרְאַת שָׁמָיִם. יְהִי רָצוֹן,
שֶׁכְּשֵׁם שֶׁנִּכְנַס לַפִּדְיוֹן, כֵּן יִכָּנֵס לְתוֹרָה, וּלְחֻפָּה,
וּלְמַעֲשִׂים טוֹבִים. אָמֵן.

I accept this money as a substitute for this child. May he grow up to live a life of love for Torah and God. Just as the act of redemption has been enacted in his behalf, so may his future lead him into a happy marriage and a life of good deeds.

10. The *Kohen* then places his hands over the child's head and pronounces the ancient Priestly Benediction:

יְבָרֶכְךָ יְיָ וְיִשְׁמְרֶךָ.

יָאֵר יְיָ פָּנָיו אֵלֶיךָ וִיחֻנֶּךָּ.

יִשָּׂא יְיָ פָּנָיו אֵלֶיךָ וְיָשֵׂם לְךָ שָׁלוֹם.

Ye-varechecha Adonai ve-yishmerecha.
Ya'er Adonai panav elecha vi-chuneka.
Yisa Adonai panav elecha ve-yasem lecha shalom.

May the Lord bless thee and keep thee.
May the Lord cause His countenance to shine upon thee and be gracious unto thee.
May the Lord lift up His face towards thee and grant thee peace.

11. The *Kohen* then raises a cup of wine and recites the appropriate blessing (see page 148). A festive meal, a *Se'udat Mitzva,* follows (see page 12).

BAR/BAT MITZVA AND CONFIRMATION

Bar Mitzva at Thirteen

When a boy has reached the age of thirteen plus one day, Jewish law considers him to be a mature adult. Thus, from that time on he is counted as part of a *minyan* (religious quorum of ten adults) and is obligated to live up to biblical and talmudic commandments, such as donning *tefilin* and fasting on Yom Kippur.

The event is generally marked at a synagogue service on the Sabbath closest to the young man's date of birth, although a formal synagogue commemoration is not required by law.

Entering the Minyan

The phrase "entering the *minyan*" is the way Sephardim refer to a Bar Mitzva boy. Once he begins donning his *tefilin,* he is counted as part of the quorum of ten who make up a *minyan.*

Bat Mitzva at Twelve

Girls, who reach physical maturity earlier than boys, are considered adult at the age of twelve years and one day. To mark the occasion, the Bat Mitzva ceremony was introduced. The first girl to become a Bat Mitzva was Judith Kaplan, daughter of Rabbi Mordecai Kaplan, founder of the Reconstructionist Movement. The ceremony was held in New York City in 1922 in the synagogue of the Society for the Advancement of Judaism.

Bar/Bat Mitzva Days

Bar/Bat Mitzva celebrations are usually held on the Sabbath, but they may be celebrated whenever the Torah is read: Mondays, Thursdays, Rosh Chodesh (the beginning of the Hebrew month), Sabbath afternoons, and holidays. A selection from the Prophets (the *haftara*) is recited only at Sabbath and holiday morning srevices.

The Bar/Bat Mitzva Sabbath

In the fourteenth century it became customary to celebrate a Bar Mitzva by calling the boy to the Torah for the final honor (the *maftir*) at the Sabbath service after his thirteenth birthday. He was also granted the privilege of reciting the *haftara*, the prophetic portion. Today, the same procedure is generally followed for the Bat Mitzva by all except Orthodox groups.

Orthodox Bat Mitzva Approaches

Orthodox congregations do not celebrate a Bat Mitzva in the synagogue as part of the formal religious service. Those who mark the occasion do so in a purely social setting. The Spanish-Portuguese Synagogue in New York City is known to celebrate the Bat Mitzva at the *Kiddush* following the service. Girls age twelve and over who have completed the required course of Jewish study deliver a talk on the significance of the occasion and pledge their loyalty to Judaism. A variety of celebrations along these lines are conducted by Orthodox Jews.

Sephardic Bar Mitzva Practice

Unlike Ashkenazim, Sephardic Bar Mitzva boys are generally not awarded the *maftir* honor and do not recite the *haftara*. Instead, they are awarded the fifth or sixth *aliya*.

Bar Mitzva of an Adopted Child

A natural parent of a son who had been given out for adoption at a young age retains all the religious paternal rights and obligations pertaining to the child. If the natural father is present at the Bar Mitzva of his son, it is he rather than the adoptive father who recites the *Baruch She-petarani* prayer (see below), and it is he who must be honored with an *aliya*.

Stepfather at a Bar Mitzva

If a woman divorces and retains the custody of the couple's son, the natural father of the child never loses his paternal rights, even if the woman remarries and the child's stepfather assists in rearing the boy. It is the natural father who is entitled to be called to the Torah at the Bar Mitzva.

A Double Aliya

When two people speak at one time, it is often difficult to understand what is being said. Therefore, the reading of the Torah or reciting of the Torah blessings as a duet is forbidden in Jewish law. If done, these actions are considered invalid.

Most non-Orthodox congregations do not subscribe to this prohibition and often honor two people at a Bar or Bat Mitzva with the same *aliya*. Sometimes one person will recite the first Torah blessing and the second person will recite the concluding blessing.

Baruch She-petarani

An old practice still current in Orthodox synagogues is for the father of a Bar Mitzva to recite the *Baruch She-petarani* prayer after his son has pronounced the second Torah blessing. The prayer expresses the father's thanks for having been freed from bearing responsibility for the young man's future actions:

בָּרוּךְ שֶׁפְּטָרַנִי מֵעָנְשׁוֹ שֶׁל זֶה.

Baruch she-petarani me-onsho shel zeh.

Blessed is He who freed me from the obligation of my son.

Because of its negative connotation, non-Orthodox congregants do not recite this prayer and have substituted the *She-hecheyanu* blessing. (See page 150 for the *She-hecheyanu*.)

Non-Jewish Father

If the father of a Bar or Bat Mitzva is Gentile (but the mother is Jewish), Jewish law does not permit him to be called to the Torah even if he is able to learn the blessings. The blessings, which speak of granting *us* the Torah, do not apply to the non-Jewish father, and it is considered inappropriate for him to utter them. While the non-Jewish father of a Bar or Bat Mitzva is not permitted to participate formally in the service, in some congregations he is permitted to stand on the pulpit.

Lavish Parties

As far back as the sixteenth century, rabbinic authorities condemned unbridled celebrating at Bar Mitzva parties which were often held just for the purpose of enabling guests to gorge themselves with food and to carry on in an uninhibited fashion. Lavish, expensive parties are discouraged by present-day rabbis as well, and families are encouraged to donate the financial savings to organizations that feed the poor. One such organization is Mazon, which has offices in many large cities in the United States.

The Institution of Confirmation

In 1849, while serving as rabbi of Temple Beth El in Albany, New York, Bohemian-born Rabbi Isaac Mayer Wise introduced a drastic modification in the synagogue ritual. The change, which upset many of his members, involved replacing the Bar Mitzva ceremony with a Confirmation service that was to be held annually for boys and girls thirteen years of age. The day designated for the ceremony was Shavuot, the holiday commemorating the giving of the Torah on Mount Sinai.

At first, only Reform congregations followed the lead of Rabbi Isaac M. Wise and embraced the Confirmation ceremony. Orthodox congregations deplored the new practice, but in time most Conservative congregations adopted it. However, unlike Reform congregations, Conservative congregations did not abandon the Bar Mitzva ceremony. Today most Reform congregations have accepted the custom of celebrating both the Bar Mitzva and Confirmation.

Age of Confirmation

In the early years after the Confirmation ceremony was introduced, the age for boy and girl confirmands was set at thirteen. Subsequently the age was advanced because it was felt that age sixteen or seventeen is a more suitable time for youngsters to assume the role of a mature adult. Most confirmands today are high school juniors or seniors who have completed a fixed course of study in a synagogue religious school.

2
Jews By Choice
CONVERTS AND THE CONVERSION PROCESS

Introduction

According to traditional Jewish law, anyone born of a Jewish mother is considered a Jew. Anyone else desiring to become part of the Jewish community must undergo conversion.

Historically, Jews have not been averse to accepting converts into the Jewish fold. However, it is expected that the decision to become Jewish be arrived at after a period of intense soul-searching and that the prospective convert be motivated by conviction rather than convenience. Paired with sincerity, a convert to Judaism is required to absorb a core of Jewish knowledge, most commonly including an overview of Jewish history, a familiarity with home and synagogue religious practices, and an ability to read Hebrew script.

Orthodox, Conservative, Reform, and Reconstructionist Jews differ as to the way that a prospective convert must demonstrate his sincerity, the course of study prescribed, and the conversion protocol. Once the requirements of the denomination have been fulfilled, the individual is deemed to be a Jew.

BECOMING A JEW

Early Attitude Toward Converts

Because the Rabbis of the Talmud were suspicious of their motives, converts (or proselytes, as they were more commonly called in earlier times) were not eagerly accepted into the Jewish fold. In fact, conversion to Judaism was discouraged. Only after a non-Jew had petitioned the court three times could he be admitted as a candidate for conversion.

Rabbi Chelbo's Attitude

One of the oft-repeated comments in the Talmud concerning prospective proselytes originated with the fourth-century scholar Rabbi Chelbo. He said: "Proselytes are as irritating to Israel as a sore [scab]." The view of Rabbi Chelbo was widely shared by many talmudic authorities who were convinced that too many converts desired to become Jews for ulterior motives rather than out of conviction.

Conversion for the Sake of Marriage

The Talmud insists that a person not be accepted as a convert if his or her motive is simply to be able to marry a Jew. To this day, all rabbinic bodies urge their members to discourage those who wish to convert for an ulterior motive. Nonetheless, the general practice is to allow such candidates to enter the conversion process. If, during the period of preparation, the rabbi discerns that the candidate is developing a sincere affinity for Judaism, and if it becomes evident that the individual will embrace Judaism unconditionally, acceptance into the Jewish fold is granted.

Treatment of Converts

One of the most famous converts to Judaism was the twelfth-century Italian Catholic priest Obadiah. Because in the Middle

Ages proselytes were still viewed with suspicion, the utterly sincere Obadiah, who had devoted himself to Jewish scholarship, was not well received by the Jewish community and was not fully accepted even by his own teacher. The convert appealed to Maimonides, who advised him, "Go tell your teacher that he owes you an apology . . . he forgot that in thirty-six places the Torah reminds us to *respect* the convert and in thirty-six places it admonishes us to love the convert. . . . Whoever maligns him commits a great sin."

Total Rejection of Converts

While today Jewish communities in general will accept converts as Jews once they have met prescribed standards, the Syrian community specifically will not accept converts into their ranks under any circumstances because they want to maintain a close-knit, unadulterated community. This policy was established in 1937 by the Syrian Sephardic Rabbinical Council. A Syrian Jew who marries a convert is totally rebuffed by the community and excluded from its religious and social life.

Like Newborn Babes

"A convert is like a newborn babe," say the Rabbis of the Talmud. This means that from the moment of conversion to Judaism a non-Jew leaves his or her past religious associations behind and begins life anew.

Who Must Undergo Conversion

All denominations consider the offspring of a Jewish woman and a Gentile man Jewish in all respects; conversion of the offspring is not required.

According to Orthodox and Conservative Judaism, the child of a Jewish man and Gentile woman must be converted in order to be Jewish. A child whose natural mother is not Jewish but who is adopted by Jewish parents must likewise undergo conversion to be considered Jewish.

Reform Judaism, which has adopted the concept of patrilineal descent in addition to the concept of matrilineal descent, considers the offspring of a Jewish father and non-Jewish mother to be Jewish if it is the desire of the parents to bring up the child as a Jew. Formal conversion of the offspring is thus not required.

Pregnant Convert

If a Gentile woman converts to Judaism while pregnant, her child is considered Jewish regardless of what the father's religion might be.

THE CONVERSION PROCESS

Finding a Rabbi

The first step in becoming a candidate for conversion is to consult a local rabbi. If none is available in your locale, get in touch with one of the religious organizations listed in the Appendix and ask for a recommendation.

Be sure you have given ample consideration to whether you want to make contact with an Orthodox, Conservative, Reform, or Reconstructionist rabbi. At present the Israeli rabbinate does not recognize conversions performed by other than Orthodox rabbis. So, if you intend to be converted by a non-Orthodox rabbi and are thinking of settling in Israel and possibly marrying there, be aware that you will have to subject yourself to the rites of conversion once again in Israel, this time under the auspices of an Orthodox rabbi.

It is important to note that if a woman is converted by a non-Orthodox rabbi, gets married, and subsequently settles in Israel, her children may have difficulty when they want to get married, for they may not be considered Jewish in the eyes of the Israeli rabbinate.

Preparing for Conversion

Candidates for conversion are required to devote themselves to concentrated study so that they will become familiar with all Jewish beliefs, prayers, and rituals. The number of months of intensive study required is dictated by the rabbi supervising the conversion, but on average the period of study ranges from six months to one year. During this time the convert is expected to start practicing some of the customs and ceremonies of Judaism.

Three Rites of Conversion

In the Bible the Children of Israel are said to have entered into a covenant with God through three rites: circumcision, immersion, and the bringing of a sacrifice. These rituals were originally to be carried out by all Jews in order to affirm their loyalty to Judaism. Later, these rites were made applicable to all Gentiles who wished to enter the Jewish fold.

When the Temple was destroyed and sacrifices were no longer offered, only immersion and circumcision remained as criteria for entry into the Jewish community.

The Bet Din

Jewish law demands that, when certain significant religious rites are performed, a court or tribunal consisting of three rabbis or three learned laymen be present to oversee and witness the events. The tribunal is called a *Bet Din*, a "court of law."

As part of the conversion procedure, a tribunal of three must be present to verify and validate that the circumcision (or the symbolic drawing of a drop of blood), and the immersion have been performed properly.

In Reform conversions, where circumcision and immersion are not mandatory, after a period of study the candidate for conversion appears before a tribunal consisting of three rabbis or one rabbi and two elders of the congregation. He or she is examined, and then, after an oral and written commitment is made, admittance into the Jewish fold is granted. At a later date, a synagogue ceremony is usually held to mark the event; and at that time a Hebrew name is bestowed on the convert.

Circumcision of Converts

Orthodox and Conservative Judaism require that all male converts be circumcised in the same manner as an infant who is circumcised on the eighth day after birth. Reform Judaism does not require circumcision for converts.

Drawing a Drop of Blood

For a convert who was born without a foreskin, and for one who was circumcised as an infant for health rather than religious reasons, it is sufficient that a drop of blood be drawn from the glans of the penis as a symbolic gesture. See page 11 for more about this procedure.

Mikva for Converts

Orthodox and Conservative practice requires all male and female candidates for conversion to submit to immersion in a ritual bath, a *mikva*. (The nature of the *mikva* is explained on page 48.) The immersion prayer for a proselyte is the same as that pronounced by a married woman who visits a ritual bath at the conclusion of her monthly menstrual period (see below).

Reform Judaism has not traditionally required the immersion of conversion candidates in a *mikva*. However, in recent years some Reform rabbis have introduced the practice.

Mikva Prayers for Converts

Men and women converts, when immersing themselves in a *mikva*, pronounce the following blessing:

בָּרוּךְ אַתָּה יְיָ, אֱלֹהֵינוּ מֶלֶךְ הָעוֹלָם, אֲשֶׁר קִדְּשָׁנוּ בְּמִצְוֹתָיו, וְצִוָּנוּ עַל הַטְּבִילָה.

Baruch ata Adonai, Elohenu melech ha-olam, asher kideshanu be-mitzvotav, ve-tzivanu al ha-tevila.

Praised art Thou, O Lord our God, King of the universe, who sanctified us through His commandments and commanded us concerning immersion.

This is followed by the *She-hecheyanu* blessing:

בָּרוּךְ אַתָּה יְיָ, אֱלֹהֵינוּ מֶלֶךְ הָעוֹלָם, שֶׁהֶחֱיָנוּ, וְקִיְּמָנוּ, וְהִגִּיעָנוּ לַזְּמַן הַזֶּה.

Baruch ata Adonai, Elohenu melech ha-olam, she-hecheyanu, ve-kiyemanu, ve-higiyanu la-zeman ha-zeh.

Praised art Thou, O Lord our God, King of the universe, who has kept us alive, and sustained us, and permitted us to enjoy this day.

Witnesses to an Immersion

The *Code of Jewish Law,* compiled in the sixteenth century, endorses Maimonides' twelfth-century view on immersion. Maimonides required that three men be present when a conversion candidate (male or female) undergoes immersion. In the case of a woman, however, for the sake of modesty the witnesses stand outside the *mikva* room and are advised by a female attendant that the ritual has been performed in the manner prescribed by law.

Immersion in the Nude

Strict compliance with Jewish law demands that the convert be nude when the immersion rite takes place. However, when a regular *mikva* is not available and the immersion is done in a river, lake, or in the ocean, the convert may wear a loose-fitting garment. This is not considered a barrier (*chatzitza* in Hebrew) because it does not prevent the water from making full contact with all parts of the body.

Swimming Pool as a Mikva

When neither a regular *mikva* or a natural body of water (lake, river, or ocean) is available, the Committee on Law and Standards of the Rabbinical Assembly (Conservative) permits the use of a swimming pool, particularly an in-ground pool. The Orthodox rabbinate is not as lenient in this regard.

Procedure for Conversion of a Female Child

The only ritual required of a female child undergoing conversion is that of immersion in a ritual bath. The procedure described above for an adult is followed for a child as well.

Procedure for Conversion of a Male Child

Conversion of a male child involves immersion in a *mikva,* as described above. However, the immersion must be preceded by the regular circumcision ceremony as described on page 32. The immersion usually takes place a few weeks after the circumcision so as to allow sufficient time for the child to heal.

As with an adult convert, if the child had already been

circumcised or if he was born without a foreskin, only a drop of blood need be drawn.

At the circumcision ceremony, the *mohel* recites two special circumcision blessings for converts.

After the Immersion

For both male and female, after the immersion ceremony has been completed, the final rite of conversion takes place, often in the synagogue during a religious service. In the presence of a *Bet Din,* the convert makes a formal declaration that he or she voluntarily accepts the faith of Israel and promises to abide by its commandments. This acceptance is known as *kabbalat ol mitzvot,* "accepting the yoke of the Law."

Conversion of Adopted Child

The conversion of a child adopted by a Jewish couple must be done by agreement with, and in the presence of, a *Bet Din.* This tribunal of three will convene when expressly requested to do so by the adoptive parents.

Naming Converts

After the declaration of faith has been made, male and female converts are named by the tribunal of three, which is present to witness and validate the procedure. Appropriate prayers are recited to mark the occasion.

Names for Converts

Male converts are usually given the Hebrew name Avraham as the first name, and females are usually called Sara (wife of Abraham) or Rut (the loyal non-Jewish daughter of Naomi). In both instances, Avraham (father of the Jewish people) is used as the patronymic. Thus, in Hebrew, a male will be called Avraham *ben* (son of) Avraham, and a female will be called Sara or Rut *bat* (daughter of) Avraham.

If preferred by the convert, so as to draw less attention to his or her status, a name other than Avraham, Sara, or Rut may be used.

RIGHTS AND OBLIGATIONS OF CONVERTS

Marriage of Kohen and Proselyte

According to Orthodox law, a *Kohen* is not permitted to marry a convert (proselyte), but the daughter of a *Kohen* may marry a convert. The Law Committee of the Rabbinical Assembly (Conservative) ruled that a marriage between a converted woman and a *Kohen* is permitted.

Showing Respect Toward Natural Parents

The Rabbis considered the fifth of the Ten Commandments, "Honor thy father and mother," to be a basic Torah commandment that applies to Jews and non-Jews alike. Although not obligated to do so, the Rabbis were in general agreement that a convert may sit *Shiva* or say *Kaddish* for his natural (non-Jewish) parents. In a 1933 responsum, Orthodox authority Rabbi Aaron Walkin ruled that a convert is obligated to recite *Kaddish* for his Christian father, but more recently Rabbi Chaim Denburg, of Montreal, ruled that a convert must not say *Kaddish* for a non-Jewish parent.

The Right to Renounce a Conversion

If a baby born to a Gentile is adopted by a Jewish couple, and the adoptive parents convert the child to Judaism, the child is considered to be a full Jew even though he or she did not consent to the conversion. However, Jewish law grants the child the right to renounce the conversion at maturity: age thirteen for a boy and twelve for a girl. If the conversion is not explicitly renounced at that time, Jewish law considers the convert a Jew forever.

Jewish Education of Non-Jewish Children

Conservative and Reform congregations, and some Orthodox ones, permit the unconverted child of a Jewish man and Gentile woman to attend their religious schools. Orthodox and Conservative synagogues, however, do not allow such children to become Bar or Bat Mitzva unless they first undergo conversion.

Reform congregations permit such children to become Bar or Bat Mitzva if they pledge to live a committed Jewish life. The ceremony marks their formal entrance into Judaism.

ABANDONING JUDAISM

Once a Jew, Always a Jew

A basic principle enunciated in the Talmud and in the later codes of Jewish law is that a Jew is a Jew forever, even if he sins and abandons Judaism in favor of another religion. As a sinner he may forfeit some privileges, but he does not lose his basic Jewish rights.

A Convert Who Abandons Judaism

A convert or any other Jew who joins a non-Jewish religious sect, such as Jews for Jesus, is not entitled to any of the privileges granted Jews under the Israeli Law of Return. This ruling was handed down in a unanimous 1989 decision of the Israeli supreme court (the High Court of Justice). It declared that the Law of Return identifies a Jew as a person born of a Jewish mother or one who has converted to Judaism, but excludes anyone who is a member of a different faith.

While a Jewish defector loses much credibility as a Jew and may be denied some privileges, he cannot be denied all rights as a Jew, for the legal principle of "once a Jew, always a Jew" still applies. Thus, a Jewish apostate may be denied the privileges of the Law of Return, but he cannot, for example, be denied the right of inheritance. Nor is the apostate freed of all obligations: he is required to give his wife a Jewish divorce (*get*) should she want to remarry.

A Returning Defector

A Jew who abandons Judaism, joins another faith, and then subsequently has a change of heart can return to Judaism without going through the conversion process.

In Jewish law, a Jew who abandons his religion in favor of another faith is still considered a Jew. He is considered no more than a sinner. The Talmud says, "A Jew, even if he sins [by abandoning his faith] is still a Jew."

Child of a Defector

A child born to a Jewish woman after she has defected to another religion is considered a Jew.

3
Marriage and Divorce

Introduction

Of the sixty-three tractates of the Talmud, four of the larger ones (Kiddushin, Ketubot, Yevamot, and Gittin) are devoted to the rules governing marriage and divorce, for next to the Sabbath there are no institutions of greater importance in Jewish law. Marriage and divorce are also given a great deal of attention in the many classics on Jewish law written in post-talmudic times, particularly Joseph Caro's sixteenth-century *Code of Jewish Law* and in the responsa literature that has appeared over the centuries. In these we find a web of law and custom regarding such matters as whom a Jewish man or woman is permitted to marry, the days in the year when weddings may be held, the nature of the marriage contract, the ring ceremony, and the relationship between religious and civil marriage law.

While silent on marriage procedure, the Bible (Deuteronomy 24:1) outlines the general procedure to be followed when a marriage is to be dissolved:

> When a man marries a woman in whom, after a time, he is displeased because he has discovered some unseemly traits in her, he may write a document of divorce and give it to her.

The Rabbis of the Talmud amplified upon this biblical law by spelling out how the divorce document *(get)* is to be written, who must be present at its writing, and how it is to be presented to the wife.

MARRIAGE LAWS AND CUSTOMS

Matchmaker, Matchmaker

One of the most honorable professions among Jews of earlier times was that of matchmaker, better known by the Hebrew term *shadchan*. The Talmud considers no job more important or difficult than that of arranging marriages. Rabbi Jose said, "It is as difficult as God's splitting of the Red Sea." In modern times, with the introduction of the computer, matchmaking has become somewhat easier.

Marriage Age

In talmudic times eighteen was considered the proper age for a man to marry. Later, authorities felt it best that people marry at an earlier age, suggesting thirteen for a boy and twelve and one-half for a girl. Where such marriages were contracted, the couple waited a number of years before living together.

Girls at Sixteen

In 1950 the Israeli rabbinate ruled it illegal for girls under age sixteen to marry.

Polygamy Banned

The Bible permits polygamy, but around the year 1000 the highly respected German authority Rabbenu Gershom ben Yehuda issued a ban on all polygamous marriages. Only the Ashkenazic communities abided by this edict. Jews who lived in

Moslem countries continued to marry more than one woman until 1950, when the Chief Rabbinate of Israel extended the ban to all Jews.

Mourners and Marriage

During *Sheloshim*—the first thirty days after the death of a close relative—mourners are not permitted to marry. An exception is made in cases where final marriage arrangements had been completed before the death occurred.

Civil Marriage of a Jewish Couple

Although a Jewish marriage ceremony must be performed for a bona fide Jewish marriage to exist, if a Jewish couple is married by a Justice of the Peace or some other governmental official, the marriage is nevertheless valid. Should the couple separate at a future date and the woman desire to remarry in a Jewish ceremony, Orthodox and Conservative rabbis require that a Jewish divorce *(get)* first be obtained.

Civil Marriage Between Jews and Gentiles

In Jewish law, a civil marriage between a Jew and non-Jew is not recognized. If a couple was so married and subsequently obtained a civil divorce, rabbis of all denominations will remarry the Jewish partner to another eligible Jew.

Living Together

Jewish tradition does not look favorably upon the prevalent practice of couples living together without having been formally married. However, there is a mistaken notion that if it is widely known that a Jewish man and woman have lived together for more than thirty days and then decide to separate, they must obtain a Jewish divorce *(get)* before either can get married to someone else. The fifteenth-century German talmudic scholar Rabbi Israel Isserlein and, in more recent times, Chief Rabbi Herzog of Israel have ruled that living together without having been formally married does not constitute a marriage and therefore a *get* is not required to end the relationship.

In-laws With a Common First Name

Marrying a woman with the same first name as one's mother was avoided by men in talmudic times. Likewise, marrying a man with the same first name as one's father was avoided by women. The Talmud puts it this way: "When he calls to his wife [by name], his mother might answer, and this would prove embarrassing." In Jewish tradition it is disrespectful to call a parent by his or her first name.

Intermarriages Prohibited

All segments of the Jewish religious community are averse to marriages between Jews and non-Jews. Orthodox and Conservative rabbis are forbidden to officiate at intermarriages, while the Reform and Reconstructionist movements leave the option with the individual rabbi. Although the official position of the Reform rabbinate is that "mixed marriages are contrary to Jewish tradition and should be discouraged," fifty percent of its members presently do, under varying circumstances, perform intermarriages.

Synagogue Membership and Intermarrieds

Orthodox and Conservative congregations do not admit non-Jews as congregational members, hence an intermarried couple is not accepted as a family unit. The Reform and Reconstructionist movements do welcome intermarried couples and their families as members.

The Ring Declaration at Intermarriage Weddings

As he places the ring on her finger, a Jewish groom says to his Jewish bride: "Behold, thou art consecrated unto me with this ring according to the laws of Moses and Israel." Since it is incumbent only upon Jews to follow the laws of Moses, it would be inappropriate for a non-Jew to make this declaration.

Intermarriage Conducted by a Rabbi

The marriage of a Jew to a non-Jew is not binding under Jewish law even if performed by a rabbi. The Jewish partner in such a "marriage" may remarry without obtaining a *get* (Jewish divorce).

Children of Interfaith Couples

The child of a Jewish woman married to a non-Jewish man is considered Jewish and hence may marry a Jew. The offspring of a marriage between a Jewish man and a non-Jewish woman is considered non-Jewish by all but Reform Jews (see page 30) and hence must be converted before becoming eligible to marry a Jew.

Contrary to popular belief, the child of an interfaith couple is not considered illegitimate (a bastard) under Jewish law.

Incestuous Marriages

The Book of Leviticus, Chapter 18, lists all relationships considered incestuous. At the top of the list are those between a man and his mother, his daughter, his sister, his granddaughter, and his aunt. A child born of any such incestuous relationship is a *mamzer* (bastard) in the eyes of Jewish law. For a full list of incestuous and other prohibited marriages, see page 559 of *Pentateuch and Haftorahs,* edited by J.H. Hertz (Soncino Press).

Amram's Marriage

The Book of Exodus (6:20) reveals that the father of Moses, Amram, married his aunt (his father's sister). Leviticus (18:12) considers such a marriage to be incestuous, but the Rabbis of the Talmud do not fault Amram because the marriage took place before the laws of incest were declared on Mount Sinai.

Marriage to a Bastard

Anyone born of an incestuous marriage is a bastard, and a Jew is not permitted to marry a bastard. Only bastards and proselytes are permitted to marry bastards.

Nieces and Nephews

In Jewish law, an uncle may marry his niece, but an aunt may not marry her nephew. American civil law does not permit a man to marry the daughter of his brother or sister but permits him to marry a niece who is the daughter of his wife's sister or brother.

Cousins

According to Jewish law, men and women may marry their cousins.

Kohen and Divorcee

The Bible (Leviticus 21:7) prescribes that a *Kohen* may not marry a divorcee. However, the Rabbis of the Talmud concluded that if the marriage has already been contracted, it is considered valid, although the *Kohen* must forego his priestly privileges. Reform and Conservative Judaism permit such a marriage in the first place, but Conservatives expect the *Kohen* to forego being called to the Torah for the first *aliya,* officiating at a *Pidyon Ha-ben,* and participating in other religious functions.

Kohen and Proselyte

The Book of Leviticus (21:7) stipulates that a Priest shall not marry a woman who is "defiled by harlotry." To the Rabbis of the Talmud the word "harlot" meant not only "prostitute" but any woman tainted for any reason. And since proselytes in ancient times came from heathen stock, they were considered tainted. In later rabbinic rulings, the marriage of a *Kohen* to a proselyte was prohibited in the first place, but once consummated was considered valid, with the *Kohen* having to forego his priestly privileges. The non-Orthodox permit the marriage of a *Kohen* to a proselyte.

Kohen and Widow

Although a *Kohen* may not marry a divorcee or a proselyte, he may marry a widow. In biblical times, only High Priests were forbidden to marry widows or divorcees (Leviticus 21:14).

THE BEST TIME TO MARRY

Weddings During Elul

Some Sephardim, primarily Syrians, arrange for marriages

to be held during the month of Elul, the month before the High Holy Days. Elul is considered a month for love because the word *Elul* is an acronym formed from the Hebrew words in the Song of Songs, *Ani Le-dodi, Ve-dodi Li,* "I am my beloved's, and my beloved is mine."

Weddings on Tuesdays

There is an old tradition that Tuesday—the third day of the week—is a lucky day on which to hold a wedding because, in describing the third day of Creation, the Bible twice uses the expression "God saw that this was good" (Genesis 1:10, 12), while in describing the other days of the week, the word "good" is used only once.

Wednesday, Thursday, and Friday Weddings

A tradition that began in talmudic times considers the best day of the week for the marriage of virgins to be Wednesday, and for widows, Thursday. Later, Friday became a preferred day for marriages.

Among the Sephardim of Morocco, weddings usually take place on Wednesday night, which is actually Thursday *(yom chamishi),* the fifth day of the week. The fifth *aliya* is one of the prestigious *aliyot* among Moroccans.

Marriage Days in Orthodox Practice

Marriages may not be performed on Sabbaths and major festivals but are permitted on minor holidays, including the New Moon (Rosh Chodesh), Chanuka, and Purim.

Marriages may not be performed on the Intermediate Days (Chol Ha-moed) of Passover and Sukkot.

With some days excepted, marriages may not be performed during the period of national mourning that extends for three weeks in summertime—from the seventeenth of Tammuz to the ninth of Av. During this time period in the year 586 B.C.E. the Babylonians breached the walls of Jerusalem and destroyed the First Temple. (See page 47 for exceptions.)

With regard to the seven-week *Sefira* period, which falls between Passover and Shavuot (see page 241), the most widely accepted practice in Orthodox Ashkenazic communities is to refrain from holding weddings until three days before Shavuot, except for Rosh Chodesh Iyyar, Rosh Chodesh Sivan, and Lag B'Omer. Recently, the fifth of Iyyar—Israel Independence Day— has been added to the list of days on which marriages may be performed.

Sephardic Sefira Practice

Sephardim by and large do not hold weddings from the beginning of Passover until Lag B'Omer but do permit them afterwards. Jews of Spanish-Portuguese extraction permit weddings during the entire month of Nissan, on Rosh Chodesh Iyyar and Sivan, on Lag B'Omer, and on the three days prior to Shavuot.

Lag B'Omer Weddings

According to tradition, the plague that decimated the ranks of Rabbi Akiba's students in the second century C.E. abated on the thirty-third day after the first day of Passover (the eighteenth day of Iyyar), and as a consequence weddings were permitted in keeping with the joyous spirit of the day. The eighteenth day of Iyyar is known as Lag B'Omer. (See page 240 for more about the Omer.)

Marriages in Conservative Practice

In 1949 the Committee on Law and Standards of the Rabbinical Assembly (Conservative) favored the eighth- and ninth-century tradition of forbidding weddings from the second day of Passover (Nissan 16) until Lag B'Omer (Iyyar 18). Subsequently, the law committee shortened to less than two weeks—from the beginning of Passover until Nissan 27 (Yom Ha-sho'ah)—the period during which weddings and other festive celebrations are prohibited. The remainder of the Sefira period is "to be considered as any other time during the year."

During the three-week period from the seventeenth of Tammuz to the ninth of Av marriages are prohibited on the two fast days, Shiva Asar B'Tammuz and Tisha B'Av, but are permitted from the eighteenth of Tammuz until the end of the month. Small, informal weddings (without music) are permitted from the first to the eighth of Av.

Marriage Days in Reform Practice

Reform Judaism does not ban weddings on *Sefira* days or on fast days, except that with regard to Tisha B'Av the *Reform Manual* says: "On the grounds of historical consciousness, marriages should be avoided by Reform rabbis on the ninth of Av, even though the Reform Synagogue does not officially recognize the day as a fast day."

Between Rosh Hashana and Yom Kippur

The Days of Awe—the ten days between Rosh Hashana and Yom Kippur—are a somber period in the Jewish calendar and are not considered an appropriate time to hold elaborate wedding celebrations. However, weddings may be held during this period.

PREPARING FOR THE CEREMONY

The Aufruf

Aufruf is a German word meaning "calling up." It is customary, on the Sabbath before his marriage, for the bridegroom to be honored with an *aliya*. In non-Orthodox congregations the bride will sometimes accompany the groom to the Torah. After the second Torah blessing has been recited by the groom, congregants often shower celebrants with candy and serenade them with song.

Talit for the Groom

A popular custom among Orthodox and some Conservative Jews is for the bride to present her groom with a gift *talit* (prayershawl) before the wedding. In many communities the wearing of a *talit* at religious services signifies that a man is married.

Use of Talit Among Sephardim

Among Sephardim, the *talit* given to the groom as a gift is sometimes used as the actual wedding canopy *(chupa)* and is held over the heads of the bride and groom during the ceremony. In some communities both sets of parents hold up the prayershawl, while in others only the fathers hold it. Often, the *talit* is held aloft by a structured canopy.

Bride and Groom Fast

Among Orthodox Jews in particular, a bride and groom will fast on their wedding day until after the ceremony. This represents an expression of penance for past misdeeds and symbolizes entry into a new phase of life with a clean slate. In Jewish tradition marriage is a watershed event in a couple's life—comparable to Yom Kippur—when sins are forgiven and the old slate is wiped clean.

Visiting Graves Prior to a Wedding

It is customary for brides and grooms who have lost parents to visit the cemetery prior to the wedding and to recite the memorial prayer, *El Malay Rachamim* (page 93). At some weddings this prayer is recited during the actual ceremony, while at others it is recited privately before the ceremony begins.

THE MIKVA

What Is a Mikva?

A *mikva* can be a body of natural water, such as an ocean, lake, or pond fed by natural springs, or it can be an in-ground pool fed by water from a natural source, such as a well, or by stored water from rains, melted snow, and melted ice.

Visiting a Mikva

Orthodox and some Conservative brides visit a *mikva* (ritual bath) during the week preceding their wedding. This introduces the bride to a practice she is obligated to follow monthly until menopause.

Purification by Immersion

In the Bible, immersion is required of an impure person if he is to be restored to a state of purity.

Sexual Intercourse and the Mikva

After the menstrual period is over, Orthodox and some Conservative couples will not engage in sexual intercourse until the wife has immersed herself in a *mikva* and pronounced the appropriate prayer. The immersion takes place on the seventh day after the woman's period has ended.

Mikva for Converts

An important aspect of the conversion process is immersion by men and women in a *mikva*. This is the same ritual bath used by married women at the end of the menstrual period.

The Physical Structure

The *mikva* structure must be a minimum of two feet square by six feet high and must be filled with at least 191 gallons of natural water, an amount sufficient for average-sized persons to immerse themselves fully. If additional water is needed to fill the *mikva*, it may be drawn from any other source.

Throughout the ages the *mikva* was generally housed in the synagogue structure, but in recent years many have been erected as independent buildings. They are sometimes referred to as ritualariums.

Modern Mikva Amenities

Modern ritual baths are equipped with amenities such as hairdryers, and those in affluent neighborhoods sometimes have cosmeticians, hairdressers, and manicurists on call to service their clients.

Summary of
WHAT TO EXPECT AT A MIKVA

- Depending on the location, the fee to use a *mikva* ranges from $5.00 to $25.00.
- One or more attendants will be available to help you and answer questions.
- In order for an immersion to be valid, it is necessary that *mikva* water come into contact with all parts of the body. Before immersing oneself, the body must be cleansed of even the most minute particles of dirt, the presence of which might prevent total contact. Bathtubs and showers are available for this purpose.
- It is expected that nails be trimmed and thoroughly cleaned and that loose body hairs and makeup be removed.
- You will be expected to enter the *mikva* totally unclothed, with all jewelry and bandages removed. A covering will be draped over you, which the attendant will remove as you descend the few steps into the warm *mikva* water, which is about four feet deep.
- Standing with your legs apart, arms hanging loose, bend over and immerse yourself completely so that every part of the body, hair included, is touched by water.
- Then, standing erect once again, recite the Immersion Blessing while still in the water:

בָּרוּךְ אַתָּה יְיָ, אֱלֹהֵינוּ מֶלֶךְ הָעוֹלָם, אֲשֶׁר קִדְּשָׁנוּ בְּמִצְוֹתָיו, וְצִוָּנוּ עַל הַטְּבִילָה.

Baruch ata Adonai, Elohenu melech ha-olam, asher kideshanu be-mitzvotav ve-tzivanu al ha-tevila.

Praised be Thou, O Lord our God, King of the universe, who has sanctified us with His commandments and commanded us concerning the immersion.

- After reciting the blessing, immerse yourself quickly two more times.

- Ascend the steps and drape yourself with the covering the attendant holds out for you.

THE WEDDING CEREMONY

Erusin, Nisuin, Kiddushin

In earlier centuries Jewish marriages were conducted in two stages. The first stage, referred to as *Erusin,* is often translated as "betrothal" or "engagement." The second stage, the marriage proper, which took place as much as one year later, is known as *Nisuin* or *Kiddushin.*

In the first stage, the wine was blessed, the bride received a ring, and the *ketuba* (marriage contract) was read. In the second stage, a cup of wine was filled and seven blessings, called the *Sheva Berachot,* were recited (see page 52). With the completion of this second step, the bride and groom were officially married and were permitted to live together as man and wife.

Two Stages of Marriage Combined

In Germany and France during the twelfth century, the two ceremonies of *Erusin* and *Nisuin* (see above) were combined, and that is how the marriage ceremony is conducted to this day. According to Maimonides, the terms *Erusin* and *Kiddushin* are synonymous, although we often refer to the combined portions of the marriage ceremony as *Kiddushin.*

The Ketuba

The Jewish marriage contract—the *ketuba*—is written in Aramaic, which was the language of the masses in talmudic times. The document guarantees to the bride that her husband will provide for all of her needs and, should the marriage be dissolved, he or his estate will provide her with a specified amount of money.

Modern Ketubot

Modern *ketubot* (plural of *ketuba*), like many in earlier centuries, frequently are rendered in beautiful calligraphy and full color and are suitable for framing and wall hanging.

Witnesses to the Ketuba

The *ketuba* must be signed by two witnesses unrelated to the bride or groom. Although the actual signing is done privately before the wedding ceremony begins, the witnesses must be present when the contract is read aloud under the wedding canopy. Sometimes a memorial prayer *(El Malay Rachamim)* for deceased parents of the bride and groom is recited at the signing.

The Reform Ketuba

In Reform Judaism, the issuance of a *ketuba*, which had fallen into disuse, has been reintroduced for couples desiring one. Modified versions of the *ketuba* which stipulate the mutual obligations of the couple rather than only those incumbent upon the male partner have also been introduced.

A Lost Ketuba

The Rabbis of the Talmud considered it sinful for a couple to live together without a *ketuba*, but a marriage is not terminated or invalidated if a *ketuba* is lost. A new document is written to replace the lost one.

The Seven Blessings

The Seven Blessings, known in Hebrew as *Sheva Berachot*, are recited by the rabbi or cantor at the conclusion of the marriage ceremony. In many traditional homes, during the week following the wedding the Seven Blessings are recited each evening as part of a special version of the Grace After Meals. Guests at the dinner are honored by being asked to recite one of the blessings. The *Sheva Berachot*, chanted over a cup of wine from which the bride and groom drink, are the following:

First Blessing

בָּרוּךְ אַתָּה יְיָ, אֱלֹהֵינוּ מֶלֶךְ הָעוֹלָם, בּוֹרֵא פְּרִי הַגָּפֶן.

Baruch ata Adonai, Elohenu melech ha-olam, boray peri ha-gafen.

Praised be Thou, O Lord our God, King of the universe, who created the fruit of the vine.

Second Blessing

בָּרוּךְ אַתָּה יְיָ, אֱלֹהֵינוּ מֶלֶךְ הָעוֹלָם, שֶׁהַכֹּל בָּרָא לִכְבוֹדוֹ.

Baruch Ata Adonai, Elohenu melech ha-olam, she-ha-kol bara li-chevodo.

Praised be Thou, O Lord our God, King of the universe, who created all things for His glory.

Third Blessing

בָּרוּךְ אַתָּה יְיָ, אֱלֹהֵינוּ מֶלֶךְ הָעוֹלָם, יוֹצֵר הָאָדָם.

Baruch ata Adonai, Elohenu melech ha-olam, yotzer ha-adam.

Praised be Thou, O Lord our God, King of the universe, Creator of man.

Fourth Blessing

בָּרוּךְ אַתָּה יְיָ, אֱלֹהֵינוּ מֶלֶךְ הָעוֹלָם, אֲשֶׁר יָצַר אֶת הָאָדָם בְּצַלְמוֹ, בְּצֶלֶם דְּמוּת תַּבְנִיתוֹ, וְהִתְקִין לוֹ מִמֶּנּוּ בִּנְיַן עֲדֵי עַד. בָּרוּךְ אַתָּה יְיָ, יוֹצֵר הָאָדָם.

Baruch ata Adonai, Elohenu melech ha-olam, asher yatzar et ha-adam be-tzalmo, be-tzelem demut tavnito, ve-hitkin lo mimenu binyan aday ad. Baruch ata, Adonai, yotzer ha-adam.

Praised be Thou, O Lord our God, King of the universe, who fashioned man in His own image, after His own likeness, and established through him enduring life. Praised be Thou, O Lord, Creator of man.

Fifth Blessing

שׂוֹשׂ תָּשִׂישׂ וְתָגֵל הָעֲקָרָה, בְּקִבּוּץ בָּנֶיהָ לְתוֹכָהּ בְּשִׂמְחָה. בָּרוּךְ אַתָּה יְיָ, מְשַׂמֵּחַ צִיּוֹן בְּבָנֶיהָ.

Sos tasis ve-tagel ha-akara, be-kibutz baneha le-tocha be-simcha. Baruch ata, Adonai, me-same'ach Tziyon be-vaneha.

May Zion, made bereft of her children, soon rejoice as they return joyfully to her. Praised be Thou, O Lord, for causing Zion to rejoice upon the return of her children.

Sixth Blessing

שַׂמֵּחַ תְּשַׂמַּח רֵעִים הָאֲהוּבִים, כְּשַׂמֵּחֲךָ יְצִירְךָ בְּגַן עֵדֶן מִקֶּדֶם. בָּרוּךְ אַתָּה יְיָ, מְשַׂמֵּחַ חָתָן וְכַלָּה.

Same'ach t'samach re'im ha-ahuvim, ke-samechacha yetzircha be-Gan Eden mi-kedem. Baruch ata, Adonai, me-same'ach chatan ve-chala.

Bring abundant joy to these dear companions, just as Thou didst bestow joy upon Thy creations in the Garden of Eden. Praised be Thou, O Lord, who bestows joy upon groom and bride.

Seventh Blessing

בָּרוּךְ אַתָּה יְיָ, אֱלֹהֵינוּ מֶלֶךְ הָעוֹלָם, אֲשֶׁר בָּרָא שָׂשׂוֹן וְשִׂמְחָה, חָתָן וְכַלָּה, גִּילָה רִנָּה, דִּיצָה וְחֶדְוָה, אַהֲבָה וְאַחֲוָה, וְשָׁלוֹם וְרֵעוּת. מְהֵרָה, יְיָ אֱלֹהֵינוּ, יִשָּׁמַע בְּעָרֵי יְהוּדָה וּבְחוּצוֹת יְרוּשָׁלַיִם

קוֹל שָׂשׂוֹן וְקוֹל שִׂמְחָה, קוֹל חָתָן וְקוֹל כַּלָּה, קוֹל
מִצְהֲלוֹת חֲתָנִים מֵחֻפָּתָם, וּנְעָרִים מִמִּשְׁתֵּה
נְגִינָתָם. בָּרוּךְ אַתָּה יְיָ, מְשַׂמֵּחַ חָתָן עִם הַכַּלָּה.

*Baruch ata Adonai, Elohenu melech ha-olam, asher
bara sason ve-simcha, chatan ve-chala, gila, rina, ditza,
ve-chedva, ahava ve-achava, ve-shalom ve-re'ut. Me-
hera Adonai Elohenu yi-shama be-aray Yehuda u-ve-
chutzot Yerushala'yim, kol sason ve-kol simcha, kol
chatan ve-kol kala, kol mitzhalot chatanim me-chu-
patam, u-ne'arim mi-mishtay neginatam. Baruch ata,
Adonai, me-same'ach chatan im ha-kala.*

Praised be Thou, O Lord our God, King of the universe,
who created joy and gladness, a groom and his bride,
mirth and merriment, dancing and delight, love and
harmony, peace and friendship. O Lord our God, may
there soon be heard again in the cities of Judah and
in the streets of Jerusalem joyful voices: the voices of
groom and bride joined in marriage under the *chupa,*
voices of young people feasting and celebrating. Praised
be Thou, O Lord, who makes the groom rejoice with
his bride.

Breaking the Glass

The custom of breaking a glass at the conclusion of the
wedding ceremony has its origin in ancient superstition. It was
believed that noise scares away demons intent upon harming
people engaged in joyous activity. A later explanation applied
a more spiritual meaning to this custom: to serve as a reminder
that our ancient Temples were destroyed and that moments
of joy must be tempered with the harsh realities of life.

Reform Judaism considers the tradition of breaking a glass
to be of little significance, and its observance is optional. A
number of outstanding modern Orthodox authorities (including
Hillel Posek of Tel Aviv and the former Sephardic Chief Rabbi
of Israel, Ben-Zion Uziel) have deprecated the practice, claiming
that it causes many in the audience to shout, clap, and cheer,
which is inappropriate, considering that the glass-breaking symbolizes the destruction of the Temple.

Yichud

In the Orthodox tradition, after the glass is broken ending the wedding ceremony, the couple leaves the gathering and spends five or ten minutes alone together in a private room. Since the bride and groom have fasted all day, they partake of a small snack at this time. Years ago, the marriage was actually consummated at this time. This custom is known as *Yichud,* meaning "togetherness."

The Bride in White

At a first marriage a bride is expected to wear a white gown. White is a symbol of purity.

The Groom in White

At some Orthodox and Conservative ceremonies the groom will wear a white gown *(kittel)* as a symbol of purity.

Veiling the Bride

The custom of the bride's face being covered with a veil during the wedding ceremony is of biblical origin. It recalls our matriarch Rebeccah, who in a gesture of modesty covered herself with a veil when her prospective husband, Isaac, approached her for the first time (Genesis 26:45). Before Orthodox and many Conservative weddings today, the groom lowers the veil over the bride's face in a private ceremony called *Badeken,* meaning "the covering."

The Handkerchief Ceremony

Among Orthodox and some Conservative Jews, a handkerchief ceremony called *Kabbalat Kinyan* is conducted before the formal wedding begins. In the presence of the two witnesses who have signed the *ketuba,* the rabbi holds one end of a handkerchief and the groom takes hold of the other. Through this symbolic act the groom expresses his willingness to fulfill all the obligations the *ketuba* places upon him. In Jewish law, "agreement by handkerchief" was one way of sealing an agreement.

The Chupa

The *chupa,* the wedding canopy, symbolizes the Jewish home that the bride and groom will establish. Generally, the canopy consists of a piece of embroidered material approximately six feet square that is mounted on vertical posts. Sometimes it is simply a *talit* which is attached to four wooden or metal staves and held up by four honorees. Occasionally, a *chupa* is constructed as a bower of leaves and flowers. In Reform practice, the use of a *chupa* is optional.

Some scholars regard the *chupa* as a symbol of the laurel wreath worn by the bride and groom during the marriage ceremony in talmudic times. The original meaning of the word *chupa* is "to cover with garlands." During the Middle Ages, when it became customary to hold weddings in the synagogue, the type of *chupa* shown above came into use.

First Under the Chupa

The groom is the first to walk down the aisle and stand under the canopy. There, the rabbi welcomes him with words of prayer, after which the groom waits to receive his bride. When the bride arrives, she is positioned to the groom's right side, the favored side in Jewish tradition.

Chupa Under the Stars

Holding an outdoor evening wedding ceremony, with the couple standing under the *chupa,* has long been popular among ultra-Orthodox segments of the Jewish community. To them, this is a way of expressing the hope that the offspring of the young couple will be as numerous as the stars in the heavens.

Carrying Lighted Candles

Among Jews of the first century, the bride was received by bridesmaids carrying torches, light being a symbol of purity. In later times, friends of the groom carried candles as they escorted him. The use of candles has been interpreted as a reminder of the lightning that pierced the heavens on Mount Sinai when God (the groom) accepted Israel (the bride).

A Minyan at a Marriage

In talmudic times the presence at weddings of a quorum of ten men (minyan) was not required. The requirement was instituted in the eighth century, when it was felt that a minyan would lend dignity to the occasion. While it is desirable to have a minyan present at a wedding today, if less than a quorum is available, the marriage is still considered valid.

Double Weddings

So as to avoid the possibility of detracting from each other's joyous celebration, it is customary for siblings not to hold weddings on the same day. One week usually separates the two ceremonies.

Non-Jewish Bridesmaids and Best Man

Jewish law has no objection to a non-Jew serving as a bridesmaid or best man at a Jewish wedding, since these honors are purely social. Nor would there be objection to Jews serving in these capacities at a Christian wedding, provided that the ceremony is held in a chapel from which Christological symbols have been removed.

Circling the Groom

At Orthodox and some Conservative weddings the bride, sometimes alone and sometimes accompanied by her mother or both parents, encircles the groom three times or seven times, depending on local custom. In some communities the bride's mother-in-law and bridesmaids join in the procession.

While many explanations have been offered for this custom, it most likely stems from the old belief that circling a person is a way of protecting him from potentially harmful demons and spirits. Just as soldiers protect a king, so do the bride and her entourage protect her husband. In Jewish tradition, three and seven are lucky numbers, hence the encirclement three or seven times.

The Wedding Ring

The wedding ring that the groom places on the bride's finger represents the sealing of the agreement spelled out in the marriage contract (ketuba). For this reason, the ring must have a value of not less than a peruta, the smallest coin of the realm in ancient Palestine.

Rings With Precious Stones

Since the average bride is a novice at evaluating gems, the Rabbis ruled that the ring the groom places on the bride's finger must be simple, without precious stones. The bride must not be left with the impression that she is receiving something of great value, when that in fact may not be the case. In Reform Judaism the use of any kind of ring is acceptable.

Borrowed Rings

Traditionally, the ring given by the groom to the bride must be his own property, not one borrowed for the occasion.

Ring on Index Finger

The groom places the ring on the index finger of the bride's right hand, the index finger being the most prominent digit. The ring is so placed in order to be visible to the witnesses who signed the ketuba. The groom should be prepared to recite these Hebrew words:

הֲרֵי אַתְּ מְקֻדֶּשֶׁת לִי בְּטַבַּעַת זוּ כְּדַת מֹשֶׁה וְיִשְׂרָאֵל.

Haray at mekudeshet li be-tabaat zu ke-dat Moshe ve-Yisrael.

Behold, you are consecrated unto me with this ring in accordance with the laws of Moses and Israel.

With this declaration, which is referred to as *Kiddushin,* meaning "sanctification," the marriage is official and binding.

Double-ring Ceremony

In recent years it has become customary for the bride to place a ring on the finger of the groom during the marriage ceremony. Although some object to this practice on the ground that it is not traditional or that it might appear as if the bride were returning the ring given to her by the groom, there is no legal basis for its prohibition.

When a double-ring ceremony is conducted, the bride places the ring on one of the groom's fingers but does not (except in the Reform tradition) utter the same words used by the groom, since he alone is *obligated* to give his mate a ring and to make a legal declaration to that effect. In many cases the bride will simply say, "Behold, you are consecrated unto me with this ring," to which she may also add some personal words.

Summary of
WHAT TO EXPECT AT A WEDDING CEREMONY

- The groom and his escorts (usually his parents, but sometimes his father and father-in-law or others who may have been designated) walk down the aisle and stand under the canopy. The groom faces the rabbi (and cantor if one is present), making room for the bride, who will later stand to his right.
- The officiating clergy welcome the groom with one or more appropriate prayers.
- The groomsmen, bridesmaids, and others in the wedding party proceed down the aisle and occupy their places.
- The bride and her escorts (usually her parents, but sometimes her mother and mother-in-law or others who may have been

designated) proceed down the aisle to the canopy. The bride positions herself to the right of the groom.

An American custom followed in many Jewish ceremonies is for the father alone to escort the bride. They stop a few feet from the canopy, and the groom comes down to escort his bride to her place under the canopy.

- All escorts station themselves under the canopy or around its perimeter.
- At this point, at some Orthodox weddings and occasionally at Conservative ones, the bride, accompanied by her mother (and sometimes by her mother-in-law as well), encircles the groom seven times.
- One of the clergy raises a goblet of wine and pronounces the prayer over wine followed by the *Erusin* blessing.
- The rabbi hands the cup of wine to the groom, who sips some of the wine and then lifts the cup to the lips of the bride, who also tastes the wine. The maid of honor usually raises the bride's veil.
- At some ceremonies the rabbi hands the wine to the father of the groom, who lifts the cup to his son's lips. The wine is then handed to the groom's mother, who brings the cup to the bride's lips so that she may drink from it.
- The rabbi may read a prayer or deliver a brief message at this point, although some rabbis do so later in the ceremony.
- The bridegroom now places the marriage band on the forefinger of the bride's right hand. The ring will reach only to the finger's second joint, and the bride keeps it in that position until the ceremony is over.
- The marriage declaration is pronounced at this point (see page 59). The bridegroom should learn the Hebrew and English in advance so that he can recite the declaration without the assistance of the rabbi.
- In many ceremonies today, the bride also places a ring on one of the groom's fingers. She recites the same words used by the groom, usually omitting the last phrase, "according to the laws of Moses and Israel," since it is not a requirement that the bride give the groom a ring.
- At this point couples occasionally choose to make statements or vows that they have composed.

- The Jewish marriage contract, the *ketuba*, is read aloud by the rabbi. After the reading he hands it to the groom, who hands it to his bride with the understanding that she keep it in her possession from that day on.
- At Reform weddings a simple Certificate of Marriage is used in place of the *ketuba*.
- The cantor or rabbi raises a second cup of wine and chants the seven concluding blessings, known in Hebrew as the *Sheva Berachot* (see pages 53 to 55).
- The groom and then the bride drink from the second cup of wine.
- The ceremony ends, sometimes with a closing prayer and/ or a blessing conferred by the rabbi upon the bride and groom.
- The rabbi places a glass wrapped in paper or cloth on the floor. The groom then crushes the glass with the heel of his foot, and all present shout *Mazal tov!* as the bride and groom kiss.
- All those under the canopy proceed down the aisle, the bride and groom going last. At some weddings, during the recessional the bride and groom are showered with rice.
- Among Orthodox and some Conservative Jews, the newlyweds then spend time alone in a private room. If they have fasted during the day, as many Orthodox and some Conservative couples do, they break their fast at this time. The custom is called *Yichud* in Hebrew, meaning "union, joining, togetherness."

REMARRIAGES

Remarriage Without a Get

A Jewish divorce *(get)* is valid only after a civil decree has been obtained. Jewish law forbids remarriage without first obtaining a *get*, a ruling by which Reform Jews do not abide.

Remarrying a Divorced Wife

A man may not remarry a woman whom he had once divorced if she had later been married to another man.

Remarriage of an Apostate's Wife

A Jew who has defected and has joined another religion is still considered a Jew under Jewish law. If he divorces his Jewish wife in a civil action, she is not free to marry unless he issues her a Jewish *get* (divorce). If he refuses to grant her a *get*, she may not remarry.

Remarriage of a Pregnant Woman

A pregnant woman who becomes widowed or divorced may not remarry before giving birth.

Remarriage of a Widow

A woman must wait ninety days after the death of her husband before remarrying. This regulation was established in order to avoid any dispute concerning the paternity of a child who might be born to a woman in the months immediately following her husband's death. In cases where the woman could not possibly be pregnant (if she is in her post-menstrual period), she may marry immediately after *Shiva*.

Remarriage of a Widower

A widower is not permitted to remarry until three festivals have elapsed after the death of his wife. (In this regard, only Pesach, Sukkot, and Shavuot are considered festivals. Rosh Hashana, Yom Kippur, and Shemini Atzeret, as well as minor holidays such as Chanukah and Purim, are not considered festivals.) However, if a widower has small children and no one to care for them, he may remarry after thirty days *(Sheloshim)*.

Deserted Women

In Jewish law, the following women are considered *agunot* (singular, *aguna*), meaning "deserted ones":

- a woman whose husband has disappeared and it has not been established whether he is living or dead
- a woman who has been divorced civilly but whose husband has refused to grant her a Jewish divorce *(get).*

These women are considered to be in limbo, for they cannot remarry without a *get.* Many proposals have been set forth by Jewish authorities to alleviate the condition of the *aguna,* but rabbinical authorities have not agreed on how to modify the law.

DIVORCE PROCEEDINGS

Civil and Jewish Divorce

Just as a Jewish marriage cannot be formalized unless a marriage license is first obtained from the State, it cannot be abrogated (by issuing a *get*) without first obtaining a divorce decree from the State.

Initiator of a Divorce

In Jewish law a man can divorce his wife by delivering into her hands a Jewish divorce *(get* in Hebrew), but a wife does not have the right to initiate such an action.

Writing the Get

The writing of a *get* is done by a Jewish scribe *(sofer).* A rabbinic court of three rabbis is convened. Also present are the scribe, two witnesses, the husband, and sometimes the wife. After a last-minute effort to effect a reconciliation, the scribe writes the *get* on a piece of parchment. In twelve lines, the provisions of the divorce are spelled out. The document is then attested to by witnesses, and the husband hands it to his wife if she is present.

Tearing the Get

After the writing of a *get* has been completed, a tear is made in it to assure that it will not be used in the future for other divorce proceedings (by erasing the script and reusing the parchment).

Delivering the Get

The husband must hand the *get* to his wife. If she is not present at the proceedings, the husband appoints an agent to deliver it to her. A member of the court of three rabbis or one of the two witnesses sometimes acts as the messenger for the husband.

Filing the Get

The actual handwritten *get* is not kept by the wife. It is kept in the files of the *Bet Din* (court), and in its stead the husband and wife are given official letters stipulating that they are divorced and may remarry.

Reform Practice

Reform rabbis will generally accept a civil divorce as sufficient and will not require the divorced person to have obtained a religious divorce decree before entering a new marriage.

4

Death and Mourning

Introduction

When a loved one dies, mourners (*avelim*; singular, *avel*) usually have little time to decide how to go about notifying relatives and friends, which chapel to use for the funeral service, which rabbi to call upon to officiate at the service, whom to honor as pallbearers, the type of coffin to be ordered, and a host of similar urgent matters. Making these decisions and attending to the many necessary details is very stressful to the immediate family. With this in mind, the first section of this three-part chapter has been designed to provide information that will enable the mourner to handle the difficult questions that arise when death strikes.

Part Two of the chapter deals with home and synagogue observances during the first year of mourning. Particular emphasis is placed on the *Shiva* period, the initial seven days of mourning when, with the exception of Sabbaths and holidays, mourners are cloistered in the home of one of the bereaved.

Some of the restrictive practices of the *Shiva* period are observed throughout the first thirty days of mourning (*Sheloshim*). The formal period of mourning ends one year after death.

The third section focuses on memorializing the deceased: the selection and unveiling of a tombstone, reciting the memorial prayer (*Yizkor*), and observing the anniversary of death (*Yahrzeit*). Virtually all practices in this category are mandated by custom rather than Jewish law.

Variations in practice exist between Orthodox and non-Orthodox Jews and within each of the denominations themselves. There are differences over matters as diverse as the placing of flowers on a grave, the presence of a Priest (*Kohen*) at a funeral, the burial of a suicide in a Jewish cemetery, the covering of mirrors in a house of mourning, and the length of time one should wait before unveiling a tombstone.

PART ONE:

MOMENT OF DEATH TO BURIAL

THE STRESSFUL DAYS

The Onen

From the moment of death until after burial an immediate relative of the deceased is called an *onen,* which means "one who is distressed." Since during this time the *onen* is terribly distraught and is busy making funeral and related arrangements, he is not obligated to observe many of the positive commandments, including reciting particular prayers, donning *tefilin,* sitting in a *sukka,* and being called up for a Torah honor. An *onen* is not counted as part of a *minyan* (quorum).

Body Watchers

As a sign of respect, the body of the deceased is never left unattended from the time of death until burial. A watcher (*shomer*; plural, *shomrim*) is always in attendance and recites selections from the Book of Psalms during this period.

Pouring Water on Floor

Some Orthodox Jews still practice the old custom of placing the body of the deceased on the floor approximately twenty minutes after death. Water is then poured on the floor as a sign to those entering the home that a death has occurred. This practice originated in the Middle Ages, when it was commonly believed that the ghost of the dead hovers about after a death and may be harmful to relatives. Spirits and ghosts, it was thought, cannot cross water.

Embalming Prohibited

Embalming, preserving the remains of the deceased, was once practiced by Jews (see Genesis 50:2, 26, where the embalming of Jacob and Joseph is described) but was abandoned because the Rabbis of the Talmud considered the procedure disrespectful to the deceased. The Rabbis believed that a person's body—including limbs, organs, and blood—should be laid to rest in its natural state. Since the blood was thought to be the very essence of life, it was not to be drained off before burial.

Autopsy Exceptions

In the Jewish tradition any form of bodily mutilation is considered a desecration of the human form and an affront to human dignity. Hence, autopsies are forbidden. Exceptions are permitted in cases where the cause of death must be ascertained for medical or legal reasons. These include homicides, suicides, and deaths caused by accident.

Autopsies to Help the Living

Rabbi Ezekiel Landau, the famous eighteenth-century rabbi

of Prague, ruled that an autopsy may be performed if there is reason to believe that doctors may learn from it how to save a seriously ill patient who is at hand and who is in dire need of help.

Chevra Kadisha

The *Chevra Kadisha*, meaning "Holy Society," consists of members of the Jewish community who devote themselves to the task of preparing the dead for burial. Their primary function is to wash the body thoroughly from head to toe while reciting appropriate prayers. Such preparation of the body is called *Tahara*, meaning "purification."

Avoiding a Chapel Service

Small families as well as families who would like to keep expenses to a minimum may prefer to avoid having a formal chapel service. They can proceed directly to the cemetery and have a rabbi conduct the service at the grave site. It will, however, be necessary to make arrangements with a funeral director to transport the body and to file the proper legal papers with the cemetery officials.

Ashes on Eyelids

Among some Jews it is customary to place ashes on the eyelids of the deceased to symbolize the sentiment expressed in the Book of Genesis (3:19), "For thou are dust, and unto dust thou shalt return."

Honoring Requests of the Deceased

Rabbinic authorities are in agreement that reasonable requests made by the deceased prior to death should be honored. Thus, if the wish that no eulogy be recited has been expressed, that wish must be respected because eulogies are in honor of the dead. However, any request that violates Jewish law may not be carried out.

Viewing the Remains

Jewish tradition considers it disrespectful to view the body of the deceased after it has been placed in the coffin. Viewing by a family member before the funeral service begins, for the purpose of identification, is considered proper.

THE RENDING OF GARMENTS

The Keria Procedure

The rending of garments, called *keria* in Hebrew, is an expression of grief. The first recorded instance of a garment being torn following the death of a family member is in the Book of Genesis (37:34). There, we are told, when Jacob learned that his son Joseph had been killed, he immediately tore his garment. David (II Samuel 1:11) did likewise when he learned of the death of Saul and Jonathan. And in the Book of Job (1:20), Job also tore his garment when he learned of the death of his children.

The rent garment (or ribbon, see below) is worn during the entire week of mourning except for the Sabbath. A garment torn in mourning for parents is never mended, but one rent for other relatives may be basted after *Shiva* and completely sewn after *Sheloshim*.

Time of Keria

Most Ashkenazim follow the practice of tearing the garment either in the funeral chapel before the service or at the cemetery before burial. Most Sephardim perform *keria* at home after the funeral.

Reform Keria Practices

In the middle of the nineteenth century, Rabbi Isaac Mayer Wise, the prominent American leader of Reform Judaism, and his followers discouraged the rite of rending one's garment as a sign of mourning. As support for their position, they cited a verse from the prophet Joel (11:13): "Tear your hearts and not your garments."

In recent years Reform rabbis have reintroduced the *keria* ceremony, and the blessing appears in the *Rabbi's Manual* of the Central Conference of American Rabbis. *Gates of Mitzvah,* a Reform guide, indicates that the choice of rending the garment or cutting a black ribbon "is left to the discretion of the family and rabbi."

Keria for Parents and Close Relatives

For parents the garment is torn on the left side, the side closest to the heart. For all other immediate relatives (spouse, son, daughter, brother, sister) the right side of the garment is torn. Today, non-Orthodox and some Orthodox Jews allow a ribbon to be attached to the garment, and this is cut with a knife. Orthodox observance demands that the garment itself be torn by hand, especially in the case of the death of a parent. The cut is started with a knife.

Sons-in-law and Daughters-in-law

Sons-in-law and daughters-in-law are not required to rend their garments or sit *Shiva,* but they may do so if their own parents do not object.

Keria by Newlyweds

If newlyweds learn of the death of a member of the immediate family within the first seven days after their wedding, they wait until the week is over before performing *keria* and sitting *Shiva.*

Keria for Infants

Keria is not performed for a child who has lived less than thirty days.

Obligation of Young Children

Boys under the age of thirteen and girls under the age of twelve are not obligated to rend a garment, but most authorities recommend that *keria* be performed on minors if they are aware of their loss.

Summary of
WHAT TO EXPECT AT THE FUNERAL CHAPEL

- About one hour before the service begins, members of the immediate family assemble in an anteroom to receive the condolences of family and friends.
- Unless he has met with members of the family beforehand, the rabbi will do so before the service begins. Family members should be prepared to tell the rabbi the Hebrew name of the deceased and that of the deceased's father. They should also be prepared to tell him something about the deceased so that a proper eulogy can be delivered. It is helpful to provide the rabbi with pertinent facts to use in his eulogy, such as organizations to which the deceased belonged, some of the deceased's unusual accomplishments, and relevant items about his or her relationship to the immediate family.
- A member of the family may be asked by the funeral director to view the body and identify it. (Errors are known to have been made.) Traditionally, the casket is not opened before the service for viewing by the public.
- After all visitors have left the anteroom and are seated in the chapel, the funeral director or rabbi will perform the *keria*, the rending of an outer garment. Do not wear new clothing. The *keria* is done on the left side of the jacket or dress for those who have lost a parent, and on the right side for other members of the immediate family.
- At Orthodox and some Conservative funerals the *actual* garment is torn (after a short cut is made with a knife). At non-Orthodox funerals (and occasionally at Orthodox ones) a black ribbon supplied by the chapel is attached to the right or left side of the garment and it, rather than the garment itself, is cut.
- After he has cut the garment or ribbon of each mourner, the rabbi or funeral director will lead the individual separately in the recitation of the *keria* blessing, or he may perform

keria on all mourners and then lead them as a group in the recitation of the blessing:

בָּרוּךְ אַתָּה יְיָ, אֱלֹהֵינוּ מֶלֶךְ הָעוֹלָם, דַּיַּן הָאֱמֶת.

Baruch ata Adonai, Elohenu melech ha-olam, da'yan ha-emet.

Praised be Thou, O Lord our God, King of the universe, who is a true Judge.

- After *keria* the family enters the chapel and is seated in the first row.
- The funeral service, consisting principally of several psalms, a memorial prayer (*El Malay Rachamim*), and one or more eulogies, is now held. Note that the *Kaddish* is not recited until after the burial.
- When the service is over, the casket is wheeled from the room, preceded or followed by the rabbi or pallbearers. During the recessional the rabbi recites a selection from the Book of Psalms. The immediate family then follows the rabbi outside and follows the hearse to the cemetery.

THE BURIAL

Attendance at the Interment

Among Ashkenazim it is customary for all members of the family to escort the deceased to the cemetery and to be present when the coffin is lowered into the grave. Sephardim follow a variety of practices.

Among Syrian Jews the sons may go to the cemetery for the burial of a mother but not the burial of a father. In Morocco women do not go to the cemetery for burials, but Moroccan Jews in America often do.

Among the Jews of Greece, Turkey, and other Balkan states, until recently women were not permitted to attend a burial, and in some of these Judeo-Spanish communities a father would not be present at a child's interment.

Until recent times the Spanish and Portuguese custom was for women not to be present at the grave site. Those who come to the cemetery wait in the cemetery chapel. In more recent times, depending on the congregation, women wanting to join the male members of the family while the actual burial takes place have been permitted to do so.

A Minyan at Burials

Although a burial service may be held with less than a quorum of ten adults, traditional Jews will not recite the *Kaddish* unless a *minyan* is present. (See page 78 for more on the *Kaddish*.)

Immediate Burial

Jewish law demands that the deceased be buried within twenty-four hours, before sunset on the day of death if at all possible. This does not apply if there are extenuating circumstances, such as the need to wait for close relatives to arrive from distant places. The passage from the Bible generally quoted as the basis for early burial is Deuteronomy 21:23: "You must bury him on the same day [as the death occurred]." All burials must take place within three days.

Burial on the Sabbath and Holidays

Burials may not be conducted on the Sabbath or on the first day of a festival but may be performed on the second day of all festivals as well as on the eighth day of Passover so as to comply with the law that the deceased be buried as soon as possible. Burial is permitted on the Intermediate Days (Chol Ha-moed) of Passover and Sukkot.

Burial of Apostates

Although a Jew who has forsaken Judaism for another faith is still considered a Jew in the eyes of Jewish law and therefore has every legal right to be buried in a Jewish cemetery, burial of apostates in Jewish cemeteries is generally discouraged.

Suicides

The Talmud says that normal burial rites are not accorded those who, in full possession of their mental faculties, deliberately take their own lives. The Rabbis, however, consider most suicides as victims of uncontrollable depression, as individuals not responsible for their actions. Most suicides are therefore accorded full burial rites.

A Widower's First Wife

A widower who had remarried should be buried next to his first wife, especially if he had children with her. The Talmud says that a man's first wife is his true love and that if she dies in his lifetime, it is as catastrophic as if the Temple had been destroyed in his lifetime.

Cremation

Jewish law forbids cremation, for it violates the principle of respect for the dead. The prohibition is based on the biblical concept that the body must revert to its original state and be buried in the earth from which it came (Genesis 3:19).

Reform Judaism does not object to cremation.

Ashes of Cremation

Although Jewish law frowns upon cremation, authoritative bodies such as the Burial Society of the United Synagogue in London (Orthodox) and the Law Committee of the Rabbinical Assembly (Conservative) do permit the ashes of cremation to be buried in a Jewish cemetery. In cases where the ashes are buried in the earth, the family is obligated to observe *Shiva*. If the ashes are kept in an urn or scattered above the earth, the family is not required to observe *Shiva*.

Burial in Shrouds

To promote the democratic ideal that all men and women—rich and poor—are equal, Rabbi Gamliel (first century C.E.) proposed that all Jews be buried in simple garments: shrouds (*tachrichim* in Hebrew) made of inexpensive muslin, cotton, or linen. This practice is followed to this day.

Pocketless White Shrouds

Although not prescribed by law, since the sixteenth century only pocketless white shrouds have been used in Jewish burials, white being a symbol of purity. The absence of pockets emphasizes that the accumulation of wealth is unimportant. Just as we enter life without material possessions, so do we leave it.

Burial in a Kittel

A *kittel* is a white garment similar to a shroud that is worn on Rosh Hashana, Yom Kippur, and at the Passover Seder. A pious person is usually buried in the *kittel* he wore during his lifetime.

Burial With a Talit

It is customary to drape the personal prayershawl *(talit)* of a male deceased over his *kittel* or shroud. However, before burial one of the fringes *(tzitziot)* is cut off to indicate that the deceased is no longer bound by the commandments of the Torah.

Burial of Religious Articles

As an expression of respect, worn-out Torah scrolls as well as sacred books and other religious articles—*mezuza* parchments and *tefilin,* for example—are not to be discarded unceremoniously. They are brought to the cemetery for burial alongside a pious individual.

Caskets

In order to comply with the verse in Genesis (3:19), "For thou art dust, and unto dust shalt thou return," simple wooden boxes (usually pine) held together with wooden pegs rather than nails are used for burial of the Jewish dead. Metal caskets disintegrate slowly, thus interfering with the return of the body to mother earth. Wooden boxes decompose relatively rapidly.

In Jewish tradition, spending an exorbitant amount of money on an elaborate casket is not considered an expression of respect for the dead.

Holes in Caskets

So that bodies will decompose more quickly, holes are drilled in the bottom of caskets. This guarantees that the words of Genesis (3:19), "Unto dust shalt thou return," will be more speedily fulfilled.

Holy Land Earth

Some Jews believe that when the Messiah appears, the dead will be resurrected and will roll underground to the Holy Land to be revived. As a symbol of this belief, some Jews place earth from Israel inside the coffin.

Coffins In Israel

Coffins generally are not used in Israel. The body is completely covered by a thin shroud. The shrouded male body is then draped with a *talit;* the shrouded female body is draped with a special cloth. The shrouded bodies are placed directly in the grave and are covered with earth and stones.

Burial on Reed Mats

In Israel, mats made of woven reeds are often placed on the floor of the grave.

Burial in Kibbutzim

Kibbutzniks bury their dead in coffins. Every kibbutz has its own tradition concerning the type of service conducted at graveside.

Filling the Grave

Once the coffin is lowered into the ground, it is immediately covered with earth. In Orthodox practice the entire grave is filled while the mourners look on. However, in extenuating circumstances—such as when family members are extremely distraught or the hour is late—the family leaves once the coffin itself has been covered with earth.

Among the non-Orthodox the coffin is covered with a small amount of earth in the presence of the mourners; after the service, cemetery personnel fill the grave with the remaining earth.

The Shovel

Using the back side of a shovel, loved ones take turns filling the grave with earth. The back of the shovel is used in order to establish a difference between the ordinary use of a shovel and its use for burying a loved one. When one person is finished shoveling, rather than pass the tool to the next person, he pushes it into the mound of earth beside the grave. Not handing the shovel directly to the next person is explained as a symbolic way of not passing trouble from one person to another.

The First Kaddish

The first time a mourner recites the *Kaddish* for a relative is immediately after the interment. While more often than not modern rabbis lead the mourner in reciting the *regular* mourner's *Kaddish* at this point, some traditional rabbis use a *special* form. In this special form several sentences are added to the first paragraph.

The Special Interment Kaddish

יִתְגַּדַּל וְיִתְקַדַּשׁ שְׁמֵהּ רַבָּא בְּעָלְמָא דְּהוּא עָתִיד
לְאִתְחַדָּתָּא, וּלְאַחֲיָא מֵתַיָּא, וּלְאַסָּקָא לְחַיֵּי עָלְמָא;
וּלְמִבְנֵי קַרְתָּא דִירוּשְׁלֵם, וּלְשַׁכְלֵל הֵיכָלֵהּ בְּגַוַּהּ,
וּלְמֶעֱקַר פּוּלְחָנָא נוּכְרָאָה מֵאַרְעָא, וּלְאָתָבָא
פּוּלְחָנָא דִשְׁמַיָּא לְאַתְרָה, וְיַמְלִיךְ קוּדְשָׁא בְּרִיךְ
הוּא בְּמַלְכוּתֵהּ וִיקָרֵהּ, בְּחַיֵּיכוֹן וּבְיוֹמֵיכוֹן, וּבְחַיֵּי
דְכָל בֵּית יִשְׂרָאֵל, בַּעֲגָלָא וּבִזְמַן קָרִיב, וְאָמְרוּ,
אָמֵן.

Yitgadal ve-yitkadash shemay rabba. Be-alma de-hu atid le-itchadeta, u-le-achya meta'ya, u-le-aska le-cha'yay alma, u-le-mivneh karta di-Yerushlem, u-le-

shachlel he-chaleh be-gava, u-le-me'ekar pulchana nuchra'a me-ara, u-le-atava pulchana di-shema'ya le-atra, ve-yamlich Kudsha Brich Hu be-malchuteh vi-ye-kareh, be-cha'yaychon u-ve-yomaychon, u-ve-cha'yay de-chol bet Yisrael, ba-agala u-vi-zeman kariv, ve-imru, Amen.

Glorified and sanctified be the great name of God in the world which He will create anew, and in which the dead will be revived and ushered into everlasting life. There, Jerusalem and the Temple will be rebuilt, the worship of idols will be eradicated, and true heavenly worship restored to its position of primacy. May this happen within your lifetime and within the lifetime of the whole house of Israel, speedily and soon, and let us say, Amen.

[Continue with the second paragraph of the regular *Mourner's Kaddish (Y'hay shmay rabba)*. See page 90.]

The First Expression of Condolence

Upon the conclusion of the funeral rites at the cemetery, visitors form two rows so that mourners may pass through and receive the first words of condolence from those assembled. Among Ashkenazim the expression used is

הַמָּקוֹם יְנַחֵם אֶתְכֶם בְּתוֹךְ שְׁאָר אֲבֵלֵי צִיוֹן וִירוּשָׁלָיִם.

Ha-Makom ye-nachem etchem be-toch she'ar avelay Tziyon vi-Yerushala'yim.

May the Lord comfort you along with all the mourners of Zion and Jerusalem.

The traditional expression of condolence among Sephardim is

מִן הַשָּׁמַיִם תְּנוּחָמוּ.

Min ha-Shamayim te-nuchamu.

May Heaven comfort you.

Disinterment of Bodies

Generally speaking, unless there are compelling reasons, disinterment of a body is considered an offense to the dead and is forbidden in Jewish law. The custom among Spanish-Portuguese Jews is to announce at the time of burial that the interment taking place is conditional *(al tenai)*, and should it be necessary in the future to disinter the body, the action will not be in violation of Jewish law.

THE PRIESTLY FAMILY

The Kohen and the Dead

Kohanim (singular, *Kohen*), members of the priestly family, are not permitted to come into contact with, or be in close proximity to, the dead. This prohibition dates to ancient times when Priests were obligated to be in a constant state of purity so that they could offer sacrifices in the Temple. The tradition has been retained and, despite the disappearance of the sacrificial system, a *Kohen* does not attend funerals or visit cemeteries unless the deceased is a member of his immediate family.

Waiting Outside the Chapel

Because a *Kohen* is forbidden to be in close proximity to a corpse unless the deceased is a member of his immediate family, the *Kohen* will generally be found waiting outside the chapel at a funeral. When in a cemetery, the *Kohen* will distance himself at least six feet from the grave.

Female Members of a Priestly Family

While male members of a priestly family may not attend funerals or come within six feet of a corpse, female members of such a family are not bound by this rule. The priesthood is transmitted only through the male lineage.

A Rabbi Kohen

An Orthodox rabbi who is a *Kohen* will not accept invitations to officiate at funerals or unveilings unless the deceased is a member of his immediate family. Most non-Orthodox rabbis do not follow this rule.

NON-JEWISH PARTICIPATION

Non-Jewish Pallbearers

Although Jewish law does not prohibit non-Jews from acting as pallbearers, it is traditional for only family members and close Jewish friends to carry the deceased to his final resting place.

Non-Jewish Funeral Parlors

If there are no Jewish funeral parlors in a city, the services of a non-Jewish undertaker knowledgeable in the requirements of Jewish law may be used. A rabbi may officiate if all Christological symbols are removed from the funeral parlor chapel.

Burial of a Non-Jewish Spouse in a Jewish Cemetery

Although there have been exceptions, the Orthodox view is that a non-Jewish spouse may not be buried in a Jewish cemetery. Conservative Judaism is in agreement but makes an exception in cases where the non-Jewish partner identified positively with the Jewish religion and community during the course of the marriage. The Reform attitude is that close non-Jewish relatives may be buried in the family plot in a Jewish cemetery.

Floral Displays

In ancient times flowers and fragrant spices were used at funerals to counteract the offensive smell of a decaying body. Since this practice is of non-Jewish origin and of no practical value in our time, sending floral gifts to adorn the casket is sometimes discouraged. Nevertheless, if flowers are sent to mourners, they are generally accepted.

The placement of flowers on graves is more acceptable in Israel than in the Diaspora. In fact, floral shops and stands are found near cemeteries in Israel.

Summary of
WHAT TO EXPECT AT THE CEMETERY

- Upon arrival of the cortege at the cemetery, the funeral director presents to the cemetery officials the legal documents required before the burial can take place.
- The hearse, followed by the mourners in their cars, then proceeds to the burial plot.
- The coffin is removed from the hearse, and the pallbearers, followed by the rabbi and the mourners, proceed slowly to the open grave.
- During the procession, Psalm 91 and the *Tziduk Ha-din* prayer are read by the rabbi. The *Tziduk Ha-din* offers justification for God's edict. During the procession the rabbi sometimes pauses seven times. These stops are said to be reminders of the vanity of life. (The word "vanity [*hevel*]" appears seven times in the Book of Ecclesiastes.)
- After the coffin is lowered into the ground, it is traditional for individual mourners to drop a few spadefuls of earth onto the coffin.
- Depending on local practice, the grave is completely filled with earth at this time, or it is partially filled and then draped with a blanket of simulated grass. The Orthodox tradition is to fill the grave completely.
- The rabbi then recites one or two Psalms, after which the memorial prayer *El Malay Rachamim* is recited or chanted by the rabbi or cantor.
- The mourners then recite the *Mourner's Kaddish* for the

first time (see page 90). The ceremony may end at this point, or the rabbi may conclude with a benediction.

- The assembly forms two lines on either side of the walkway. As the immediate family passes through, the assembly recites the appropriate expression of condolence. See page 79.
- As all leave the cemetery, they wash their hands at the spigot provided near the exit of the cemetery. The cup that is used is not passed directly from person to person; this is explained as a symbolic way of not passing trouble from one individual to another. If handwashing is not done at this point, the hands are washed before reentering the house of mourning.
- The immediate family assembles at the home of the deceased (or the home of some other family member), and the observance of *Shiva* begins.

PART TWO:

OBSERVANCES DURING THE FIRST YEAR OF MOURNING

RETURN FROM THE CEMETERY

Washing the Hands

If the hands were not washed upon exiting the cemetery, they should be washed before entering the house where *Shiva* is to be observed. The custom is connected with the ancient practice of purifying oneself through washing after being in close proximity to the dead.

Sitting Shiva

Upon returning from the cemetery, all immediate family

members proceed to observe seven days of mourning, popularly known by the Hebrew name *Shiva*, meaning "seven." In Jewish law the immediate family includes father and mother, brother and sister, son and daughter, and spouse.

Origin of Shiva

The earliest reference to an initial mourning period of seven days is found in the Bible (Genesis 50:10), where we are told that Joseph mourned for his father, Jacob, for seven days.

How the Days of Shiva Are Counted

In Jewish tradition the day starts at sundown and ends twenty-four hours later, at nightfall. This is based on the wording of verse 5 in the first chapter of Genesis, where it says, at the conclusion of the first day of Creation, "And there was evening and there was morning, a first day."

In Jewish law part of a day is equal to a full day. Therefore, if a mourner sits *Shiva* for as little as an hour before dark on the day of the burial, he is considered to have completed the first day of the seven-day mourning period. *Shiva* ends on the morning of the seventh day. (See page 94 for more on the last day of *Shiva*.)

Note that although the Sabbath is counted as one of the seven days of *Shiva,* the mourning rites are not observed on that day (see page 93).

Curtailment of Shiva

If a family has started sitting *Shiva* and one of the major holidays (Rosh Hashana, Yom Kippur, Passover, Shavuot, or Sukkot) intervenes, the *Shiva* period is immediately cancelled with the advent of the holiday, and the *Shiva* process does not continue after the holiday. Sitting even a few minutes before the holiday begins is considered as having sat for the full seven days.

Shiva After Cremation

Although cremation is an action not sanctioned by Jewish law, if the ashes of cremation were buried in the earth, the family is required to sit *Shiva*. (See page 75 for more on cremation.)

Shiva for Apostates

Although the ruling in the Talmud is that a Jew is a Jew forever and that even if a Jew abandons his religion in favor of another faith, he is still a Jew, the sixteenth-century *Code of Jewish Law* declares that one should not sit *Shiva* for an apostate.

Converts and Shiva

There is a difference of opinion among authorities as to whether a convert should or may sit *Shiva* for non-Jewish parents. See page 36.

Minors and Shiva

Boys under the age of thirteen and girls under the age of twelve are not obligated to sit *Shiva*. They may, however, do so if they wish.

Newlyweds and Shiva

If a bride or groom learns of the death of a close relative during the honeymoon period, he or she does not begin mourning until after returning from the honeymoon, at which time the tearing of the garment *(keria)* is done and the seven-day mourning period *(Shiva)* begins.

Delayed News

If a person learns of a death in the family after the burial has taken place, he or she begins to observe all the laws and practices of mourning from the moment of hearing the news. However, if the family is still sitting *Shiva*, the mourner may join them and conclude *Shiva* with them.

Thirty-day Delay

If a person learns of a death in the family thirty days or more after the day of death, *Shiva* is observed for only one hour. The mourner is required only to remove his or her shoes, sit on a low seat, and recite the *Baruch Da'yan Emet* blessing (page 73).

Meal of Condolence

It is an old tradition for neighbors to prepare a meal for mourners who are returning from burying their dead. Neighbors who fail to do this are considered insensitive to grief felt by a fellow human. The first meal after returning from the funeral is called *Se'udat Havra'a,* "Meal of Condolence" or "Meal of Healing."

Meal of Condolence Menu

The menu of the Meal of Condolence is very simple. It includes round rolls, bagels, and eggs—all symbolizing the unending cycle of life. Among some Sephardim the basic fare of a Meal of Condolence is eggs, olives, and bread, which the mourners eat while seated on the floor.

Wine for Mourners

In the Ashkenazic tradition, mourners are given a cup of wine (or a shot of hard liquor) to drink upon their return from the cemetery. This practice has been attributed to an interpretation of Proverbs 31:6, which implies that wine was created specifically for the purpose of comforting mourners. Syrians and other Sephardim abstain from drinking wine during *Shiva* because wine is associated with joyous occasions, and most abstain from meat for the same reason.

Casual Greetings

Tradition demands that, in greeting mourners during the *Shiva* period, use of such expressions as "Hello," "Good morning," and "How are you?" be avoided. Casual, everyday greetings of this type are considered inappropriate during this stressful mourning period.

Telephone Condolences

It is considered improper to make a condolence "call" via telephone unless it is absolutely unavoidable. Grief is best ameliorated by the personal touch.

Expressing Sympathy

Traditional Jews do not use the everyday expressions of farewell when leaving a house of mourning after a *Shiva* call. The same condolence expressions used after the cemetery service are used when leaving the house of mourning. See page 79.

Comforting Mourners

The proper time to make a condolence call is after the first two days of mourning. The Rabbis of the Talmud advised, "Do not comfort a mourner while his deceased relative is still before him." During the first two days of mourning, grief is most intense and therefore, except for the very closest of friends, visitors should wait until the third day before making a condolence call.

HOME AND SYNAGOGUE OBSERVANCES

Memorial Candles

A memorial lamp or a candle is kept burning in the house of mourning during the first week (*Shiva* period). The flame represents the soul, which is believed to ascend to the heavenly spheres. This custom was first mentioned in Jewish literature of the thirteenth century. Today, some Sephardim keep a memorial lamp or candle burning for the entire first year of mourning.

Covering Mirrors in Shiva Home

Immediately after a death, observant Jews cover mirrors in the home where the deceased lies. They also cover mirrors in homes where *Shiva* is observed. The regulation was introduced so that mourners will not be tempted to pay attention to appearance at this tragic moment in the life of a family. In some homes a cloth is spread over the mirrors; in others sudsy water is applied to cloud them over; and in still others mirrors are turned around or removed completely.

Reform Jews generally do not adhere to this ritual.

Low Stools

In talmudic times it was customary for mourners to sit on inverted beds during the week of *Shiva*. This practice fell into disuse, and for many centuries the practice among Ashkenazim has been to sit on low stools. Most Sephardim sit on the floor, sometimes on a small pillow. Reform Jews do not adhere to this ritual.

Shiva Footwear

Mourners in observant homes do not wear leather shoes during the first week of mourning, for such footwear is a sign of comfort and luxury. More appropriately, mourners wear plain slippers.

Haircutting and Shaving

Although at one time cutting one's hair and shaving were forbidden during the entire first thirty days of mourning *(Sheloshim)*, the prohibition has been eased in modern times and applies only to *Shiva*, the first week of mourning.

Torah Honors

During the week of *Shiva,* mourners are not called to the Torah. The Torah blessings contain sentiments of joy that are not consonant with the inner feelings of grief and sadness being experienced.

Torah in House of Mourning

A Torah scroll may be borrowed from a synagogue and be brought into a house of mourning if it is to be read on three separate occasions: Monday, Thursday, and Sabbath morning or Sabbath afternoon. It must remain there throughout the week, for it is considered disrespectful to transport a Torah to and from the synagogue for each reading. Some Sephardim, particularly Syrians, do not bring a Torah into a house of mourning under any circumstances.

Synagogue Seating of Mourners

Mourners do not occupy their customary synagogue seats during the mourning period. New seats are selected and occupied during the first twelve months of mourning for parents and during the first thirty days of mourning for other close relatives.

Working During Shiva

Going to work or engaging in business during the *Shiva* period is forbidden, but exceptions are made where a person's livelihood is at stake. In such cases a person may leave his home for such purposes on the third day of mourning.

THE KADDISH

Essence of the Kaddish

The *Kaddish* makes no reference to death, and the basic reason for its recitation is to enable mourners to express their faith in God despite their grievous loss. The *Kaddish* prayer is primarily an echo of the sentiment expressed in the Book of Job: "Though He [God] slay me, I will trust in Him."

Recitation of Kaddish

Kaddish—the mourner's prayer—which begins with the Hebrew word *yitgadal,* meaning "may He [God] be glorified," is recited for the first year (which is actually eleven months, as explained on page 95) after the loss of a parent and for thirty days after the loss of a brother, sister, son, daughter, or spouse.

Among Ashkenazic Jews all sons (and often daughters) recite the *Kaddish* for a parent during the first year of mourning. Among some Sephardim, particularly Moroccans, only the first-born and youngest son in a family are obligated to recite *Kaddish* for a parent during the first year. Subsequently, when observing *Yahrzeit,* it is obligatory upon all sons to say *Kaddish.*

A Minyan for Kaddish

Wherever possible, a quorum of ten adults (minyan) assembles in the house of mourning for morning and evening services so that the Kaddish may be recited. (Kaddish may not be recited without a minyan.) When assembling a minyan in the house of mourning is not feasible, mourners are permitted to attend services in a synagogue.

Orthodox and many Conservative congregations count only men over thirteen years of age to a minyan. Reform, Reconstructionist, and some Conservative congregations count women of post-Bat Mitzva age to the quorum of ten.

Mourner's Kaddish

יִתְגַּדַּל וְיִתְקַדַּשׁ שְׁמֵהּ רַבָּא בְּעָלְמָא דִי בְרָא
כִרְעוּתֵהּ, וְיַמְלִיךְ מַלְכוּתֵהּ בְּחַיֵּיכוֹן וּבְיוֹמֵיכוֹן
וּבְחַיֵּי דְכָל בֵּית יִשְׂרָאֵל בַּעֲגָלָא וּבִזְמַן קָרִיב,
וְאִמְרוּ, אָמֵן.

יְהֵא שְׁמֵהּ רַבָּא מְבָרַךְ לְעָלַם וּלְעָלְמֵי עָלְמַיָּא.

יִתְבָּרַךְ וְיִשְׁתַּבַּח, וְיִתְפָּאַר וְיִתְרֹמַם, וְיִתְנַשֵּׂא
וְיִתְהַדָּר, וְיִתְעַלֶּה וְיִתְהַלַּל שְׁמֵהּ דְּקֻדְשָׁא, בְּרִיךְ
הוּא, לְעֵלָּא (וּלְעֵלָּא) מִן כָּל בִּרְכָתָא וְשִׁירָתָא
תֻּשְׁבְּחָתָא וְנֶחֱמָתָא, דַּאֲמִירָן בְּעָלְמָא, וְאִמְרוּ אָמֵן.

יְהֵא שְׁלָמָא רַבָּא מִן שְׁמַיָּא, וְחַיִּים עָלֵינוּ וְעַל כָּל
יִשְׂרָאֵל, וְאִמְרוּ, אָמֵן.

עֹשֶׂה שָׁלוֹם בִּמְרוֹמָיו, הוּא יַעֲשֶׂה שָׁלוֹם עָלֵינוּ
וְעַל כָּל יִשְׂרָאֵל, וְאִמְרוּ, אָמֵן.

Yit-gadal ve-yit-kadash shmay rabba be-olma di-vera chiru-tay. Ve-yamlich malchutay be-cha'yaychon u-ve-yomaychon u-ve-cha'yay de-chol bet Yisrael ba-agala u-vi-zeman kariv, ve-imru, Amen.

Ye-hay shmay rabba me-vorach le-olam u-le-olmay olma'ya.

Yit-barach ve-yishtabach, ve-yit-pa'ar ve-yit-romam, ve-yit-nasay ve-yit-hadar, ve-yit-aleh ve-yit-halal shmay de-kudesha, b'rich Hu. Le-ayla min kol birchata ve-shirata tushbechata ve-nechemata, da-amiran be-olma, ve-imru, Amen.

Y'hay shelama rabba min she-ma'ya ve-cha'yim alenu ve-al kol Yisrael, ve-imru, Amen.

Oseh shalom bi-meromav, Hu ya'aseh shalom alenu ve-al kol Yisrael, ve-imru, Amen.

Glorified and sanctified be God's great name throughout the world, which He has created according to His will. May He establish His kingdom within your lifetime and within the lifetime of the whole house of Israel, and let us say, Amen.

May His great name be a blessing unto all eternity.

Exalted and praised, glorified and adored, extolled and revered be the name of the Holy One, blessed be He, and let us say, Amen.

May life and peace descend from heaven upon us and all Israel, and let us say, Amen.

May the Creator of heavenly peace bestow peace upon us and all Israel, and let us say, Amen.

Language of the Kaddish

For nearly a thousand years—from the time of Ezra in the fifth century B.C.E. until the Talmud was finalized in the fifth century C.E.—the vernacular of the Jewish people was Aramaic. The *Kaddish* was therefore written in Aramaic, the everyday, spoken language of the masses.

Women and Kaddish

Jewish law does not require women to recite the *Kaddish,* but today female mourners in Conservative, Reform, and some

Orthodox congregations stand to recite *Kaddish* along with the men.

Kaddish for Minors

Authorities are not agreed on how long the deceased must have lived for *Kaddish* to be recited for him or her. Some believe the age should be twenty while others believe *Kaddish* should be recited even for infants who have lived for one month. Each locality has its own custom.

Kaddish for Adoptive Parents

An adopted child is required to recite *Kaddish* for his adoptive parents, just as he would have done for his natural parents. Some authorities require this only when the deceased has no natural sons who will be saying *Kaddish* for him.

Kaddish for an Apostate Father

There is a difference of opinion among authorities as to whether the child of apostate parents may recite *Kaddish* for such parents. The consensus is that the commandment to honor one's father and mother (Exodus 20:12) must be obeyed under all circumstances.

Kaddish for a Convert's Parents

Authorities do not agree on whether a convert should or is permitted to say *Kaddish* for his or her parents. See page 36 for the opposing views.

The Aleph Bet Psalm

Psalm 119, the longest chapter in the Bible, consists of twenty-two sections of eight verses each, a total of 176 verses. Each group of eight starts with a different letter of the Hebrew alphabet, beginning with *aleph* and ending with *tav*.

Psalm 119 is a paean expressing man's loyalty to the Torah and his acceptance of it as a source of salvation. To memorialize the dead, Sephardim use this psalm often in their prayers, selecting verses and putting them in a sequence so that the first Hebrew letter of each verse spells out the name of the deceased.

Syrians read verses from Psalm 119 when they visit the cemetery after *Shiva* and after *Sheloshim.*

Moroccans read verses when important persons are being prepared for burial (during the *Tahara*) and also during the unveiling ceremony.

Memorial Prayers

Among Ashkenazim the most popular memorial prayer is the *El Malay Rachamim,* meaning "God of Mercy." The prayer is recited at the chapel funeral service and again when the body is interred. It is also recited when the grave of a loved one is visited and in the synagogue when *Yizkor* is recited or when an individual is memorialized.

Sephardim use a similar prayer, known as *Hashkaba,* meaning "Rest in Peace." The version used for males begins with the words *Tov shem mi-shemen tov,* "A good name is more precious than the choicest oil." For women the prayer opens with the words of Proverbs 31: *Eshet cha'yil mi yimtza?,* "A woman of valor who can find?"

MOURNING AND THE SABBATH

No Mourning on Sabbath

The Sabbath is a day of delight (Isaiah 58:13), and all outer expressions of grief (sitting on a low stool, wearing a rent garment, and so on) are discontinued on that day. The *Shiva* period resumes on Saturday night after evening prayers have been recited. Although mourning rites are suspended on the Sabbath, it is nevertheless counted as one of the seven days of mourning.

Sabbath Services During Shiva

On the Sabbath, mourners are permitted to leave their homes to visit a synagogue. They are not awarded Torah honors *(aliyot),* but should accept one if proffered. A mourner may not officiate as cantor.

THE END OF SHIVA

Last Day of Shiva

Just as sitting *Shiva* for as little as an hour on the first day (after the funeral) is the equivalent of sitting for a whole day, so sitting for one hour after the morning service (or the hour when the morning service would normally be held) on the last (seventh) day is considered the equivalent of sitting for a full day. (See page 84 for the rationale.)

When Sabbath Is the Last Shiva Day

Should the seventh day of mourning be a Sabbath, *Shiva* ends an hour or so before sundown on Friday, allowing mourners sufficient time to prepare for the Sabbath.

The Shiva Walk

It is customary to conclude the *Shiva* period on the seventh day of mourning by walking around the block or for some short distance immediately after the morning service, an activity symbolizing the mourner's return to the real world.

POST-SHIVA PERIOD

Holidays Reduce the Mourning Period

If a major holiday falls during the *Shiva* period, the remaining days of *Shiva* are cancelled. If a mourner sits *Shiva* for even a few moments before a holiday begins, it is considered as if he had sat for the full week and needs not continue to sit *Shiva* after the holiday is over.

Restricted Activity for Thirty Days

Some of the restrictions that prevail during the first week of mourning continue in force for the entire first month (Sheloshim). These prohibitions include getting married; getting one's hair cut; wearing new garments; and attending parties, weddings, dances, or other joyous celebrations. Listening to music on radio and television are included in the ban, although some Orthodox authorities permit listening to mood music that has a soothing effect or watching television performances that are serious and thought-provoking.

The mourning period for all relatives except parents ends after thirty days.

When a Holiday Cancels Sheloshim

If the full seven days of mourning (Shiva) have been observed and soon thereafter one of the five major holidays (Rosh Hashana, Yom Kippur, Sukkot, Passover, and Shavuot) occurs, the restrictions pertaining to Sheloshim are completely cancelled.

Twelve-month Mourning Period

The Talmud stipulates that the mourning period for parents should be twelve months. In the sixteenth-century, however, legal authority Rabbi Moses Isserles ruled that Kaddish should be recited for only eleven months. This was based on the belief, prevalent in talmudic times, that the wicked are consigned to hell (gehenna) and are subject to punishment for a maximum of twelve months. To avoid the possibility of people thinking that the parent for whom Kaddish was being recited (for a twelve-month period) was wicked, Isserles reduced the requirement for the recital of the Kaddish for parents to eleven months. By ruling that Kaddish for a parent should not be recited for more than eleven months, Rabbi Isserles was removing all possibility of ascribing wickedness to the parent. Even when the Jewish year has thirteen months, as in leap years, Kaddish, according to Isserles, should be recited only for eleven months.

Most Jews follow the ruling of Isserles.

PART THREE:
MEMORIALIZING
THE DECEASED

ERECTING A TOMBSTONE

The First Tombstone

The erection of a tombstone for the deceased dates back to biblical times when Jacob "set up a pillar" on the grave of his wife Rachel, who had died on the road to Bethlehem (Genesis 35:20). While it has become traditional for Jews to memorialize their dead in this manner, it is not mandated in Jewish law.

Two Views on Monuments

The second-century C.E. Rabbi Simeon ben Gamaliel said: "We need not erect monuments for the righteous; their good deeds are their memorials." But the thirteenth-century Spanish authority Rabbi Solomon Adret believed that erecting a monument was a worthy way of honoring the dead, and this practice became normative in Judaism.

When to Erect a Tombstone

It is wise to allow sufficient time for the earth that had been dug up at the burial site to settle before setting the heavy tombstone upon it. Among many Sephardim, a monument is erected as soon as possible after *Shiva*, but Ashkenazim generally wait from six to twelve months. In Israel, a tombstone is generally erected before the first thirty days *(Sheloshim)* of mourning have ended.

Inscriptions on Tombstones

Generally, the Hebrew and English names of the deceased are inscribed on the stone, along with the dates of birth and death. Sometimes a brief, loving sentiment is added.

Before the monument is transported to the cemetery, it is advisable to make sure that no errors in spelling or dates have been made.

Tombstone Inscriptions in Israel

Generally, only Hebrew inscriptions are permitted on the face of tombstones in Israel. However, in more liberal localities, such as Holon, inscriptions in foreign languages do appear on the obverse side of monuments.

Symbols on Tombstones

Symbolic engravings on tombstones are found most often on graves of a *Kohen* or *Levi*. The symbol of the *Kohen* is outstretched palms, for that was the gesture used when the *Kohen* blessed the people in ancient times. The symbol generally used on the tombstone of a *Levi* is a pitcher; it is with this type of container that he poured water on the hands of Priests before they pronounced the priestly blessings in Temple times. (This ceremony is still practiced today in Orthodox synagogues.)

Photos on Tombstones

Although placing a photograph of the deceased on a tombstone is not prohibited in Jewish law, it is discouraged as being in poor taste and out of place in a cemetery.

Pebbles on Tombstones

A popular symbolic act is the placing of small stones on top of a tombstone after having visited a grave. This serves as notice that the deceased has not been forgotten by relatives and friends. Some express this same sentiment by depositing a clump of grass on the monument.

THE UNVEILING

Origin and Purpose of Unveilings

Although monuments have been erected over graves for many centuries, the custom of conducting a special ceremony at which the tombstone is unveiled to friends and loved ones is relatively new. The practice was instituted toward the end of the nineteenth century both in England and the United States in order to formalize and dignify the erection of the monument. Americans refer to the ceremony as an "unveiling," whereas the British call it the "tombstone consecration."

Religious Significance

There is no religious obligation to hold a formal unveiling ceremony, and many families prefer an informal visit and private meditation to mark the occasion.

Unveiling Date

Most families wait about one year before holding an unveiling, but the ceremony may be held any time after the monument has been erected.

The Ceremony

A cloth is draped over the monument, and after the recitation of appropriate prayers and selected Psalms a member of the family removes the cloth, thus revealing the inscription on the stone. The leader of the service (who may or may not be a rabbi) reads the inscription and then recites the memorial prayer (*El Malay Rachamim*) and delivers a brief eulogy.

Minyan at Unveilings

In order for *Kaddish* to be recited at an unveiling service it is necessary for a *minyan* to be present. *Kaddish* may not be recited at any service if less than a quorum of ten is present.

Food at Unveilings

Jewish law discourages the serving of food in a cemetery because such activity is considered disrespectful to the deceased. In communities where the practice is acceptable, the food is generally limited to wine and liquor (as well as cookies and cake) to satisfy those who would like to raise a glass of spirits and wish others *le-cha'yim,* "to life."

UNVEILING CHECKLIST

In planning for an unveiling, one should

- visit the firm preparing the monument and check to be sure names and dates are correct.
- be sure the tombstone will be in place before the date set for the ceremony.
- clear the date with the rabbi.
- submit to the rabbi in writing the English and Hebrew names of the deceased and pertinent personal information so that the rabbi can prepare a meaningful eulogy.
- advise the cemetery officials of the exact date and hour of the ceremony.
- send out announcements to family members and friends.
- bring along a cheesecloth (or another kind of covering) and drape it over the wording on the tombstone before the ceremony begins. Cemetery officials will often take care of this if requested.
- try to have a *minyan* present so *Kaddish* can be recited.
- avoid bringing wine, liquor, or refreshments to the cemetery. This is no longer accepted practice.

Grave Visitations

Although grave visitations are permissible at any time, it is common practice among Ashkenazim for mourners to wait a full year, or at least until a tombstone has been erected, before visiting the grave. Some Sephardim make it a practice of visiting the cemetery immediately after *Shiva*, while others wait until *Sheloshim* (thirty days) has passed.

THE YIZKOR SERVICE

Meaning of Yizkor

Yizkor, which means "May He [God] remember," is a service recited in memory of the dead.

Scholars believe that *Yizkor* was introduced as a formal part of the synagogue service during the Crusades of the eleventh century, when many thousands of European Jews were murdered· indiscriminately. It was a way of restoring faith and expressing hope that God would bring relief from suffering.

Objections to Yizkor

The eminent Babylonian scholar of the early eleventh century, Hai Gaon, along with some of his disciples, was opposed to the custom of praying for the dead (reciting *Yizkor* prayers) or donating charity on their behalf on Yom Kippur and festivals. They contended that each person must perform good deeds in his own lifetime and that one cannot be saved through the good deeds of one's parents or relatives.

Sephardic Yizkor Practice

Sephardim today generally subscribe to the view of Hai Gaon (see above) and do not recite *Yizkor.* Since the Holocaust, after the Torah reading on *Yizkor* days, some congregations have introduced the custom of reciting an *El Malay Rachamim* prayer in behalf of the six million martyrs. In recent years, to satisfy members who may also have Ashkenazic antecedents, some congregations have introduced a *Yizkor* service after the formal *Musaf* service has been completed. A special *Yizkor* booklet is distributed, since the traditional Sephardic prayerbook does not include a memorial service.

When Yizkor Is Recited

Originally, *Yizkor* was recited by Ashkenazim only on Yom Kippur, but later it was included in the synagogue service for Shemini Atzeret (the holiday that follows immediately after Sukkot), the last day of Passover, and the second day of Shavuot. It is customary to light a memorial candle in the home or synagogue in observance of *Yizkor*.

Reform Yizkor Days

Most Reform Jews recite *Yizkor* prayers only on Yom Kippur and on the last day of Passover, but some follow the general practice of reciting *Yizkor* on other holidays as well.

Legal Requirement

Unlike *Kaddish,* there is no legal requirement that one recite *Yizkor.* Each person is free to make that decision for himself.

YIZKOR PRAYERS

Yizkor Prayer for a Father

יִזְכֹּר אֱלֹהִים נִשְׁמַת אָבִי מוֹרִי שֶׁהָלַךְ לְעוֹלָמוֹ.
אָנָּא, תְּהִי נַפְשׁוֹ צְרוּרָה בִּצְרוֹר הַחַיִּים, וּתְהִי
מְנוּחָתוֹ כָבוֹד. אָמֵן.

Yizkor Elohim nishmat avi mori she-halach le-olamo. Ana, tehi nafsho tzerura bi-tzeror ha-cha'yim, u-tehi menuchato kavod. Amen.

Heavenly Father: Remember with love the soul of my dear departed father whose life I recall in this solemn hour of remembrance. May his spirit ever abide among us, and may his memory be a blessing as he rests in peace. Amen.

Yizkor Prayer for a Mother

יִזְכֹּר אֱלֹהִים נִשְׁמַת אִמִּי מוֹרָתִי שֶׁהָלְכָה לְעוֹלָמָהּ.
אָנָּא, תְּהִי נַפְשָׁהּ צְרוּרָה בִּצְרוֹר הַחַיִּים, וּתְהִי
מְנוּחָתָהּ כָּבוֹד. אָמֵן.

*Yizkor Elohim nishmat imi morati she-halcha le-olama.
Ana, tehi nafsha tzerura bi-tzeror ha-cha'yim, u-tehi
menuchata kavod. Amen.*

Heavenly Father: Remember with love the soul of my
dear departed mother whose life I recall in this solemn
hour of remembrance. May her spirit ever abide among
us, and may her memory be a blessing as she rests
in peace. Amen.

For Other Relatives

Consult your prayerbook for *Yizkor* for other family members.

Leaving the Synagogue During Yizkor

There is a popular misconception that persons who have
not lost loved ones must leave the synagogue while *Yizkor*
is being recited. To do otherwise, they believe, would be tempt-
ing fate.

Yizkor at Home

Yizkor may be recited at home, but the *Kaddish* prayer must
be omitted, for *Kaddish* may be recited only in the presence
of a *minyan*. Reform Judaism does not require the presence
of a *minyan* for the recitation of *Kaddish*.

Yizkor Before the First Anniversary of a Death

Many Jews are under the impression that it is forbidden
to recite *Yizkor* during the first year after the death of a loved
one, but this belief has no basis in fact. Actually, *Yizkor* may
be recited on the very first holiday after a death.

YAHRZEIT OBSERVANCE

Yahrzeit Origin

The word *Yahrzeit* (in German, *Jahrzeit*), meaning "anniversary," was first used in the writings of the fourteenth-century German scholar Rabbi Jacob Mollin (Maharil) to denote the anniversary of a death. Sephardim use the word *Nachala,* meaning "inheritance," for *Yahrzeit.*

The concept of observing the anniversary of a death as a sign of reverence for the deceased goes back to talmudic times. In Ashkenazic synagogues, particularly among the Orthodox, at the Sabbath service before the *Yahrzeit* date a special memorial prayer known as *El Malay Rachamim* is recited to memorialize the deceased. Sephardim recite a similar prayer, which is called the *Hashkaba.* Some Jews fast to commemorate the day.

Yahrzeit Observance

All Jews observing a *Yahrzeit* for the death of a close relative light a twenty-four-hour memorial candle or lamp in the home and attend synagogue services to recite the *Kaddish.* Sephardim light a memorial candle in the synagogue as well as the home.

Many synagogues have electrified memorial plaques inscribed with the names of loved ones. On the day of *Yahrzeit* a bulb adjacent to the name of the individual is lighted.

Yahrzeit Light Rationale

The custom of lighting a candle or lamp on the anniversary of death dates back to the Middle Ages. Scholars believe that the practice may derive from the Christian custom of lighting votive candles. It is also believed that the flame, which ascends heavenward, encourages the soul to reach higher spheres. This concept is based on the verse in the Book of Proverbs (20:17): "The lifebreath of man is the lamp of the Lord."

Electric Yahrzeit Lamps

Today, for safety reasons, electric lamps are often used

instead of candles, especially by the elderly in hospitals and nursing homes.

Yahrzeit Day

In Jewish law a day begins on the previous evening and extends for twenty-four hours. Therefore, for example, a *Yahrzeit* to be commemorated on the fifteenth of Adar begins after sunset on the fourteenth of Adar, at which time the *Yahrzeit* lamp is lighted.

Under normal circumstance, *Yahrzeit* is observed on the Hebrew date of death. In exceptional cases, such as when the date of burial is more than three days after the date of death, the first *Yahrzeit* is observed on the date of burial, and the subsequent ones on the date of death. If the date of burial is known but the date of death is unknown, *Yahrzeit* is observed on the date of burial.

The First Yahrzeit

In most Ashkenazic and Sephardic communities the first *Yahrzeit* is always observed on the Hebrew date of burial, and in subsequent years on the Hebrew date of death. Moroccans observe *Yahrzeit* on the date of death even in the first year.

Yahrzeit in Leap Years

In the Jewish calendar ordinary years have twelve months and leap years thirteen. The twelfth month of the year is Adar, and the thirteenth month, when added, is called Adar II (Adar the Second). In leap years *Yahrzeit* is always observed in Adar II regardless of whether the actual date of death was in Adar I or Adar II. If a death occurred in Adar II, and the year in which *Yahrzeit* is to be observed has only one Adar, Yahrzeit is observed in Adar I.

Observance for a First Wife

Although it is not forbidden, authorities discourage a man who remarried after the death of a first wife from observing her *Yahrzeit* by reciting *Kaddish* in the synagogue or by lighting a memorial lamp at home, lest his new wife be offended. Jewish law does not discuss the propriety of a woman observing *Yahrzeit* for her first husband.

5
The Foods We Eat

Introduction

The animal foods a Jew may or may not eat are prescribed in the Bible (Leviticus 11 and Deuteronomy 14), and the manner in which they are to be made fit to eat and served is spelled out in various parts of the Talmud and the codes of Jewish law. (No restrictions are placed on nonanimal foods.) The degree to which a Jew adheres to these dietary regulations often is considered indicative of his or her loyalty to traditional Judaism.

The Bible specifies that the following may be consumed: domestic fowl, animals that chew the cud and have split hooves, and fish that have both fins and scales. The Talmud goes one step further and establishes laws pertaining to the manner in which an animal must be slaughtered to be considered kosher. It also details the various facets of the koshering process, for meat is not considered kosher until it has been washed and salted according to prescribed procedure.

Health is not offered in Jewish tradition as a reason for not eating certain foods. The reason given is holiness: to make the Jewish people a holy one with a distinct and separate way of life. Thus, Jewish law mandates that meat and milk not be eaten at the same time, that there be a waiting period between eating meat and dairy, and that separate sets of dishes be used for each.

The Rabbis of the Talmud were not without opinions on nutrition, and this chapter concludes with some of their dietary advice.

THE MEANING OF KOSHER

Kashrut vs. Kosher

The Hebrew word *kashrut* (also pronounced *kashrus*), which means the state of being "ritually correct" or "ritually fit," is a form of the Hebrew word *kasher*. "Kosher" is an Anglicized form of *kasher*.

The Scope of Kashrut

Although when we use the word kosher we think mostly of food products, the concept also applies to food utensils and to religious articles. A Torah scroll, a *talit,* and a pair of *tefilin* can also be kosher or nonkosher.

The process of making food and food utensils kosher is called *kashering* or *koshering.* The procedure is designed to remove as much blood as possible from animal flesh and to cleanse food utensils that have come in contact with nonkosher items. (See page 117 for more on this process.)

In the food sphere, the terms kosher and nonkosher are applied only to animal life. All food that is grown—that is, plant life—is kosher and may be eaten without further treatment.

Rationale for Dietary Laws

The Bible (Leviticus 11:45) offers a single reason for the dietary laws: to help Israel become a holy nation. By following a distinctive diet, Israel was encouraged to remain apart, separate from its idol-worshipping neighbors. This lifestyle insured that the adoption of idolatrous ways by Jews would be kept to a minimum.

The twelfth-century scholar Moses Maimonides is one of a number of authorities who viewed the dietary laws as having health value and as being a vehicle to teach compassion. These points are not made in the Bible.

KOSHER CERTIFICATION

Function of the Rabbinate

The Orthodox rabbinate generally supervises the *kashrut* of manufactured foods, although in some communities Conservative rabbis and organizations have assumed that role. There are more than fifty *kashrut*-certifying entities in the United States, ranging from the largest, the Union of Orthodox Jewish Congregations, which certifies thousands of products manufactured by eleven hundred firms, to one individual rabbi in Pittsburgh who certifies a single product: a brand of soft drinks.

Certifying Agencies

Each of the rabbinic agencies, communal organizations, and individual rabbis called upon by food manufacturers to certify their products as kosher has its own identifying symbol. The symbol is printed on the box or label of the product receiving certification.

Occasionally, a P or D will appear near the symbol of the certifier. The P stands for *pareve* and the D for dairy. On items that are kosher for Passover, one will sometimes find a P next to the symbol, in which case the P stands for Passover. When the Passover product is neutral, the word *pareve* will be spelled out. Food items certified as kosher are not necessarily kosher for Passover, unless so stated on the box or label.

The K Symbol

Some kosher food products carry the letter K on their packaging to indicate that they are under rabbinic supervision, but the name of the certifying agent cannot be known unless one writes directly to the manufacturer. The manufacturer will provide a copy of the certification upon request.

MOST POPULAR KOSHER SYMBOLS

Ⓤ Union of Orthodox Jewish
Congregations
45 West 36th Street
New York, NY 10018

Kosher Supervision Service
1444 Queen Anne Road
Teaneck, NJ 07666

National Kashruth
One Route 306
Monsey, NY 10952

Ⓚ Organized Kashrus
Laboratories
P.O. Box 218
Brooklyn, NY 11204

Vaad Hakashrus of the
Orthodox Jewish Council of
Baltimore
7504 Seven Mile Lane
Baltimore, MD 21209

Kehila De Los Angeles
186 North Citrus
Los Angeles, CA 90030

Rabbi Joseph Ralbag
225 West 85th Street
New York, NY 10024

Central Rabbinical Congress
(Hisachdus Harabonim)
85 Division Street
Brooklyn, NY 11211

Board of Rabbis
143 Bay Street
Jersey City, NJ 07303

KAJ Kahal Adas Jeshurun (Breuer's)
85-93 Bennett Avenue
New York, NY 10033

Chicago Rabbinical Council
3525 West Peterson Avenue
Chicago, IL 60659

MK Montreal Vaad Hair
5491 Victory Avenue
Montreal, Quebec, Canada

Kashruth Alliance (Igud
Harabonim)
156 Fifth Avenue
New York, NY 10010

Kosher Le'Mhadren Supervision
Service
P.O. Box 48 (Blythe Station)
Brooklyn, NY 11219

Ⓚ Kosher Overseers Association
of America
P.O. Box 1321
Beverly Hills, CA 90213

United Kosher Supervision
P.O. Box 122
Monsey, NY 10952

"Menora K" Kosher Supervision
P.O. Box 48 (Blythe Station)
Brooklyn, NY 11219

Synagogue Center
7214 Park Heights Avenue
Baltimore, MD 21215

Wholesome & Kosher
689 Adams Avenue
West Hempstead, NY 11552

Rabbi Solomon B. Shapiro
73-09 136th Street
Flushing, NY 11367

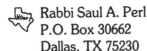 Rabbi Saul A. Perl
P.O. Box 30662
Dallas, TX 75230

KO Kosher Service
5871 Drexel Road
Philadelphia, PA 19131

Rabbi Harry Cohen
165 West 91st Street
New York, NY 10024

Sephardic Rabbinical Council
of America
2030 Ocean Parkway
Brooklyn, NY 11223

Metropolitan Kashruth Council
of Michigan
6533 Post Oak Drive
West Bloomfield, MI 48033

Rabbinical Council of California
244-13 Hendrick Avenue
Lomita, CA 90717

Kashruth Supervision Service
7111 Park Heights Avenue
Baltimore, MD 21215

Kashruth Inspection Service of
the Vaad Hoier of St. Louis
4 Millstone Campus
St. Louis, MO 63146

Canadian Jewish Congress of
Toronto
4600 Bathurst Street
Downsview, Ontario, Canada
M2R 3V2

Vaad Hakashrus of Buffalo
P.O. Box 755
Williamsville, NY 14221

Denver Association of Intensive
Torah Education
1560 Winona Court
Denver, CO 80204

The Vaad Harabbonim of
Flatbush
1618 Coney Island Avenue
Brooklyn, NY 11230

The Syracuse Vaad Ha'ir
4905 Onondaga Road
Syracuse, NY 13215

Vaad Horabonim (Vaad
Hakashrus) of Massachusetts
80 Boylston Street
Boston, MA 02116

Vaad Harabonim of Queens
90-45 Myrtle Avenue
Glendale, NY 11385

Kashrus Department of the Beth
Din of Johannesburg
24 Raleigh Street
Johannesburg, South Africa

Vaad Horabonim of Greater
Detroit
17071 West Ten Mile Road
Southfield, MI 48075

Rabbi Bernard Poupko
5715 Beacon Street
Pittsburgh, PA 15217

Vancouver Kashrus
3476 Oak Street
Vancouver, BC, Canada
V6H 2L8

Dallas Kashruth Council
P.O. Box 30511
Dallas, TX 75230

Kosher Style

Use of the term "kosher style" can mislead people into thinking that the food being served is kosher. Some states, such as New York, prohibit the use of such terminology in restaurant advertising.

KOSHER AND NONKOSHER ANIMALS

The Word Trefa

The word *trefa* (also spelled *terefa*) referred originally to an animal that was "torn" by another animal and for this reason was not fit for food (Exodus 22:30). In time, the concept was extended to include all unfit foods and utensils. *Trayf* is the colloquial way of pronouncing *trefa*.

What Makes an Animal Kosher?

Chapter 11 of the Book of Leviticus and Chapter 14 of the Book of Deuteronomy list the characteristics of a kosher animal: it must have hooves that are fully split, thus forming two toes, and it must chew its cud. If only one of these characteristics is present in an animal, it is not kosher. Thus, animals such as camels, horses, badgers, and hares—which chew the cud but do not have genuine split hooves—are not kosher; nor are animals such as pigs, which have split hooves but do not chew the cud. On the other hand, animals such as oxen, sheep, deer, and goats fulfill both requirements and are therefore kosher.

Aversion to Swine Flesh

The special aversion of Jews to the flesh of the swine goes back to the Hasmonean period in Jewish history (second century B.C.E.) when the Syrian-Greeks, who had occupied Palestine, tried to force Jews to sacrifice pigs in the Temple and to eat their flesh. The Talmud says: "Cursed is he who raises pigs."

KOSHER AND NONKOSHER FISH AND FOWL

Kosher Fish

All fish that have fins and scales are kosher.

Koshering Fish

Because fish contain a small amount of blood, they need not be koshered. Animals that live out of water must be koshered to remove excess blood. See below.

Fish Roe

Fish roe is kosher only if it comes from a kosher fish.

Shellfish

All shellfish are not kosher, for they have neither fins nor scales.

Substitutions for Shellfish in Recipes

Cut into small pieces, the following substitutions of fish for shellfish have been suggested:

- flounder for shrimp
- halibut, haddock, or cod for scallops
- halibut or sole for crabmeat salad
- haddock or halibut for lobster

Most Popular Kosher Fish

- anchovy
- bass
- bluefish
- carp
- cod
- flounder
- grouper
- haddock
- hake
- halibut
- herring
- locus (lokus)
- mackerel
- perch
- pike
- plaice
- pollack
- pompano
- porgy
- redfish
- red snapper
- sable
- salmon
- sardines
- shad
- smelt
- St. Peter's fish
- sunfish
- tilefish
- trout
- tuna
- turbot (Pacific only)
- whitefish
- white snapper
- yellowtail

Swordfish and Sturgeon

Swordfish and sturgeon have fins and scales, but at some point in the development of the fish, before they are taken from the water, the fins and scales fall off. The Orthodox rabbinate does not permit the use of these fish, but the Conservative rabbinate has approved them.

Kosher Birds

The Bible does not specifically name which birds may be eaten, but it does state that any "clean" bird is fit for consumption. Birds traditionally accepted as kosher are chickens, turkeys, ducks, geese, and pigeons, among others. In many localities rabbis classify the pheasant as kosher.

Nonkosher Birds

The Bible lists the wild birds and birds of prey that are not kosher. These include the ostrich, hawk, raven, eagle, owl, pelican, and stork.

Kosher Eggs

Eggs of forbidden birds are not kosher. Kosher eggs are generally broad at one end and smaller at the other.

Unborn Eggs

Undeveloped eggs found in kosher poultry, regardless of size, must be koshered in the same manner as other pieces of meat, but the washing and salting is done separately. These eggs may not be eaten with dairy foods.

Winged Swarming Things

"Locusts of every variety, crickets of every variety, and grasshoppers of every variety" are considered kosher according to Leviticus 11:22, but the Rabbis have generally disapproved of their use. It is interesting to note that the Jews of Rabat and other communities in Morocco do eat grasshoppers (chagavim).

MEAT AND DAIRY PRODUCTS

Fleishidig and Milchidig

Fleishig is a Yiddish word meaning "made of meat" or "associated with meat," and it applies to all foods that contain or that have come in contact with meat in any form. *Milchig* is a Yiddish word that means "made of milk" or "associated with dairy products."

One who observes the dietary laws does not mix meat and dairy products when preparing food or when serving it at one meal. This is based on the biblical prohibition in Exodus 23:19. Flatware, pots, pans, and dishes used in conjunction with meat products are said to be *fleishidig,* and those associated with dairy products are said to be *milchidig.*

Pareve Food

Food that is neutral—that contains neither meat nor dairy ingredients—is called *pareve* in Yiddish. All naturally grown products such as fruits, vegetables, cereals, coffee, nuts, and the like are *pareve,* as are artificial milk products that are so marked and inorganic food enhancers such as salt and synthetic sweetener.

Nonkosher Cheeses

Orthodox law prohibits the consumption of cheeses made with rennet, an extract of the enzyme renin, which is used in cheesemaking to hasten the coagulation of the milk. Rennet is derived from the lining of an animal's stomach, and its use is prohibited even if the animal from which the substance is obtained is kosher. This prohibition is based on the law forbidding the mixture of meat and milk products.

Conservative Jews do not classify rennet as a meat product, because in the course of manufacture the character of the substance changes totally. The processed rennet—which is inert, without active properties—is no longer considered an animal product.

Superkosher Milk

Many Orthodox Jews use only milk that has been under careful surveillance by a Jew from the moment of milking to the time of bottling. Such close supervision offers assurance that at no time during processing was the milk of a nonkosher animal or some other prohibited ingredient mixed in with it. Milk carefully guarded in this manner is called *chalav Yisrael,* "milk of Israel."

Reform Dietary Practice

Reform Jews do not feel bound by the laws of *kashrut,* but some maintain kosher homes either out of respect for parents, to accommodate other family members, or as an expression of solidarity with the Jewish community as a whole. Many Reform Jews, and many Conservative Jews for that matter, are selective in their observance of the dietary laws and will abstain only from certain foods, such as pork or shellfish.

KOSHER SLAUGHTERING

Ritual Slaughtering

For its meat to be considered kosher, an animal must be slaughtered by a ritual slaughterer *(shochet).* The purpose of such slaughtering is to drain off as much blood as possible, for the Bible considers blood to be the very essence of life (Leviticus 3:17). The mandatory removal of blood applies to all animals except fish.

The Shochet

The *shochet,* the ritual slaughterer, must be well versed in the laws of slaughtering and be technically trained to perform the procedure. He is expected to be an observant Jew.

Slaughtering Procedure

Shechita is the Hebrew word for slaughtering. When the *shochet* performs this act, he draws a razor-sharp knife *(chalif)* across the throat of the animal, severing the trachea and esophagus in one swift motion.

The Chalif

The *chalif* is the knife used by the *shochet* to slaughter animals. A large *chalif* (with a twenty-inch blade) is used for mammals, and a smaller knife (with a six-inch blade) is used for fowl. The knife must be razor-sharp and free of all nicks.

Hunting for Food

The Talmud discourages hunting, which it considers an unnecessary activity that can result in the cruel treatment of animals. Kosher animals, such as deer, when killed by hunters, may not be used for food because they have not been ritually slaughtered.

Glatt Kosher

The word *glatt,* Yiddish for "smooth," refers to the lung of an animal, particularly a mammal. Lungs that have incurred some sort of damage carry scar tissue, rendering the lung no longer smooth. Many persons who are fastidious about religious observance believe that an animal whose lungs are not perfectly smooth should not be used as food. Such strictness goes beyond the requirement of the law, which considers an animal kosher as long as there is no puncture in its lungs.

The term "glatt kosher" does not apply to fowl, the lungs of which are very small.

Glatt Kosher Fictions

Dairy or vegetable products—such as cheese, butter, bread, candy, and cookies—are sometimes misleadingly labeled *"glatt kosher."* The term is correctly applied only to the flesh of an animal with lungs.

KOSHERING FOOD

Why Meat Is Koshered

After an animal (including fowl but excluding fish) has been ritually slaughtered as explained above, its meat is then koshered to further draw off as much blood as possible. This procedure is followed in order to comply with the biblical commandment "You shall eat no manner of blood" (Leviticus 7:26). Leviticus 17:11 explains the prohibition when it says, "for the life of the flesh is in the blood."

The Koshering Process

To kosher meat, the flesh is rinsed off and placed in a large receptable filled with water to soak for one-half hour. The meat is then removed, rinsed off again (the soaking softens the meat, releasing the blood), salted with kosher (coarse) salt on all surfaces, and placed on a grooved board set on an incline so the blood can run off. The meat sits on the board for one full hour. It is then rinsed off twice, at which point it is deemed kosher.

Animal Hindquarter

The hindquarter of an otherwise kosher animal is unfit for use unless all the blood vessels have been removed, since this is the only way to purge the flesh of sufficient blood to make it kosher. This is a tedious operation, and most butchers are neither capable nor desirous of executing it. For this reason, kosher meat markets generally sell only the forequarter of an animal. (In some communities outside the United States, specially trained butchers take the trouble to remove all the veins, arteries, and forbidden fat from the hindquarter of an animal, thus making it kosher.)

Nonkosher Meat

Meat (including fowl) that has been left unwashed and unsalted for more than three days after slaughtering cannot be koshered, since the blood has congealed. The only way of salvaging such meat is to treat it as liver—namely, to broil it.

Delayed Koshering

If unkoshered meat is rinsed off before three days have elapsed from the time the animal was slaughtered, the meat may still be koshered within the next three days.

Removing Feathers

A fowl that is dipped in hot water in order to facilitate the removal of its feathers is not kosher because the blood in the bird will congeal when the bird is removed from the hot water. The regular koshering process of soaking and salting will no longer extract the blood.

Koshering Liver

Liver contains so much blood that it cannot be koshered in the normal manner. To kosher liver, broil it under an open flame in the oven or over hot coals. Although it is unnecessary to do so, some people sprinkle salt on the liver before broiling it.

Koshering and Freezing

Before meat is put into a deep freeze, it should be koshered (soaked in water for one-half hour and then salted for one hour). It may then be cooked after it has been removed from the freezer and thawed; it need not first be washed or koshered again, even if more than three days have elapsed since it was originally frozen.

In 1934 the chief rabbi of Palestine ruled that meat frozen without having been koshered may be koshered by soaking and salting after it has been removed from the freezer and thawed. However, some authorities believe that such meat may be koshered only by broiling.

Pâté de Foie Gras

Geese are force-fed to fatten them, thus enlarging their livers. From such oversized livers the delicacy called *pâté de foie gras* ("goose liver paste") is made.

Authorities are divided about the propriety of using such livers, since force-feeding is painful to animals and Jewish law prohibits inflicting pain on living creatures. The chief rabbi of Israel ruled that force-feeding is permissible because the pain inflicted is negligible and the economic gain considerable.

MIXING FISH, MEAT, AND DAIRY

Eating Fish With Meat

Fish may be eaten at a meat meal, but those who are particularly fastidious about religious observance eat bread or soup between fish and meat courses, to separate the tastes. Some Sephardim do not serve fish even at dairy meals, but most Ashkenazim do.

Waiting Period Between Meat and Dairy

Since the taste of meat stays on the palate for a while, a waiting period is required before eating dairy foods. The precise interval is not specified in the Talmud, and one therefore finds considerable variations from community to community. The length of the waiting period often depends on the type of meat eaten.

The waiting time after eating a meat product and before eating a dairy food can extend from one to six hours. After eating meat, Orthodox Jews who have their roots in Holland wait one hour. German Jews wait three hours, and East European and most Sephardic Jews wait a full six hours. The same waiting period applies to the eating of dairy foods after eating fowl.

Waiting Period Between Dairy and Meat

Most rabbinic authorities call for a waiting period of at least thirty minutes from the time one eats soft cheeses and other dairy products to the time one consumes meat. Hard cheeses, unlike soft varieties, cling to one's teeth and palate, and some strict authorities require that one wait a full six hours before consuming meat products.

Two Sets of Dishes

The biblical prohibition against the cooking of meat with milk (Exodus 23:19) was extended by the Rabbis of the Talmud to include the use of the same utensils for preparing or eating dairy and meat products. The kosher home therefore has separate dishes, cookware, and flatware for the preparation and eating of dairy and meat products.

Koshering Cookware and Flatware

Pareve or dairy cookware that had mistakenly been used to boil, broil, bake, or fry a meat preparation can be koshered— that is, made fit for use in the kosher home—by exposing it to the intense heat of an open fire. Silverware is sometimes koshered by inserting it into the earth and allowing it to remain there for several hours.

Koshering Dishes and Utensils

Pots, pans, dishes, and utensils made of porous materials such as wood, earthenware, and plastic cannot be koshered because they absorb food particles and odors which cannot be expunged. Once they have been used for meat meals, they may not be used for dairy meals and vice versa.

Dishwashers

The same dishwasher may be used to cleanse both meat and dairy dishes and utensils. The water is so hot that the machine actually koshers itself. Those more fastidious about observance do not machine-wash meat and dairy dishes together. In fact, the empty machine is run through one full cycle between meat and dairy washings. Members of the ultra-Orthodox community often have two dishwashers (and sinks and refrigerators) in their homes.

Glass Dishes

Most rabbinic authorities consider glass dishes to be non-absorbent and hence technically suitable for use with either meat or dairy foods after a thorough washing. This is particularly so if the dishes are used only for cold food. Nevertheless, those who are more observant will keep separate sets of glass dishes for serving meat and milk products. Drinking tumblers that are used primarily for cold water or beverages may be used interchangeably at meat and dairy meals.

Hot and Cold Dishes

Hot kosher food when placed on nonkosher dishes becomes nonkosher. This is so because some of the flavors that had been absorbed by the nonkosher dishes are released by the heat of the kosher food. However, when cold kosher food is placed on a cold nonkosher dish, the food remains kosher and may be eaten.

Accidental Mixing of Meat and Dairy

If a meat product is accidentally placed on a nonabsorbent dish (such as glass) that has been used for dairy foods, or if a dairy product is placed on a nonabsorbent dish previously used for meat products, the dish may be used again after a thorough cleaning and rinsing.

If a spoon, fork, or knife designated for meat meals is accidentally used with dairy foods (or vice versa), the flatware can be koshered by inserting it into soil (either in your backyard or in a flower pot) and leaving it there for several hours.

These procedures apply only to accidental mixing. It is not proper to mix dairy and meat products and utensils knowingly.

Facts to Remember
WHEN STARTING A KOSHER HOME

- Begin by purchasing two sets of dishes, two sets of flatware, and two sets of pots and pans. Select two distinct patterns and designs so that it can be recognized at a glance which are to be used for dairy foods and which for meat.
- For the preparation of *pareve* ("neutral") foods—those that contain neither meat nor dairy ingredients—a special set of

pots and pans should be purchased. *Pareve* foods include fruits, vegetables, grains, and the foods made from them.

- If *pareve* food is cooked in a meat pot, it must be served on meat dishes. If it is cooked in a dairy pot, it must be served on dairy dishes.

- Although glass dishes (which includes Pyrex) technically may be used for the preparation and serving of both meat and dairy foods, two sets are ordinarily required, for the concept of *kashrut* involves the separation of meat and dairy dishes and implements as well as foods.

- Drinking glasses and glass salad plates can be used interchangeably at dairy and meat meals. Thorough washing is necessary after each use.

- Separate sponges and dish towels should be kept for meat and dairy. In many homes one color is used for meat and another color for dairy.

- An electric can opener can be kept neutral by using it only for such items as canned vegetables, canned fish, canned fruits and *pareve* soups. Hand can openers can then be used for dairy and meat products.

- Separate sink receptacles should be used for washing dairy and meat dishes. Meat and dairy dishes should not be placed on the floor of the sink. Use wooden or plastic receptacles and racks.

- Serving meat and dairy foods to different persons at the same table should be avoided. If unavoidable, use a different colored place mat for each.

- When *pareve* substitutes for butter or cream are served at a meat meal, the substitute should be kept in its original wrapper or container and placed directly on the table so that everyone will recognize that the item is *pareve*. The substitute should have a P (the kosher/pareve symbol) on it, for some items—particularly margarines—contain ingredients derived from milk and hence are not *pareve*.

- If kosher meat is purchased in the kosher department of a supermarket, make sure that the product is certified to be kosher. The label must so state.

- Most kosher butchers sell meat that they have already koshered (washed and salted). Meat that has not been koshered by the butcher will have to be koshered at home. See Chapter 9 for the procedure.

• Separate dietary rules apply to Passover. See Chapter 9 for details.

Nonkosher Wines

Talmudic law states that wine used in connection with idol worship is forbidden to Jews, as is wine so much as touched by idolators. The prohibition was extended by the Rabbis to include wine made by Gentiles that was never intended for idolatrous purposes, and that ban has been carried over to this day despite the fact there are no longer idolators in our midst. According to the Orthodox rabbinate, wine handled by non-Jews, known in Hebrew as *ya'yin* (or *yayn*) *nesech*, may not be consumed.

Conservative Attitude Toward Wine

For the most part, winemaking in the United States is automated from the time grapes are fed into vats until wine appears in sealed bottles. Based on the fact that no person has contact with the wine during this automated process, the Committee on Law and Standards of the Rabbinical Assembly (Conservative) has ruled that wines manufactured in this manner in the United States are kosher, although some have expressed concern about the use of so-called "fixing agents" of nonkosher origin.

Since wine that had been boiled was not permitted to be used in pagan worship, the presumption was that wine that had been boiled could not be associated with pagan use. Many producers of kosher wines therefore boil their wine after the pressing stage. Such wine is considered kosher regardless of who has processed it. The words *ya'yin mevushal,* "cooked [boiled] wine," often appear on bottles of kosher wine so processed.

The Nature of Gelatin

Gelatin is considered nonkosher by Orthodox authorities because it is made of the bones, hooves, and tissue of nonkosher animals. Conservative authorities, however, consider gelatin kosher because it has been so completely altered in the course of manufacture that it can no longer be characterized as a food product.

RECOMMENDED FOODS AND EATING HABITS

Vegetables Recommended

The Talmud suggests that "one should not live in a city that does not have a vegetable garden." The diet of most Jews in past centuries was primarily vegetarian, meat being eaten only on the Sabbath, holidays, and festive occasions.

Maimonides Recommends

For a wholesome diet, the twelfth-century scholar and physician Moses Maimonides recommends that one eat bread baked from flour that is neither too old nor too fine. He also recommends cheese, butter, white-meated fish with firm flesh, goat and sheep meat, and chicken. He considers fresh fruits to be unwholesome, but dried fruits and wine are recommended.

Olives and Olive Oil

Olives in general were extremely popular in talmudic times, although white olives, it was believed, affected one's memory. Olive oil was recommended as being good for old men, as the old aphorism has it, "Bread for young men, oil for old men, and honey for children."

Radishes and Onions

Radishes are good for one's health, says the Talmud, but onions should be avoided because of the pungent odor.

Aphrodisiacs

The Talmud suggests that the following foods have a positive effect on sexual potency: eggs, fish, garlic, wine, milk, cheese, and fatty meats. On the other hand, salt and egg barley are said to diminish potency. Ezra the Scribe decreed that garlic be eaten on Friday nights because "it promotes and arouses sexual desires."

Garlic Favored

Garlic is highly recommended in the Talmud: "It satisfies, it warms the body, it makes the face shine, it increases seminal fluids, and it cures tapeworm."

Popularity of Nuts

Nuts were always popular in Jewish tradition. Aside from their use in baking, they were popular with children, much as lollipops are today. The Midrash refers to nuts as "playthings for children and kings."

Rendering Chicken Fat

Rendered chicken fat, known in Yiddish as *shmaltz,* gives Jewish foods such as chopped liver, *kasha varnishkes* (buckwheat groats and bowtie noodles), and *kugels* (puddings) much of their special taste.

To prepare *shmaltz,* remove the skin and all fat from the bird. Cut the skin and fat into small pieces, transfer to a heavy pot, and add cold water to cover. Cook uncovered until almost all the water has evaporated. Lower the heat and add chopped onion—about one onion to one cup of fat. Some like to add a few slices of raw potato at this point.

The *shmaltz* is ready when the onions and potato are nice and brown and the chicken skin (called *griben, gribenes,* or *grivenes* in Yiddish) is light and crispy. After the pot cools a little, strain the chicken fat into a jar and store in the refrigerator. The *gribenes* can be stored in the freezer.

Talmudic Dietary Advice

The Talmud, advising that one should be careful about diet and eating habits, recommends that fluids be drunk at mealtime and that one engage in physical exercise after meals.

On Eating Breakfast

The Talmud encourages one to eat a hearty breakfast. Persons who follow such a regimen, it explains, will enjoy good health and renewed vigor.

6

Basic Rituals, Customs, and Blessings

Introduction

Jews often speak of a certain action—visiting the sick, comforting a mourner, giving charity—as being a *mitzva* (plural, *mitzvot*), a good deed, a meritorious act. In a theological sense, however, the term *mitzva* carries greater significance. A *mitzva* is a religious obligation either mandated in the Bible or based upon the interpretation of a biblical mandate.

According to tradition, there are 613 biblical commandments, of which 248 are affirmative and 365 negative. "Honor thy father and mother is one of the best known of the former; "Thou shalt not steal," the latter. Both men above age thirteen and women above age twelve are considered to be bound by the biblical commandments, with one important exception: women are exempt for those affirmative commandments that must be performed at a particular time of day (such as the donning of *tefilin* [phylacteries], which must be done in the morning) because such commandments might interfere with their household duties. The 365 prohibitions, on the other hand, are incumbent upon all Jews. Although the Rabbis of the Talmud considered all commandments to be of equal importance, many have lost their relevance with the passage of time.

125

Many *mitzvot* are associated with symbols: donning *tefilin,* mentioned above; putting on a *talit* (prayershawl); attaching a *mezuza* to the doorpost of one's home; sitting in a *sukka* (thatched hut) and waving a palm branch (*lulav*) during the Sukkot holiday; and lighting Sabbath candles on Friday night. The performance of virtually all of these commandments is preceded by the recitation of a blessing, as is the consumption of food. Interestingly, the wearing of the most prominent of Jewish symbols, the skullcap or *yarmulke,* has no theological roots and no blessing associated with it.

THE MEZUZA: SYMBOL OF THE JEWISH HOME

Significance of the Mezuza

The outstanding twelfth-century Jewish philosopher Moses

שמע ישׂראל יהוה אלהינו יהוה אחד ואהבת את
יהוה אלהיך בכל לבבך ובכל נפשך ובכל מאדך והיו
הדברים האלה אשר אנכי מצוך היום על לבבך ושננתם
לבניך ודברת בם בשבתך בביתך ובלכתך בדרך
ובשכבך ובקומך וקשרתם לאות על ידך והיו לטטפת
בין עיניך וכתבתם על מזוזת ביתך ובשעריך
והיה אם שמע תשמעו אל מצותי אשר אנכי
מצוה אתכם היום לאהבה את יהוה אלהיכם ולעבדו
בכל לבבכם ובכל נפשכם ונתתי מטר ארצכם בעתו
יורה ומלקוש ואספת דגנך ותירשך ויצהרך ונתתי
עשב בשדך לבהמתך ואכלת ושבעת השמרו לכם
פן יפתה לבבכם וסרתם ועבדתם אלהים אחרים
והשתחויתם להם וחרה אף יהוה בכם ועצר את
השמים ולא יהיה מטר והאדמה לא תתן את יבולה
ואבדתם מהרה מעל הארץ הטבה אשר יהוה נתן לכם
ושמתם את דברי אלה על לבבכם ועל נפשכם וקשרתם
אתם לאות על ידכם והיו לטוטפת בין עיניכם ולמדתם
אתם את בניכם לדבר בם בשבתך בביתך ובלכתך
בדרך ובשכבך ובקומך וכתבתם על מזוזות ביתך
ובשעריך למען ירבו ימיכם וימי בניכם על האדמה
אשר נשבע יהוה לאבתיכם לתת להם כימי השמים
על הארץ

These twenty-two handwritten Hebrew lines appear on all *mezuza* parchments. The white space at the beginning of the seventh line (from the top) is the spot where *Shaddai,* the Hebrew word for God, appears on the obverse side of the parchment.

Maimonides wrote, "By the commandment of the *mezuza*, one is reminded of the unity of God and is aroused to love Him. . . . This thought will make him mindful that he must walk in the path of righteousness."

Mezuza Biblically Mandated

The *mezuza* (literally, "doorpost") consists of a piece of parchment inserted into a small receptacle. This is affixed to the doorpost of the home. Two passages from the Book of Deuteronomy (Chapter 6, verses 4-9 and Chapter 11, verses 13-21) are inscribed upon the parchment and explain the rationale for the *mezuza*.

The first selection begins with the familiar words, *Shema Yisrael, Adonai Elohenu, Adonai Echad*, "Hear, O Israel, the Lord our God, the Lord is One," and ends with the verse, "And you shall write them [the commandments of God] on the doorposts of your house and upon your gates." The second selection begins with the words *Ve-ha'ya im shamoa*, "And

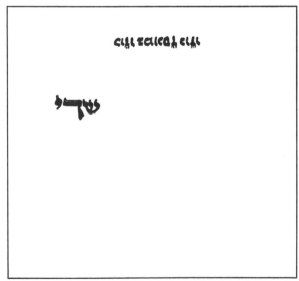

This is the obverse side of the *mezuza* parchment. The single word on the right side is *Shaddai*. When the parchment is rolled up and placed inside the *mezuza* receptacle, the word *Shaddai* is visible if there is an aperture in the receptacle (see the illustration on page 129). The three words towards the top, *kozu be-muchsaz kozu*, are mystical "'nonwords" that represent the Hebrew words *Adonai Elohenu Adonai*, meaning "the Lord our God is Lord."

if you will obey [the commandments]," and goes on to express the same sentiment as the first selection—specifically that a *mezuza* be affixed to the doorposts of every Jewish home.

The two passages from Deuteronomy must be handwritten by a scribe on parchment made from the skin of a kosher animal. If the passages are printed, the *mezuza* is considered invalid, as is the case if the passages are inscribed on paper.

Mezuza Called Shema

Since the first word inscribed on the *mezuza* parchment is *shema,* some people refer to the *mezuza* as "The *Shema.*"

The Obverse Side of the Parchment

When the scribe *(sofer)* prepares a *mezuza,* he letters the word *Shaddai* on the obverse side, opposite the open space (indentation) that appears before the beginning of the second paragraph. When the parchment is rolled up and inserted into its container, the word *Shaddai* ("God") can be seen through the aperture of the receptacle (see below).

The Mezuza Receptacle

The receptacle in which the *mezuza* parchment is housed serves to protect the writing on parchment from being erased. The casing may be made of metal, wood, or ceramic and is affixed to a doorpost with nails or glue. Most casings have a small aperture near the top.

Rolling Up the Mezuza Parchment

To roll up a *mezuza* parchment so that it will fit into the receptacle, place the parchment on a flat surface with the twenty-two lines of Hebrew lettering facing up. Roll up the parchment from the left side to the right side so that the Hebrew word *Shaddai* is visible when the parchment has been rolled up.

Positioning the Mezuza

The *mezuza* is positioned on the right doorpost, one-third down from the top. The upper portion of the *mezuza* is slanted

Mezuza receptacles, such as the one on the right, are often very simple in design, and made of inexpensive metals. Through the aperture near the top the Hebrew word *Shaddai* can be seen. More elaborate *mezuza* receptacles, such as the one on the left, usually do not have an aperture; in this case the word *Shaddai* appears in raised letters on the receptacle itself.

toward the inside of the house or room as one enters it. A *mezuza* may also be placed vertically if there is insufficient space to angle it, a practice common in many Balkan Sephardic communities.

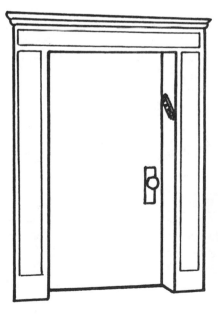

After the *mezuza* parchment is placed in its receptacle, the *mezuza* is affixed to the right doorpost. In earlier centuries, when houses were made of stone, the parchment was placed in a niche cut into the stone doorpost. To this day, such a niche is still visible in the doorpost of the stone house in Gerona, Spain, where Nachmanides (born 1194) is said to have lived.

Why the Right Doorpost?

The right side and right hand are favored in Jewish tradition. It is for this reason that the *mezuza* is affixed to the right doorpost (as one enters) of a house or room. Most persons are righthanded, and it is natural for them to reach up with the right hand to touch the *mezuza*.

Kissing the Mezuza

As a gesture of reverence and love, Jews customarily kiss holy objects such as a Torah, a prayershawl, and a prayerbook. Following an ancient talmudic custom, many Jews reach up and touch their fingers to the *mezuza*, then bring the fingers to their lips as they enter or leave the home. As they do, some will recite, "May God protect my going out and my coming in, now and forever." However, no special blessing need be recited when kissing a *mezuza*.

Where a Mezuza Is Not Required

A *mezuza* is affixed to the doorpost of every room in a home except the bathroom. Only permanent buildings and rooms in which one eats and/or sleeps require *mezuzot* (plural of *mezuza*). Thus, buildings such as garages, even when attached to a home, or beach cabanas used only for undressing and dressing do not require *mezuzot*. A building owned jointly by Jews and non-Jews does not require a *mezuza*.

Mezuza on a Sukka

A *sukka* ("tabernacle") is a temporary dwelling, and it is therefore not proper to post a *mezuza* on its entrance.

The Synagogue Mezuza

The sanctuary of the synagogue is reserved for prayer, and posting a *mezuza* on its doorpost is not required. The holiness of the sanctuary is self-evident, and there is no need for an additional reminder. Nevertheless, many synagogues do have *mezuzot* affixed to their doorposts. Rooms in the synagogue that serve social and other purposes must have *mezuzot* on their doorposts.

Mezuza Inspection

Maimonides, in his writings on Jewish law, ruled that *mezuzot* affixed to the doorposts of private homes must be inspected once every seven years. Other authorities believe that inspection should take place twice every seven years. If letters on the parchment are discovered to be faded or erased, they must be corrected by a scribe.

Removing Mezuzot

When a Jew moves out of a residence, he is expected to leave the *mezuzot* for the new occupants if he knows them to be Jews. Rabbi Moses Isserles, in his notes to the *Code of Jewish Law* (sixteenth century), states that the *mezuzot* should be left on the doorposts even if the new residents are Gentiles. This will prevent any ill-feeling that might result from removal of the *mezuzot*.

The Mezuza as a Charm

Many people wear a small facsimile of a *mezuza* as a charm. There is no religious significance to this practice but, as with the Star of David and Chai charms, wearing a *mezuza* charm is an expression of pride in one's heritage.

Yemenite Mezuza Custom

In order to alleviate the suffering of a terminally ill patient, Yemenites remove the *mezuza* from the room in which a dying person is bedded. They believe that the *mezuza* possesses protective powers and that by removing the *mezuza* the Angel of Death has easier access to the patient and will take his life sooner, thus sparing him unneccessary pain and anguish.

Ceremony for Affixing a Mezuza

No formal ceremony for affixing a *mezuza* exists in Jewish tradition. Generally, the *mezuza* is attached to the doorpost and the blessing on page 134 is recited.

When *mezuzot* are affixed to several rooms in a home at the same time, a blessing need be recited only once, before the first *mezuza* is attached.

The following ceremony is designed to make the occasion more meaningful:

Leader:

We have come together to share a happy occasion in the lives of _____ [family name] as we prepare to affix a *mezuza* to the doorpost of this new home. Placing a *mezuza* on a doorpost is a deeply cherished Jewish tradition which has its origin in Chapter 6 of the Book of Deuteronomy.

"Write them upon the doorposts of thy house and upon thy gates," says the Bible, and we honor that commandment this day. The commandment reminds us to be aware of God's law which demands that we live useful, constructive lives; lives that are kind, caring, and compassionate; lives that reveal concern for the good and welfare of our fellow man.

[The leader holds up the *mezuza* parchment.]

A participant continues:

This is the message inscribed on this handwritten *mezuza* parchment which we are about to mount on our doorpost. It begins with the words that have, over the centuries, been our pledge of allegiance to God, a pledge we repeat in prayer every morning and evening, throughout the year:

שְׁמַע יִשְׂרָאֵל, יְיָ אֱלֹהֵינוּ, יְיָ אֶחָד.

Shema Yisrael, Adonai Elohenu, Adonai Echad.

Hear, O Israel, the Lord our God, the Lord is One.

A participant continues:

What do these words of the *Shema* mean, and what is their significance? By emphasizing that God is One, they teach us that just as the physical world, the world of nature, is governed by only one set of rules, so the moral world can survive only if there is one standard to govern our lives. The prophet Micah (6:8) expressed very clearly what this moral code must be. He asked, "What does God require of thee?" And he answered his own question with this simple but precise statement: "God requires only that we do justice, that we love goodness, and that we be modest." This is the wise course for man to follow, concludes Micah, for this is how we walk with God.

A participant continues:

The *Shema* also reminds us that we must not only treasure the belief in God for ourselves but that we must pass its meaning on to our children. The message is articulated in these words:

וְאָהַבְתָּ אֵת יְיָ אֱלֹהֶיךָ בְּכָל לְבָבְךָ וּבְכָל נַפְשְׁךָ
וּבְכָל מְאֹדֶךָ. וְהָיוּ הַדְּבָרִים הָאֵלֶּה, אֲשֶׁר אָנֹכִי
מְצַוְּךָ הַיּוֹם עַל לְבָבֶךָ. וְשִׁנַּנְתָּם לְבָנֶיךָ, וְדִבַּרְתָּ בָּם
בְּשִׁבְתְּךָ בְּבֵיתֶךָ, וּבְלֶכְתְּךָ בַדֶּרֶךְ, וּבְשָׁכְבְּךָ וּבְקוּמֶךָ.
וּקְשַׁרְתָּם לְאוֹת עַל יָדֶךָ, וְהָיוּ לְטֹטָפֹת בֵּין עֵינֶיךָ.
וּכְתַבְתָּם עַל מְזֻזוֹת בֵּיתֶךָ וּבִשְׁעָרֶיךָ.

Ve-ahavta et Adonai Elohecha be-chol levavecha u-ve-chol nafshecha u-ve-chol me'odecha. Ve-hayu ha-devarim ha-eleh, asher anochi metzavecha ha-yom al levavecha. Ve-shinantam le-vanecha, ve-dibarta bam be-shivtecha be-vetecha, u-v'lechtecha va-derech, u-ve-shochbecha u-ve-kumecha. U-keshartam le-ot al yadecha, ve-hayu le-totafot bayn enecha. U-chetavtam al mezuzot betecha u-vi-she'arecha.

All read in unison:

You shall love the Lord your God with all your heart, with all your soul, and with all your might. Take to heart these words with which I charge you this day. Teach them to your children and speak of them when you are at home and when you are on the road. Pronounce them when you lie down to sleep at night and when you rise up in the morning. Bind them for a sign upon your hand and let them serve as a symbol between your eyes. Inscribe them on the doorposts of your house and on the gates of your cities.

A participant continues:

And so as we are about to affix this *mezuza* (holds up *mezuza*) to our doorpost, we are mindful of its significance. We recognize it as a reminder of the Ten Commandments spoken at Mount Sinai in the presence of the whole community of Israel, commandments that teach us and demand of us

- that we respect father and mother and the stranger in our midst
- that we refrain from injuring our fellow man or denying him that which is rightfully his
- that we deal fairly and honestly at all times and never compromise with the truth.

[The master or mistress of the home now rolls up the *mezuza* parchment and places it in its container. It is then affixed to the doorpost with nails, screws, or glue. The assembled then pronounce the *mezuza*-affixing blessing:]

בָּרוּךְ אַתָּה יְיָ, אֱלֹהֵינוּ מֶלֶךְ הָעוֹלָם, אֲשֶׁר קִדְּשָׁנוּ בְּמִצְוֹתָיו, וְצִוָּנוּ לִקְבּוֹעַ מְזוּזָה.

Baruch ata Adonai, Elohenu melech ha-olam, asher kideshanu be-mitzvotav, ve-tzivanu likboa mezuza.

Praised be Thou, O Lord our God, King of the universe, who has sanctified us with His commandments and commanded us to affix a *mezuza*.

Leader concludes:

With placement of the *mezuza* on the doorpost of this home, we pray that all who enter its portals be ever mindful of its message and that they be blessed with peace and happiness. May all who dwell in it live in harmony and enjoy a life of blessing and good health. *Amen. Mazal tov!*

[Everyone joins in singing *Siman Tov* and other appropriate songs found in the Appendix. See Appendix.]

COVERING THE HEAD

Headcoverings for Men

Although the wearing of a headcovering is not mandated in the Bible or Talmud, in recent centuries the practice of covering the head upon rising in the morning and keeping it covered throughout the day has become widespread among Orthodox and many Conservative Jews. The skullcap, the headcovering widely used by men, is called a *yarmulke* in Yiddish and a *kipa* in Hebrew.

In Orthodox and Conservative synagogues today, males are expected to cover the head. In Reform congregations the practice is optional.

Headcoverings for Women

In biblical and talmudic times, as a sign of modesty and chastity, women covered their heads with scarves. A scarf used for this purpose is referred to in Yiddish as a *tichl*. The sixteenth-century *Code of Jewish Law* states: "Married women always keep their heads covered," for the sake of modesty and to make their marital status perfectly clear.

Toward the end of the eighteenth century, despite opposition from some Orthodox rabbis, the *sheitel* (also spelled *shaytel*; Yiddish for "wig") was introduced as a headcovering for women.

In the synagogue, although not mandatory, it has become the practice for women to cover the head, particularly in Orthodox and Conservative congregations. Among the Reform it is optional.

Non-Jews and the Headcovering

It is considered desirable for a non-Jew to wear a skullcap when present at a Jewish religious service.

THE PRAYERSHAWL

Why a Prayershawl Is Worn

At the first prayer service of each day a *talit* (prayershawl; also pronounced *talis*) is worn. The *talit* was created as a garment to hold the fringes (*tzitziot*; singular, *tzitzit*) that are attached to each of its four corners. The basic law appears in the Book of Numbers (15:37-41): "Speak to the Children of Israel and bid them to affix fringes to the corners of their garments" so that when the Israelites see them, they will be reminded of God's commandments.

The Stripes on the Talit

Talitot (plural of *talit*) are made primarily of wool, silk, or rayon and are decorated with black or blue stripes. Blue has long been a color favored by Jews and, in fact, the Bible (Numbers 15:38) specifies that one of the eight threads of each

The fringes (*tzitziot*; singular, *tzitzit*) on the four corners of a *talit* are the most important part of that garment, as is evident from the fact that the blessing recited (see page 138) when donning the prayershawl refers to the *tzitziot* rather than the *talit*. The *talit* is merely the medium to hold the fringes.

The band that runs along the top of the prayershawl may merely be decorative or may contain the *talit* blessing. *Talitot* (plural of *talit*) distributed in synagogues are generally eighteen by sixty-six inches and made of rayon. Many Jews wear larger *talitot* that are made of wool.

fringe be dyed blue, which is no longer a requirement. The Talmud comments that blue is the appropriate color for *talit* stripes because "blue resembles the sea and the sea reflects the sky. . . ."

Black stripes for the *talit* may have been introduced when the Romans controlled Palestine: for the Romans blue was a color reserved for royalty, and therefore Jews of that time were forbidden to use it as a *talit* color.

When the Talit Is Worn

The *talit* is worn during morning worship, whether at home

or in the synagogue. The sole exception is Tisha B'Av, on which day the *talit* is worn only during the afternoon service *(Mincha)*.

In the synagogue the wearing of a *talit* is mandatory when an individual leads the congregation in prayer or is honored with an *aliya*.

The Talit Not Worn at Night

The *talit* is not worn at night because the biblical commandment (Numbers 15:39) specifically states that the fringes must be *seen*, and at night objects are not easily visible. The *talit* is worn at the *Kol Nidre* (night) service only because the service begins before nightfall; the congregants drape themselves in their prayershawls while there is still daylight.

Unmarried Men and the Talit

In talmudic times only married men wore prayershawls. It later became customary for synagogues to establish their own individual practices. Today, in most synagogues a prayershawl is worn by all men at morning services. In Reform congregations the wearing of a *talit* is optional.

Talitot Worn by Women

As in the case of *tefilin*, women are not obligated to fulfill positive Torah commandments that must be observed at specific times. Since the *talit* with its *tzitziot* was to be worn during the day, when it can be seen, women were freed from this obligation. However, women who decide that they wish to abide by the *tzitzit* commandment on a regular basis are permitted to do so under Jewish law.

Non-Jews and the Talit

Because the *talit* with its four fringes *(tzitziot)* symbolizes the commandments only a Jew is obligated to fulfill, the wearing of a prayershawl by a non-Jew is considered improper.

The Talit Blessing

After draping oneself with a *talit,* a blessing recalling the commandment to place fringes on the four corners of one's garment is recited. This blessing refers only to the fringes, not to the *talit*, for the Torah commandment applies only to the fringes.

בָּרוּךְ אַתָּה יְיָ, אֱלֹהֵינוּ מֶלֶךְ הָעוֹלָם, אֲשֶׁר קִדְּשָׁנוּ בְּמִצְוֹתָיו, וְצִוָּנוּ לְהִתְעַטֵּף בַּצִּיצִית.

Baruch ata Adonai, Elohenu melech ha-olam, asher kideshanu be-mitzvotav, ve-tzivanu le-hitatef ba-tzitzit.

Praised be Thou, O Lord our God, King of the universe, who has sanctified us by His commandments and commanded us to drape ourselves with a fringed garment.

Kissing the Fringes

It is customary to gather up the fringes from the four corners of the *talit* and to kiss them when reciting certain prayers. Most worshippers kiss the fringes whenever the word *tzitzit* is mentioned during the recitation of the third paragraph of the *Shema*. Some worshippers, particularly Sephardim, cover their eyes with the fringes of the *talit* when reciting the *Shema Yisrael*. This serves to enhance their concentration.

THE SMALL PRAYERSHAWL

Arba Kanfot

Observant Jews wear a small *talit (talit katan)* under their shirts all day long. Some, particularly *Chassidim*, allow the fringes to hang outside their clothing to comply fully with the biblical commandment which requires that the fringes be visible. Yemenite Jews wear the *talit katan* over their shirts but under their coats. The small *talit* is also referred to as *arba kanfot*, meaning "four corners."

Arba Kanfot Blessing

When donning the small prayershawl in the morning, recite the following blessing, which in a minor way differs from the blessing recited when donning the larger *talit*:

בָּרוּךְ אַתָּה יְיָ, אֱלֹהֵינוּ מֶלֶךְ הָעוֹלָם, אֲשֶׁר קִדְּשָׁנוּ בְּמִצְוֹתָיו, וְצִוָּנוּ עַל מִצְוַת צִיצִת.

Baruch ata Adonai, Elohenu melech ha-olam, asher kideshanu be-mitzvotav, ve-tzivanu al mitzvat tzitzit.

Praised be Thou, O Lord our God, who has sanctified us by His commandments and commanded us to wear a fringed garment.

THE TEFILIN

The Biblical Tefilin Requirement

Just as the Bible mandates the wearing of fringes on one's outer garment, so does it (Exodus 13:9 and 13:16; Deuteronomy 6:8 and 11:18) require that one place a "sign" upon the hand and forehead as a reminder to fulfill God's commandments. To carry out this law *tefilin* were created by the Rabbis of the Talmud.

The Word "Phylacteries"

For *tefilin*, the New Testament (Matthew 23:5) uses the word "phylacteries," derived from the Greek word meaning "safeguard." *Tefilin* (singular, *tefila*) were once erroneously thought to be amulets worn to protect the wearer from evil spirits.

What Are Tefilin?

Tefilin consist of two black leather boxes (cubes), generally ranging from one to two inches. Attached to the boxes are black leather straps two to three feet in length. Inside the boxes are pieces of handwritten parchment.

The leather used to make *tefilin* must be from a kosher animal.

The Difference Between the Two Cubes

One of the cubes is embossed on two sides with the Hebrew letter *shin*, which stands for *Shaddai*, a synonym for God. This cube, known as the "head cube" (the *shel rosh*, "belonging to the head"), is worn slightly above the forehead.

The second cube, smooth on all sides, is known as the "hand cube" (the *shel yad*, "belonging to the hand"). The *tefilin* straps are used to hold the cubes in position.

What's Written on the Parchments

The cube of the hand *tefila* contains four references from the Bible, all handwritten on one piece of parchment. These passages are from Exodus 13:1-10; Exodus 13:11-16; Deuteronomy 6:4-9; and Deuteronomy 11:13-21.

1. Ten verses from Exodus, Chapter 13, beginning with verse 1.

וידבר יהוה אל משה לאמר קדש לי כל בכור פטר כל רחם בבני ישראל באדם ובבהמה לי הוא ויאמר משה אל העם זכור את היום הזה אשר יצאתם ממצרים מבית עבדים כי בחזק יד הוציא יהוה אתכם מזה ולא יאכל חמץ היום אתם יצאים בחדש האביב והיה כי יביאך יהוה אל ארץ הכנעני והחתי והאמרי והחוי והיבוסי אשר נשבע לאבתיך לתת לך ארץ זבת חלב ודבש ועבדת את העבדה הזאת בחדש הזה שבעת ימים תאכל מצת וביום השביעי חג ליהוה מצות יאכל את שבעת הימים ולא יראה לך חמץ ולא יראה לך שאר בכל גבלך והגדת לבנך ביום ההוא לאמר בעבור זה עשה יהוה לי בצאתי ממצרים והיה לך לאות על ידך ולזכרון בין עיניך למען תהיה תורת יהוה בפיך כי ביד חזקה הוצאך יהוה ממצרים ושמרת את החקה הזאת למועדה מימים ימימה

2. Six verses from Exodus, Chapter 13, beginning with verse 11.

והיה כי יבאך יהוה אל ארץ הכנעני כאשר נשבע לך ולאבתיך ונתנה לך והעברת כל פטר רחם ליהוה וכל פטר שגר בהמה אשר יהיה לך הזכרים ליהוה וכל פטר חמר תפדה בשה ואם לא תפדה וערפתו וכל בכור אדם בבניך תפדה והיה כי ישאלך בנך מחר לאמר מה זאת ואמרת אליו בחזק יד הוציאנו יהוה ממצרים מבית עבדים ויהי כי הקשה פרעה לשלחנו ויהרג יהוה כל בכור בארץ מצרים מבכר אדם ועד בכור בהמה על כן אני זבח ליהוה כל פטר רחם הזכרים וכל בכור בני אפדה והיה לאות על ידכה ולטוטפת בין עיניך כי בחזק יד הוציאנו יהוה ממצרים

3. Six verses from Deuteronomy, Chapter 6, beginning with verse 4.

שמע ישראל יהוה אלהינו יהוה אחד ואהבת את יהוה אלהיך בכל לבבך ובכל נפשך ובכל מאדך והיו הדברים האלה אשר אנכי מצוך היום על לבבך ושננתם לבניך ודברת בם בשבתך בביתך ובלכתך בדרך ובשכבך ובקומך וקשרתם לאות על ידך והיו לטטפת בין עיניך וכתבתם על מזוזת ביתך ובשעריך

4. Nine verses from Deuteronomy, Chapter 11, beginning with verse 13.

והיה אם שמע תשמעו אל מצותי אשר אנכי מצוה אתכם היום לאהבה את יהוה אלהיכם ולעבדו בכל לבבכם ובכל נפשכם ונתתי מטר ארצכם בעתו יורה ומלקוש ואספת דגנך ותירשך ויצהרך ונתתי עשב בשדך לבהמתך ואכלת ושבעת השמרו לכם פן יפתה לבבכם וסרתם ועבדתם אלהים אחרים והשתחויתם להם וחרה אף יהוה בכם ועצר את השמים ולא יהיה מטר והאדמה לא תתן את יבולה ואבדתם מהרה מעל הארץ הטבה אשר יהוה נתן לכם ושמתם את דברי אלה על לבבכם ועל נפשכם וקשרתם אתם לאות על ידכם והיו לטוטפת בין עיניכם ולמדתם אתם את בניכם לדבר בם בשבתך בביתך ובלכתך בדרך ובשכבך ובקומך וכתבתם על מזוזות ביתך ובשעריך למען ירבו ימיכם וימי בניכם

The head cube contains the same four passages, except that they are written on four individual pieces of parchment and are inserted in four separate compartments within the cube.

When Tefilin Are Worn

In Talmudic times *tefilin* were worn all day long, but this practice was abandoned after the Roman government banned their use.

Since then, *tefilin* have been worn (with very few exceptions) when reciting morning prayers *(Shacharit)*, whether at home or in the synagogue.

Tefilin on the Sabbath and Holidays

Tefilin are not worn on the Sabbath and festivals because the reason for donning them is to be reminded of the commandments of the Torah, and since the Sabbath and holidays are in themselves reminders of the bond between God and Israel, no additional signs or symbols are needed.

Tefilin on Chol Ha-moed

On the Intermediate Days (Chol Ha-moed) of Passover and Sukkot *tefilin* are not worn by Sephardim and Chassidim.

Talit Before Tefilin

At weekday morning prayers, before one puts on *tefilin*, he dons a *talit*. This is based on the Jewish principle which states that a ritual that is performed on a regular basis takes precedence over one that is performed less often. A *talit* is worn every day, but *tefilin* are worn only on weekdays.

Who Wears Tefilin?

Traditionally, *tefilin* are worn by boys once they have reached Bar Mitzva age. Some boys start wearing *tefilin* several months before their thirteenth birthday so as to become proficient at the practice.

Since the wearing of *tefilin* is considered a joyful commandment, one is absolved of this obligation from the time of learning of a death in one's family until after burial.

Women and Tefilin

Since *tefilin* must be put on every morning on a regular basis, women, who have many home responsibilities, were exempted from complying with this commandment. Nevertheless, those who wish to accept the obligation may do so. The Talmud tells us that Michal, wife of King David, wore *tefilin* all day. History tells us that the daughters of the French scholar Rashi donned *tefilin*.

HOW TO DON TEFILIN

- The straps of the hand *tefila* (singular of *tefilin*) are unwound, and the left hand is slipped through the strap opening. The cube is moved up the arms to the bicep, where it is pulled tight. The following blessing is then recited:

בָּרוּךְ אַתָּה יְיָ, אֱלֹהֵינוּ מֶלֶךְ הָעוֹלָם, אֲשֶׁר קִדְּשָׁנוּ בְּמִצְוֹתָיו, וְצִוָּנוּ לְהָנִיחַ תְּפִלִּין.

Baruch ata Adonai, Elohenu melech ha-olam, asher kideshanu be-mitzvotav ve-tzivanu le-haniach tefilin.

Praised be Thou, O Lord our God, King of the universe, who has sanctified us through His commandments and commanded us to wear *tefilin*.

- The strap is wound around the arm seven times; the unused part of the strap is then wound around the palm. Ashkenazim wind the strap around the arm in an overhand (clockwise) direction, while Sephardim wind it counterclockwise.
- The straps of the head cube are unwound, and the cube is placed on the forehead just below the hairline. The straps are left to dangle over the shoulders. The following blessing is then recited:

בָּרוּךְ אַתָּה יְיָ, אֱלֹהֵינוּ מֶלֶךְ הָעוֹלָם, אֲשֶׁר קִדְּשָׁנוּ בְּמִצְוֹתָיו, וְצִוָּנוּ עַל מִצְוַת תְּפִלִּין.

Baruch ata Adonai, Elohenu melech ha-olam, asher kideshanu be-mitzvotav ve-tzivanu al mitzvat tefilin.

Ashkenazim, which includes most East European and American Jews, wind the hand *tefila* in a clockwise motion.

Chassidim and Sephardim use a counterclockwise motion when donning the *tefila* placed on the arm.

A special type of knot is made in the strap of the head *tefila*.

The cube of the head *tefila* is placed on the forehead so that the front edge of the cube meets the beginning of the hairline.

Praised be Thou, O Lord our God, King of the universe, who has sanctified us with His commandments and commanded us concerning the law of *tefilin*.

• The handstrap, which is wound around the palm, is now unwound and rewound around the palm, the middle finger, and the fourth (ring) finger in such a way as to form the letter *shin,* which is the first letter of *Shaddai* (God).

Righthanded vs. Lefthanded People

Righthanded people place the hand *tefila* on the left arm whereas lefthanded people place it on the right arm. This is done so that the hand of the stronger can be used to wind the *tefilin* straps. The principle established by the Rabbis is: "The hand that writes [the words of the Torah on the parchment] should be the hand that winds [the *tefila* on the arm]."

STARTING THE DAY

Ritual Handwashing

Traditional Jews wash their hands ritually upon arising in the morning and before eating a full meal. The handwashing ritual is conducted as follows: a full cup of water is taken in the right hand and then transferred to the left hand. With the left hand some of the water is poured onto the right hand. The cup is then transferred to the right hand and some of the water is poured onto the left. This procedure is repeated two more times, after which the handwashing blessing is recited.

Handwashing Blessing

בָּרוּךְ אַתָּה יְיָ, אֱלֹהֵינוּ מֶלֶךְ הָעוֹלָם, אֲשֶׁר קִדְּשָׁנוּ בְּמִצְוֹתָיו, וְצִוָּנוּ עַל נְטִילַת יָדָיִם.

Baruch ata Adonai, Elohenu melech ha-olam, asher kideshanu be-mitzvotav, ve-tzivanu al netilat yada'yim.

Praised be Thou, O Lord our God, King of the universe, who has sanctified us by His commandments and commanded us to wash the hands.

Modeh Ani

In the first prayer of the day, the *Modeh Ani,* one gives thanks for having been restored to consciousness after a night of slumber:

מוֹדֶה אֲנִי לְפָנֶיךָ,

מֶלֶךְ חַי וְקַיָּם,

שֶׁהֶחֱזַרְתָּ בִּי נִשְׁמָתִי בְּחֶמְלָה,

רַבָּה אֱמוּנָתֶךָ.

Modeh ani le-fanecha,
melech chai ve-ka'yam,
she-hechezarta bi nishmati b'chemla,
raba emunatecha.

I thank Thee,
O living Ruler of the universe,
for having restored my life to me.
Your faithfulness is unbounded.

Formal Morning Prayers

Before breakfast, a traditional Jew recites the morning prayer service *(Shacharit)* either at home or in the synagogue. At this time he dons a *talit* and *tefilin* (see above).

ENDING THE DAY

Bedtime Prayer

The *Shema,* which is recited at every morning and evening service, is also a popular bedtime prayer. This Jewish affirmation of faith, found in Deuteronomy 6:4, is sometimes followed by the recitation of verses 5 through 9 of the same chapter (see page 126 and page 174).

שְׁמַע יִשְׂרָאֵל, יְיָ אֱלֹהֵינוּ, יְיָ אֶחָד.

Shema Yisrael, Adonai Elohenu, Adonai Echad.

Hear, O Israel, the Lord our God, the Lord is One.

GIVING THANKS AT MEALTIME

Beginning the Meal

A blessing over bread, known as the *Ha-motzi*, is recited at the beginning of any meal at which bread is served. Bread is the staff of life, and the prayer recited over it covers all food items eaten in the course of the meal.

The *Ha-motzi* blessing is:

בָּרוּךְ אַתָּה יְיָ, אֱלֹהֵינוּ מֶלֶךְ הָעוֹלָם, הַמּוֹצִיא לֶחֶם
מִן הָאָרֶץ.

Baruch ata Adonai, Elohenu melech ha-olam, ha-motzi lechem min ha-aretz.

Praised be Thou, O Lord our God, King of the universe, who brings bread from the earth.

In order to recite this prayer, observant Jews will consume bread at each meal. If bread is not eaten as part of the meal, it is required that individual blessings be recited for each category of food that is eaten. See page 148.

CONCLUDING THE MEAL

Grace After Meals

After eating a full meal (one that includes bread), the Grace After Meals is recited. The full Grace can be found in all daily prayerbooks. The following is an abbreviated version.

Whereas ten or more adults constitute a *minyan* for a regular prayer service, three or more adults constitute a quorum for the recitation of Grace After Meals. (The *minyan* for a meal is called a *mezuman*.) When three or more are present at mealtime, Grace begins with a special introduction, starting with the words *Rabotai ne-varech*, meaning "People, let us say Grace." These words are spoken by one of the three and responded to by the others.

בָּרוּךְ אַתָּה יְיָ, אֱלֹהֵינוּ מֶלֶךְ הָעוֹלָם, הַזָּן אֶת־
הָעוֹלָם כֻּלּוֹ בְּטוּבוֹ, בְּחֵן, בְּחֶסֶד, וּבְרַחֲמִים. הוּא
נוֹתֵן לֶחֶם לְכָל־בָּשָׂר, כִּי לְעוֹלָם חַסְדּוֹ. וּבְטוּבוֹ
הַגָּדוֹל תָּמִיד לֹא חָסַר לָנוּ וְאַל יֶחְסַר לָנוּ מָזוֹן
לְעוֹלָם וָעֶד, בַּעֲבוּר שְׁמוֹ הַגָּדוֹל. כִּי הוּא אֵל זָן
וּמְפַרְנֵס לַכֹּל, וּמֵטִיב לַכֹּל, וּמֵכִין מָזוֹן לְכָל־
בְּרִיּוֹתָיו אֲשֶׁר בָּרָא. בָּרוּךְ אַתָּה יְיָ, הַזָּן אֶת־הַכֹּל.

Baruch ata Adonai, Elohenu melech ha-olam, ha-zan et ha-olam kulo be-tuvo, be-chen, be-chesed, u-ve-rachamim. Hu noten lechem le-chol basar ki le-olam chasdo. U-ve-tuvo ha-gadol tamid lo chasar lanu ve-al yechsar lanu mazon le-olam va-ed, ba-avur shemo ha-gadol ki hu zan u-me-farnes la-kol, u-me-tiv la-kol, u-me-chin mazon le-chol beriyotav asher bara. Baruch ata, Adonai, ha-zan et ha-kol.

Praised be Thou, O Lord our God, King of the universe, who sustains the whole world with goodness, kindness, and mercy. Thou providest food for all creatures; Thy lovingkindness extends forever. Because of thine abundant goodness we have never been in need and, we pray that we shall never be in need. Thou, O God, in Thy great goodness, providest for all Thy creatures. Praised be Thou, O Lord, who sustains all life.

[On Sabbath add:]

הָרַחֲמָן הוּא יַנְחִילֵנוּ יוֹם שֶׁכֻּלּוֹ שַׁבָּת וּמְנוּחָה לְחַיֵּי
הָעוֹלָמִים.

Ha-rachaman hu yanchilenu yom she-kulo shabbat u-menucha le-cha'yay ha-olamim.

May the All-merciful grant us a day of true rest, reflecting the life of eternity.

וְנִשָׂא בְרָכָה מֵאֵת יְיָ, וּצְדָקָה מֵאֱלֹהֵי יִשְׁעֵנוּ.
וְנִמְצָא חֵן וְשֵׂכֶל טוֹב בְּעֵינֵי אֱלֹהִים וְאָדָם.
עֹשֶׂה שָׁלוֹם בִּמְרוֹמָיו, הוּא יַעֲשֶׂה שָׁלוֹם עָלֵינוּ
וְעַל כָּל־יִשְׂרָאֵל, וְאִמְרוּ, אָמֵן.

Ve-nisa ve-racha me-et Adonai, u-tzedaka me-Elohay yishenu. Ve-nimtza chen ve-sechel tov be-enay Elohim ve-adam.

Oseh shalom bi-meromav, hu ya-aseh shalom alenu ve-al kol Yisrael, ve-imru, Amen.

May we receive blessings from the Lord, lovingkindness from the God of our deliverance. May we find grace and good favor before God and all man.

May He who brings peace to His universe bring peace to us and to all the people Israel, and let us say, Amen.

FOOD BLESSINGS BETWEEN MEALS

For Wine

בָּרוּךְ אַתָּה יְיָ, אֱלֹהֵינוּ מֶלֶךְ הָעוֹלָם, בּוֹרֵא פְּרִי
הַגָּפֶן.

Baruch ata Adonai, Elohenu melech ha-olam, boray peri ha-gafen.

Praised be Thou, O Lord our God, King of the universe, who created the fruit of the vine.

For Vegetables

בָּרוּךְ אַתָּה יְיָ, אֱלֹהֵינוּ מֶלֶךְ הָעוֹלָם, בּוֹרֵא פְּרִי
הָאֲדָמָה.

Baruch ata Adonai, Elohenu melech ha-olam, boray peri ha-adama.

Praised be Thou, O Lord our God, King of the universe, who created the fruit of the earth.

For Fruit

בָּרוּךְ אַתָּה יְיָ, אֱלֹהֵינוּ מֶלֶךְ הָעוֹלָם, בּוֹרֵא פְּרִי הָעֵץ.

Baruch ata Adonai, Elohenu melech ha-olam, boray peri ha-etz.

Praised be Thou, O Lord our God, King of the universe, who created the fruit of the tree.

For Cakes and Pastries

בָּרוּךְ אַתָּה יְיָ, אֱלֹהֵינוּ מֶלֶךְ הָעוֹלָם, בּוֹרֵא מִינֵי מְזוֹנוֹת.

Baruch ata Adonai, Elohenu melech ha-olam, boray minay mezonot.

Praised be Thou, O Lord our God, who created many types of food.

For Other Foods and Beverages

Recite this blessing before consuming beverages other than wine and before consuming food that does not come from the soil. This includes meat, fish, milk, and cheese.

בָּרוּךְ אַתָּה יְיָ, אֱלֹהֵינוּ מֶלֶךְ הָעוֹלָם, שֶׁהַכֹּל נִהְיֶה בִּדְבָרוֹ.

Baruch ata Adonai, Elohenu melech ha-olam, she-ha-kol ni-he'yeh bi-devaro.

Praised be Thou, O Lord our God, King of the universe, by whose word all things came into being.

SPECIAL BENEDICTIONS OF THANKSGIVING

The She-hecheyanu Prayer

The following prayer of thanksgiving, the *She-hecheyanu*, is recited on many occasions in the course of the year, including

- when the candles are blessed and when *Kiddush* is recited on the first two days of all major holidays
- when one puts on a garment for the first time
- when one tastes a food for the first time in the year
- when celebrating a *Brit*

The *She-hecheyanu* blessing is:

בָּרוּךְ אַתָּה יְיָ, אֱלֹהֵינוּ מֶלֶךְ הָעוֹלָם, שֶׁהֶחֱיָנוּ,
וְקִיְּמָנוּ, וְהִגִּיעָנוּ לַזְּמַן הַזֶּה.

Baruch ata Adonai, Elohenu melech ha-olam, she-hecheyanu, ve-kiyemanu, ve-higiyanu la-zeman ha-zeh.

Praised be Thou, O Lord our God, King of the universe, who has kept us alive, and sustained us, and permitted us to enjoy this day.

The Ha-gomel Prayer

According to the Talmud, four types of persons who have escaped harm should recite a prayer of thanksgiving: one who has safely completed a sea trip, one who has crossed the desert successfully, one who has recovered from a serious illness, and one who has been released from prison.

Although the benediction may be recited at any time, traditionally it is recited after one has received an *aliya* and completed reciting the second Torah blessing.

The blessing is as follows:

בָּרוּךְ אַתָּה יְיָ, אֱלֹהֵינוּ מֶלֶךְ הָעוֹלָם, הַגּוֹמֵל
לְחַיָּבִים טוֹבוֹת, שֶׁגְּמָלַנִי כָּל טוֹב.

Baruch ata Adonai, Elohenu melech ha-olam, ha-gomel l'cha'yavim tovot, she-gemalani kol tov.

Praised be Thou, O Lord our God, King of the universe, who grants favors unto the undeserving and has shown kindness unto me.

[When recited in the presence of a congregation, the congregation responds:]

מִי שֶׁגְּמָלְךָ (שֶׁגְמָלֵךְ) כָּל טוֹב, הוּא יִגְמָלְךָ (יִגְמְלֵךְ) כָּל טוֹב, סֶלָה.

Mi she-gemalcha (she-gemalech for females) *kol tov, Hu yigmalcha (yigmalech* for females) *kol tov, sela.*

May He has shown you kindness now favor you with kindness forever.

7

In the Synagogue

Introduction

The synagogue as we know it today has its roots in the two Temples that once existed in Jerusalem. The main activity in the Temples was the offering of sacrifices as a way of worshipping God, showing loyalty to Him, and imploring Him for forgiveness. Although psalms were sung by the Levites when sacrifices were brought, no formal service in which the masses could participate had yet developed.

After the destruction of the First Temple in 586 B.C.E., the Jews were exiled to Babylonia. Since sacrifices could not be brought anywhere but in the Temple in Jerusalem, the Jews of Babylonia began to feel a spiritual vacuum and yearned for a form of religious expression. Gradually, they began to assemble informally on the Sabbath and holidays. Prophets and Priests began to preach and teach the masses, instructing them in the laws of the Torah. Little by little a worship service developed, and psalms that had been sung by the Levites in the Temple were recited along with newly introduced prayers.

When the Second Temple was built seventy years later and the sacrificial system was resumed, the prayer services continued concurrently. Consequently, when the Second Temple was destroyed by the Romans in 70 C.E., a body of familiar prayers was already in place for use in the synagogues that began to spring up. Sacrifices, which had been the "service of the altar" in Temple times, were now replaced by prayers, which collectively were characterized as the "service of the heart."

Over the centuries the function of the synagogue changed. In addition to serving as a house of prayer *(Bet Tefila)*, it became a house of assembly—a community meeting hall—and hence took on the name *Bet Knesset* ("House of Assembly"). In time the synagogue became a place for study as well. Thus, the name *Bet Midrash* ("House of Study") was applied to it. Today, the synagogue is very much a house of prayer, assembly, and study.

This chapter describes the modern synagogue, its physical makeup and the various types of religious services held in it on weekdays, the Sabbath, and holidays. It explains the functions of the rabbi, cantor, and others who lead and assist in conducting these services. Finally, it explores the elements of the Torah reading service, explaining how, why, and when the Torah is read. For the less knowledgeable person, practical information on what to expect when receiving a Torah honor is presented.

THE PHYSICAL MAKEUP OF THE SYNAGOGUE

The Holy Ark

The ark was the centerpiece of the Tabernacle that the Children of Israel carried with them during their forty-year trek through the desert. In it were kept the two tablets on which were inscribed the Ten Commandments.

Today, after the Torah itself, the ark is considered the most sacred object in Jewish life. It is the focal point of every synagogue, and the most important rites and rituals of Judaism center about it.

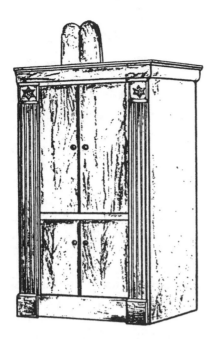

The gifted biblical craftsman Bezalel built the first ark. It was housed in the Tabernacle carried by the Children of Israel during their forty-year trek through the desert on the way to the Promised Land. The ark contained the Ten Commandments received by Moses on Mount Sinai.

A seven-branched *menora* (candelabrum) graced the Tabernacle in the desert and later the Temples in Jerusalem. The Rabbis forbade duplication of the Temple holy objects, and, for this reason, on the middle branch of a synagogue candelabrum one often sees a Star of David rather than a candle holder.

The ark curtain above is of the traditional type once seen in many synagogues. Today many new artistic designs are commonplace. The first mention of an ark curtain is found in the Book of Exodus (26:31-33), where we are told that it was made of "blue, purple, and crimson yarns. . . ." These are the popular curtain colors for ark curtains used during the year. On holidays, particularly the High Holidays, white is the color commonly used.

Location of the Ark

Traditionally, no matter where Jews live they direct their prayers toward Jerusalem, the place where the Temple of Solomon once stood. Since Jews face the ark when praying, in most Western countries, the ark is found along the synagogue's eastern wall.

The Ark and Its Curtain

The ark in Ashkenazic synagogues is called the *Aron Kodesh* ("Holy Ark"). Usually a velvet or silk curtain *(parochet)* hangs in front of it. In Sephardic congregations the ark is called the *Hechal.* An ark curtain hangs behind its doors.

In Exodus 40:21, Moses is described as having "brought the ark into the Tabernacle and set up the curtain and screened the ark." In the days of the First and Second Temples the *parochet* separated the Holy of Holies from the rest of the Temple.

Multiple Torot in Each Ark

In the average synagogue ark one will find several Torot (plural of Torah), since there are occasions when two or even three scrolls are read on a particular Sabbath or holiday. Each Torah housed in the ark is covered with a mantle.

Synagogue Candelabra

The candelabrum *(menora)* that was the centerpiece of the Tabernacle in the wilderness and of the First and Second Temples in Jerusalem had seven branches. After the Temples were destroyed, it became a tradition that the appurtenances of the Temple should not be duplicated exactly, and seven-branched *menorot* should therefore not be constructed. Consequently, the six-branched *menora* became popular, but any number of branches other than seven was permissible. A Star of David is often affixed to the center arm of the six-branched *menora.*

The original eternal light (*ner tamid*) was the westernmost branch of the seven-branched *menora* that was the centerpiece of the First and Second Temples. It was fed with oil each day and burned continuously. An eternal light of the type illustrated above was introduced in the eighteenth century as an overhead fixture.

In Temple times, the Ten Commandments, known also as the Two Tablets of the Law, were stored in the Holy of Holies, an area off-limits to everyone except the High Priest, who entered it only once yearly, on Yom Kippur. The Ten Commandments have become a popular synagogue decorative motif. They made be found above the ark, on the doors of the ark, on the outside of synagogue edifices, and as the embroidered design on ark curtains and Torah mantles.

The Eternal Light

The eternal light *(ner tamid)*, which hangs above the ark in most synagogues and burns perpetually, was originally the westernmost light of the seven-branched candelabrum of the Temple in Jerusalem. That light, fed constantly with oil, burned continuously, its chief function being to serve as a source from which the other six branches would be lighted. The other six lights were extinguished daily for cleaning purposes. The source branch was known in Hebrew as the *shamash,* meaning "that which serves." The eternal light in the modern synagogue represents the *shamash* of the Temple *menora.*

The Ten Commandments

According to the Bible (Exodus 34), the Ten Commandments—the two tablets of the Law—were brought down by Moses from Mount Sinai. These were placed in the ark, which accompanied the Jewish people during the entire post-Exodus period.

The Ten Commandments has become a popular synagogue decorative motif. Sometimes it is made of wood or stone and mounted above the ark or on the outside of the synagogue building. Oftentimes it is embroidered on the ark curtain or Torah mantle.

The Star of David

The six-pointed star is called *Magen David* in Hebrew, meaning "Shield of David." There is no mention of it in the Bible, nor is there a clear connection between it and King David. The earliest use of the six-pointed star as a decorative piece was in the synagogue of Capernaum in the third century C.E., and its first known use on a tombstone dates back to sixth-century Italy.

In seventeenth-century Prague, the *Magen David* appeared for the first time on the official seal of a Jewish community and in printed prayerbooks. Thereafter, the Star of David appeared more and more often as a decoration on arks and Torah covers and on the doors and walls of synagogues.

In modern times, the Star of David has become popular as an article of jewelry, usually worn on a neckchain.

The Lion as a Symbol

In the synagogue, representations of the lion often appear embroidered on Torah mantles and on the ark curtain. Sculpted lions are sometimes seen flanking the Ten Commandments that are mounted above the ark.

More than any other animal, the lion is mentioned in the Bible as a symbol of strength. In fact, Judah, the fourth son of Jacob, was nicknamed "The Lion" because of his strength of character.

The Pulpit

The platform on which the cantor officiates and the Torah reading is conducted is called the *bima* by Ashkenazic Jews. Sephardim refer to the platform as the *tayva,* a term also used to designate the ark.

In Orthodox synagogues the pulpit is traditionally located in the center of the room, while in non-Orthodox synagogues the pulpit is located near the ark area.

Rabbi Moshe Feinstein, considered the foremost Orthodox authority of the last generation, ruled that there is no reason why a service and Torah reading must be conducted from a platform in the center of the synagogue; the *bima* may be situated elsewhere if convenient. He says, however, that large synagogues would be well advised to position the platform in the center of the room to offset the conduct of Reform Jews, who introduced the idea of locating the *bima* near the ark.

Women's Section

Because women might distract men during prayer, in Orthodox synagogues mixed seating is not permitted. Women sit either in a gallery or, if on the same level as the rest of the congregation, behind a divider, which in Hebrew is called a *mechitza.* Dividers vary in height and design.

In Conservative and Reform congregations men and women sit together.

THE SYNAGOGUE STAFF

The Rabbi

The rabbi is basically a teacher. In fact, the Hebrew word *rabi* means "my teacher." In post-talmudic times (after the sixth century C.E.) the rabbi would preach only twice a year: on the Sabbath before Passover *(Shabbat Ha-gadol)* and on the Sabbath between Rosh Hashana and Yom Kippur *(Shabbat Shuva)*. During the last century it became customary for rabbis to deliver a weekly Sabbath sermon.

Although it is not required that a rabbi be present for a religious service to be held, in the modern synagogue he plays a crucial role. Aside from preaching, the rabbi leads religious services, conducts an educational program for synagogue members, and officiates at rites of passage for members of the congregation.

Orthodox seminaries accept only men as candidates for the rabbinate. Non-Orthodox schools have been granting ordination to women since the early 1970s.

The Cantor

The person who chants the service and leads the congregation in prayer is called the cantor *(chazan* in Hebrew). Technically, any layman can serve as cantor, but on Sabbaths and holidays most congregations employ a professional with a pleasing voice to lead the service. A layman acting as cantor is called a *baal tefila,* "prayer leader."

In most congregations today, the professional cantor also trains children for their Bar and Bat Mitzva ceremonies and performs at weddings and funerals.

Traditionally, only men have served as cantors, but today many women serve in that capacity in non-Orthodox synagogues.

Gabbaim

A person who assists in the running of congregational services is known as a *gabbai* (plural, *gabbaim*). If the individual is salaried, he is usually called the sexton *(shamash)* of the congregation, whereas volunteers are usually simply referred to as *gabbaim*. The latter may serve as ushers who show people to their seats, distribute Torah honors to congregants, or stand on either side of the reading table while the Torah is being read.

The Torah Reader

Although most congregations employ a specially trained person to read the Torah at all services, some encourage individual members to read their own portions when called to the Torah. An official Torah reader is called a *baal koray* or *baal keria*.

THE TORAH SCRIBE

Function of the Scribe

The scribe, or *sofer* as he is called in Hebrew, is a skilled calligrapher who is involved in preparing the most sacred ritual articles and documents connected with the Jewish home and synagogue. He hand-letters sheets of parchment that are sewn together to form Torah scrolls; he writes parchments that are placed inside phylacteries *(tefilin)* and *mezuzot;* and he writes divorce documents *(gittin,* plural of *get).*

Jewish law requires that a scribe be both learned and pious.

Immersion in a Mikva

A scribe engaged in the writing of a Torah scroll immerses himself in a *mikva* (ritual bath) at the beginning of the task and also on those days on which he will be writing God's name. See page 49 for more on the *mikva*.

Women as Scribes

Although it is males who have traditionally served as scribes, women have never been legally banned from the profession. Two celebrated Yemenite women—Miriam, daughter of the famous fourteenth-century Yemenite scribe Bena'yahu, and Shama'a, daughter of Shabazi—were well-known scribes.

THE SYNAGOGUE SERVICE

Public Prayer Services

For a public prayer service to be held, a quorum of ten adults must be present. A quorum of ten is called a *minyan*.

Traditionally, although no such ruling appears in the Talmud, only males above the age of maturity (thirteen) have been counted as part of a quorum. The ineligibility of women was first mentioned one thousand years later in the sixteenth-century *Code of Jewish Law*.

Today, many non-Orthodox congregations count women to a *minyan*.

Why Ten for a Minyan?

Based upon the biblical (Numbers 41:26) characterization of the group of ten spies sent by Moses to scout the land of Canaan as a "congregation" *(ayda)*, the Rabbis of the Talmud decided that ten is the proper number of persons to constitute a *minyan*.

When a Quorum Is Required

It is mandatory that a *minyan* be present in order to:

- conduct a public Torah reading
- recite the *Barechu* prayer
- recite the *Kaddish* prayer
- recite the *Kedusha* prayer of the Silent Devotion
- recite the Priestly Benediction.

When a Quorum Is Recommended

A *minyan* is recommended but not mandatory for:

- a circumcision ceremony
- a *Pidyon Ha-ben* ceremony
- a marriage ceremony
- the recitation of *Yizkor*
- recitation of prayers at graveside.

Three Daily Prayer Services

Traditional Jews pray three times each day, either at home or in the synagogue. The Talmud suggests that Abraham introduced the morning prayers *(Shacharit),* Isaac the afternoon prayers *(Mincha),* and Jacob the evening prayers *(Maariv).* Rabbi Gamaliel II, head of the Sanhedrin (supreme court) in the first century C.E., postulated a much later date for the introduction of these prayer services. He associated them with Daniel, who "knelt down and prayed three times a day" (Daniel 6:11), and with the psalmist who declared, "As for me, I call to God . . . evening, morning, and noon" (Psalms 55:18).

Historically, however, the prayer services are associated with the sacrificial system of the First and Second Temples. Animal sacrifices were offered every morning and afternoon, and the *Shacharit* and *Mincha* services are reminders of these offerings. *Maariv,* the third daily service, has no connection with this system.

Structure of the Morning Service

The weekday morning service *(Shacharit)* begins with the donning of the *talit* and *tefilin* by adult members of the congregation and the recitation of appropriate prayers to accompany the performance of these rites. In traditional congregations a series of prayers called the *Pesukay De-zimra,* "Verses of Praise," most of which are selections from the Book of Psalms, is then recited. This lengthy segment of the morning service begins with the *Baruch She'amar* ("Blessed Is He Who Said") prayer and introduces the main body of prayers of the morning service.

The core of the *Shacharit* service consists of the *Barechu,* a call to prayer; the *Shema* ("Hear, O Israel . . ."); and the *Amida,* the Silent Devotion. The *Amida* ends with *Sim Shalom,* a prayer for peace, preceded by the Priestly Benediction *(Birkat*

Kohanim), which is recited daily in Jerusalem synagogues and on the Sabbath and/or holidays in the Diaspora.

On the Sabbath and holidays the morning service is supplemented by special prayers. See Chapter Eight, The Sabbath, for additional information.

The more prominent morning prayers are described below.

The Additional Service

On the Sabbath, Rosh Chodesh, and holidays, extra prayers are recited as a supplement to the *Shacharit* service. The origin of this segment, known as the *Musaf* ("additional") service, can be traced to the additional animal sacrifices that were brought on the altar on the aforementioned days. See Chapter Eight for more information.

Structure of the Afternoon Service

In Temple days, the afternoon sacrificial offering was called *mincha* ("gift"), and the same appellation was given to the afternoon synagogue prayer service that replaced it. The main feature of the *Mincha* service is the silent recitation of the *Amida* by the congregants and its repetition aloud by the cantor. Psalm 145 *(Ashray)*, a song of praise to God, was later added as an introductory prayer. The afternoon service concludes with the recitation of the *Alenu,* another song of praise to God, and the recitation of the *Kaddish* by mourners.

At the *Mincha* service on the Sabbath and holidays, after the *Ashray* an additional prayer *(U-va Le-Tziyon)*—which consists of verses from the Torah, the Prophets, and the Holy Writings—is recited. On Sabbaths only, this is followed by the reading of the Torah.

The more prominent afternoon prayers are described below.

Structure of the Evening Service

Since sacrifices were offered in the Temple only during daylight hours, some of the Rabbis of the Talmud express the view that it is unnecessary to hold an evening prayer service. However, since the Bible (Daniel 6:11) speaks of Daniel praying "three times a day" and the Book of Psalms (55:18) refers to prayers "evening, morning, and noon," the idea of introducing a formal evening prayer service prevailed.

This third service, called *Maariv* (literally, "evening"), is longer than the *Mincha* service but much shorter than the *Shacharit* service. It begins with the *Barechu* call to prayer and is followed by a short prayer which introduces the *Shema*. This is followed by the recitation of the *Amida* silently by the congregation. The cantor does not repeat the *Amida* at any evening service.

Maariv concludes with the recitation of the *Alenu* and the recitation of the *Kaddish* by mourners.

On the Sabbath and holidays, special prayers plus the *Kiddush* are recited as well. The service generally concludes with the singing of the *Yigdal* hymn.

The more prominent evening prayers are described below.

Prayer Posture

The formal posture for prayer is the standing position. As the synagogue service grew longer, it became difficult for congregants to stand for prolonged periods, so only the more important prayers were recited while standing.

There are no hard-and-fast rules as to which prayers must be said while standing, although it is generally accepted that the *Barechu,* the *Hallel,* and the *Kedusha* are sufficiently important to warrant the formal posture.

Some authorities maintained that prayers of biblical origin that were studied in academies of learning should be recited in a sitting position because sitting is the normal position for study. This will explain why one does not have to stand while the Torah is read and why in Orthodox synagogues one does not stand for the recitation of the *Shema.*

The Prayerbook

Siddur means "order [of prayers]" and *Machzor* means "cycle [of prayers]." At first these words were used interchangeably to refer to the prayerbook. Scholars of the seventh to tenth centuries used the term *Seder Tefila* ("order of prayers") for their prayerbook, which contained the liturgy of the entire year.

As the centuries passed, more and more prayers and poems *(piyutim)* were composed for holiday services, and these found their way into the prayerbook. As a result, the prayerbook became rather heavy for worshippers to hold while at prayer, and so in recent centuries individual prayerbooks were printed for each holiday (Rosh Hashana, Yom Kippur, Pesach, Shavuot, and Sukkot). These were called *Machzorim* (singular, *Machzor*). The weekday and the Sabbath prayerbooks were called *Siddurim* (singular, *Siddur*). The name designations are completely arbitrary.

PRIMARY PRAYERS

The prayers described below are among the best known and most frequently recited in the daily, Sabbath, and holiday liturgies.

Adon Olam

Composed by the illustrious eleventh-century poet and philosopher Solomon Ibn Gabirol, the *Adon Olam* ("Master of the Universe") prayer was added to the morning *(Shacharit)* liturgy in the fifteenth century. It emphasizes the belief that as long as we trust in God, we have no cause to fear. The *Adon Olam* became exceedingly popular as the concluding hymn for Sabbath and holiday morning services.

Al Chet

Al Chet, meaning "For the Sin [we have committed before Thee]," was composed in the post-talmudic period (sixth to tenth centuries). This Confession of Sins, included in each of the five Yom Kippur services, mentions forty-four transgressions for which the individual seeks forgiveness. Particular emphasis is placed on sins of speech. It is traditional to beat one's breast as each of the transgressions is recited. (See also *Ashamnu,* page 167).

Alenu

Alenu means "It is our duty [to praise God and proclaim

his sovereignty]," and the prayer so named expresses the hope that ultimately *all* people will accept His omnipotence and that God will thus "reign forever and ever."

Because of its beautiful sentiments, the *Alenu* has won the hearts of Jews and has become a favorite concluding prayer at all formal religious services.

Al Ha-nisim

Since miracles played a central role in the Purim and Chanuka stories, in the eighth century the *Al Ha-nisim* ("For the Miracles") was added to each *Amida* prayer when recited on these holidays. It was also added to the Grace After Meals on these holidays.

The Amida

One of the oldest and most important prayers in Jewish liturgy was originally called the *Tefila*, meaning "Prayer." It originated with the men of the Great Synagogue, an institution that predates the Talmud.

Because the *Tefila* consisted of eighteen benedictions, it also became known as the *Shmoneh Esray*, literally "Eighteen." When a nineteenth benediction was added at a later date, the prayer came to be called the *Amida*, the "Standing [prayer]." *Amida* is the more accurate of the designations, because on the Sabbath and holidays this prayer contains only seven benedictions.

Because this prayer is so important and personal, it is always recited silently while standing, and therefore it acquired the additional name "Silent Devotion."

Maimonides summarized the content of the *Amida* when he wrote, "the first three benedictions deal with praise of God, the last three with thanksgiving, and those in the middle with petitions for personal and communal needs."

See also the discussion of *Kedusha* on page 171.

An'im Zemirot

Orthodox congregations conclude the Sabbath and festival *Musaf* service with *An'im Zemirot* ("I Will Chant Sweet Hymns"), which is chanted responsively by the prayer leader and the congregation. This hymn, popularly known as *Shir*

Ha-kavod ("Hymn of Glory"), was composed by Yehuda Hechasid, a prominent twelfth-century German mystic. The content of the poem is reflected in its opening couplets:

> I will chant sweet hymns and compose songs;
> For my soul yearns after Thee,
> My soul longs to be under the shadow of
> Thy hand,
> To know all Thy mysteries.

Ashamnu

Like the *Al Chet* (page 165), the *Ashamnu* ("We Have Sinned") is a Confession of Sins recited on Yom Kippur. Consisting of only twenty-eight words, it lists alphabetically, in general terms, the sins we as members of the community may have committed and for which we seek forgiveness. Traditionally, as each sin is mentioned, worshippers beat their left breast (over the heart) as a symbolic expression of remorse.

In Orthodox congregations, at most morning services the *Ashamnu* prayer is recited after the *Amida,* but it is particularly associated with Yom Kippur, when all Jews repeat it several times in the course of the day.

Ashray

The *Ashray,* a song of praise to God expressing complete confidence in His concern for all His creatures, is recited twice during every morning service and once during every afternoon service. Consisting of the twenty-one verses of Psalm 145, the song is introduced by two additional verses, one from Psalms 84:5 and one from Psalms 144:15, both of which begin with the word *Ashray,* meaning "praiseworthy, fortunate," hence, the name of the prayer.

The Rabbis of the Talmud said that anyone who recites the *Ashray* faithfully three times a day is assured of a share in the world-to-come.

Avinu Malkenu

One of the most popular prayers recited during the Ten Days of Penitence (from Rosh Hashana through Yom Kippur) is *Avinu Malkenu* ("Our Father, Our King"). The forty-four verses that comprise this prayer, usually recited responsively by cantor and congregation, are an expression of remorse for sins that have been committed and a plea for forgiveness. *Avinu Malkenu* is not recited on the Sabbath.

Barechu

Barechu ("Praised") is the first word of the proclamation that the cantor recites morning and evening when summoning the congregation to engage in public prayer. To the words *Barechu et Adonai Ha-mevorach*, "Praised be God, the Blessed One," the congregation responds, *Baruch Adonai Ha-mevorach le-olam va-ed*, "Praised be God, the Blessed One, forever and ever." If a quorum of ten adults *(minyan)* is not present in the synagogue, the *Barechu* is omitted from the service.

Baruch She-amar

The *Baruch She-amar* ("Blessed Is He Who Said") is the opening prayer of the *Pesukay De-zimra* ("Verses of Praise") section of each morning service. It expresses the same sentiment found in the first chapter of Genesis—namely, that God created the world by proclamation.

Birkat Kohanim

In the Bible (Numbers 6:22-27), the Priests were commanded to bless the Children of Israel:

> May the Lord bless thee and keep thee.
> May the Lord cause his countenance
> to shine upon thee and be gracious unto thee.
> May the Lord lift his countenance toward
> thee and grant thee peace.

The Priestly Benediction is called *Birkat Kohanim* in Hebrew (see page 168 for the Hebrew text), and the ceremony during which it is recited is popularly known as *duchening*. The word *duchening* is derived from the Hebrew *duchan*, meaning "platform." The Temple Priests would mount a platform each day and bless the assembled congregation.

In Jerusalem synagogues today this rite is performed by a *Kohen* each morning. In the Diaspora it is performed in most Orthodox Ashkenazic synagogues only on the more important

When pronouncing the Priestly Benediction, the *Kohen* stretches forward both arms and extends the fingers of each hand, separating the little finger and the ring finger from the others, thus forming a V. The Rabbis in talmudic times believed that the custom stems from the verse in the Song of Songs (2:9), "My beloved [Israel] is like a young deer who stands behind our wall and looks through our windows; he peers through the latticework." The windows, said the Rabbis, are the Priest's shoulders and arms; the latticework his fingers.

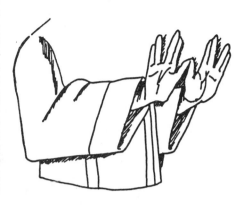

holidays in the Jewish calendar: Rosh Hashana, Yom Kippur, Passover, Sukkot, and Shavuot. Sephardim *duchen* at every Sabbath service as well.

Today, rabbis who are not Priests sometimes use the *Birkat Kohanim* as a blessing for a Bar or Bat Mitzva or for a bride and groom. This benediction is also sometimes recited at the conclusion of a service.

El Adon

El Adon ("God, the Lord of All"), a poem *(piyut)* extolling the greatness of God, was added to the Sabbath morning service in the post-talmudic period (after the sixth century C.E.). The first letter of each of this popular hymn's twenty-two phrases form the Hebrew alphabet.

El Malay Rachamim

El Malay Rachamim ("God Full of Mercy"), a memorial prayer evoking tender memories of the dead, is recited at funeral services, at *Yizkor* services, and when visiting a grave. See page 93 for more about this prayer.

En Kamocha

At Sabbath and festival services in Ashkenazic synagogues, when the Torah is removed from the ark for a public reading, the *En Kamocha* ("There is None Like Thee [among the gods, O Lord]") is recited. Sephardim recite this same prayer, which consists of verses from the Book of Psalms (86:8, 145:13, and 29:11), but introduce it with a verse from Deuteronomy (4:35) which begins with the words *Ata hareta la-daat* ("You have been taught to know [that the Lord alone is God, and there is none beside Him]").

En Kelohenu

En Kelohenu ("There Is None Like Our God") is the opening phrase of a very popular hymn sung at the conclusion of Sabbath and festival services. The first of its five stanzas reads:

> There is none like our God,
> There is none like our Master,
> There is none like our King,
> There is none like our Deliverer.

The stanzas that follow repeat the same words with only the first word changed.

When the letters beginning each of the stanzas are put side by side, they form the words *Amen ba*, "Amen is coming," meaning that the service is about to conclude.

In all Sephardic and Chassidic congregations the *En Kelohenu* is sung at the conclusion of all weekday services as well as on the Sabbath and holidays.

In most traditional synagogues a sixth stanza, which recalls the sacrificial system, has been appended to the *En Kelohenu*.

Hallel

In Second Temple days, the *Hallel* ("Psalms of Praise"), which was comprised of six selections from the Book of Psalms (113-18), was recited only at the Seder on the first night of Passover and on Sukkot and Chanuka. Subsequently the Rabbis ruled that *Hallel* should also be recited on Shavuot, the third of the three pilgrim festivals.

In Babylonia, during the Exile, the recitation of the *Hallel* throughout the Passover holiday as well as on Rosh Chodesh was introduced. To indicate that this practice deviated from established Palestinian practice, Babylonian Jewry omitted verses 1-11 of Psalm 115 and verses 1-11 of Psalm 116 when *Hallel* was recited on Rosh Chodesh and on the last days of

Passover. This abbreviated *Hallel* is popularly known as *Half Hallel.*

The Kaddish

Kaddish is a form of the word *kadosh,* meaning "holy." Originally, the Aramaic prayer so named was recited after the completion of study sessions in school and synagogue. Later, this prayer extolling God's holiness was introduced into the synagogue worship service and was recited by the prayer leader in various forms at the conclusion of various sections of the service.

In the thirteenth century the *Kaddish,* which declares man's submission to the will of God, was considered an appropriate prayer for mourners to recite aloud during the synagogue service, particularly at its conclusion, after the *Alenu.*

See Chapter Four, Death and Mourning, for more about the *Kaddish.*

Kedusha

The most important part of the *Amida* prayer is the *Kedusha* (literally, "Holiness" or "Sanctification"). As the name implies, this is an expression of praise of God, who is exalted above material existence.

As the *Kedusha* is recited by congregation and cantor, it is traditional for participants to keep their feet together as a sign of respect.

Depending on whether it is a Sabbath or weekday and whether the service in question is *Shacharit* (morning), *Mincha* (afternoon), or *Maariv* (evening), the wording of the *Kedusha* varies. There is also a difference between the *Kedusha* recited by Ashkenazim and Sephardim.

Kiddush

The *Kiddush* ("Sanctification") is one of the most important prayers associated with the Jewish home and synagogue, for this blessing over wine is recited both on the Sabbath and holidays. The exact wording of the *Kiddush* dates back to talmudic times (first to fifth century C.E.), but its origin is ascribed

to the men of the Great Assembly of the sixth to fourth centuries
B.C.E.

See page 201 for the wording of the Sabbath *Kiddush* and
page 245 for the *Kiddush* recited on festivals.

Kol Nidre

On Yom Kippur five distinct services are conducted, the
first being the *Kol Nidre,* which begins before sunset on the
tenth of Tishri. This Yom Kippur eve service is so named
because it begins with the cantor chanting a prayer that starts
with the words *Kol Nidre* ("All Vows [renunciations, promises
. . . may we be absolved of them . . ."]. Once this legal declaration
has been pronounced three times, congregants are considered
to have absolved themselves from unintentional sins and vows
rashly taken and can thus enter the day of fasting spiritually
clean and with a clear conscience.

Lecha Dodi

In the sixteenth century, Solomon (Shlomo) Alkabetz of Safed
composed a religious poem that is sung every Friday evening
at the conclusion of the *Kabbalat Shabbat* section of the service
(see *Lechu Ne-ranena* below). The poem's opening words—
Lecha dodi, "Come, my beloved friend [to greet the bride.
Let us welcome the Sabbath presence.]"—personify the Sabbath as a bride.

When the first letter of each of the eight verses of the poem
are placed side by side, they spell out the author's first name
and lineage: Shlomo Halevi.

Lechu Ne-ranena

In the sixteenth century, late each Friday afternoon Rabbi
Isaac Luria and his disciples would go to the hills on the outskirts
of Safed in the northern part of Palestine, and there they would
welcome the Sabbath. By way of welcome, they recited six
selections from the Book of Psalms (95-99; 29), which were
later transferred to the synagogue and were referred to as
Kabbalat Shabbat ("Welcoming the Sabbath").

The first of these psalms, which begins every Friday evening
service, opens with the words *Lechu ne-ranena* ("Come, let

us sing unto the Lord [let us acclaim in joy the Rock of our salvation]."

Ma Tovu

The *Ma Tovu* ("How Goodly [are thy tents, O Jacob, thy tabernacles, O Israel]") is the first prayer recited by a worshipper upon entering the synagogue in the morning. Oddly, these words of reverence were first spoken by the heathen prophet Balaam, who, when urged by Balak, king of Moab, to curse Israel, could only speak words of praise (Numbers 24:5). The *Ma Tovu* consists of this verse from Numbers plus four verses from the Book of Psalms (5:8; 26:8; 95:6; 69:14) which express reverence for the synagogue, the house that symbolizes God's presence.

Modeh Ani

This is the first prayer recited upon awakening in the morning. See page 145 for the wording of this prayer.

Modim

The popular prayer beginning with the words *Modim anachnu lach* ("We gratefully thank Thee") introduces the concluding section of the *Amida* recited at all services. (See above for a description of the *Amida*). While the prayer leader chants this prayer acknowledging our acceptance of God's sovereignty, members of the congregation recite a shorter version silently.

Nishmat

Nishmat kol chai ("The soul of all living beings [will bless Thy name]") is recited on Sabbath and holidays as the conclusion of the introductory segment *(Pesukay De-zimra)* of the morning *(Shacharit)* service. It expresses man's total dependence on God's mercy and his utter inability to laud Him sufficiently.

Shalom Alechem

Shalom Alechem ("Peace Unto You") are the opening words of the popular hymn chanted upon returning home from the synagogue on Friday night. Composed by the Kabbalists of the seventeenth century, this song of welcome to the "angels of peace" expresses the hope that their spirit will be present throughout the day of rest.

Shema

In Second Temple times, toward the end of the sixth century B.C.E., after the daily morning sacrifice had been offered, the Priests *(Kohanim)* would conduct a prayer service which consisted of a recitation of the Ten Commandments and the three paragraphs of the *Shema*. Today, the *Shema* is recited at every morning and evening service and often at bedtime.

The first and best-known section, taken from Deuteronomy 6:4-9, begins with the words *Shema Yisrael* ("Hear, O Israel [the Lord our God, the Lord is One]"). It implores Israel to love God and obey His commandments.

The second section (Deuteronomy 11:13-21) begins with the words *Ve-ha'ya im shamo'a* ("And it shall come to pass if you will obey [God's commandments]"). Here, the rewards for following the teachings of the Torah and the penalties for neglecting them are specified.

The third section of the *Shema* (Numbers 15:37-41) contains the commandment which directs Israelites to wear fringes on the four corners of their garments so as to be ever mindful of the obligation to live a holy life.

See page 126 for more information about the *Shema*.

Shemoneh Esray

See the description under *The Amida,* page 166.

Sim Shalom

Sim Shalom ("Establish Peace"), which concludes the *Amida* at every morning service, appears immediately after the Priestly Benediction and expands upon the peace theme with which that benediction ends.

At the afternoon and evening service an abbreviated prayer for peace beginning with the words *Shalom rav* ("Establish much peace") is substituted for the *Sim Shalom* because a formal benediction is not pronounced by the Priests at these services.

U-netaneh Tokef

One of the most popular of all Rosh Hashana and Yom Kippur prayers is *U-netaneh Tokef* ("Let Us Declare the Mighty [holiness of the day]"). This liturgical portion of the High Holiday service, which emphasizes the utter dependence of man upon God, is ascribed to the martyred Rabbi Amnon, who lived and died in Mainz, Germany, in the eleventh century and who resisted all attempts to be forcibly converted.

Ya-aleh Ve-yavo

The *Ya-aleh Ve-yavo* ("May Our Prayer [for deliverance and merciful treatment] Ascend and Come [before Thee on this holy day]") is recited on Rosh Chodesh and on all Pilgrim Festivals as part of the *Amida*. The first mention of this prayer is found in the minor talmudic tractate Soferim (19:7), where it is said to be based on the verse in the Book of Numbers (10:10): "On your festivals and New Moon days you shall sound the trumpets. . . . They shall be a reminder to you before your God."

Yigdal

The hymn *Yigdal,* which opens with the words *Yigdal Elohim chai ve-yishtabach* ("Extolled and praised be the living God"), summarizes the Thirteen Principles of Faith first expounded by Moses Maimonides in the twelfth century.

The *Yigdal* is recited as part of all morning services, and in many congregations it is sung as the closing hymn of the evening service. The Thirteen Principles referred to in the *Yigdal* include belief in one God who created and guides the world, and who alone is worthy of worship.

Yizkor

Yizkor ("May He [God] Remember") is a memorial prayer recited primarily in Ashkenazic synagogues on Yom Kippur and on the three Pilgrim Festivals. See page 100 for more about the *Yizkor.*

THE TORAH

What Is in the Torah

The Torah consists of the first five books of the Bible: Genesis, Exodus, Leviticus, Numbers, and Deuteronomy. These five books are referred to as the Five Books of Moses or the *Chumash*. In Hebrew, the word *chumash* means "five." The Latin (derived from the Greek) word for the Five Books of Moses is *Pentateuch*, meaning "five books."

What Is in the Rest of the Bible

In addition to the Torah, there are two other parts to the Bible: the Prophets *(Nevi'im)*, which consists of twenty-one books, including Joshua, Kings, Isaiah, Jeremiah, and Hosea; and the Holy Writings, or Hagiographa (*Ketuvim* or *Ketubim*), which consists of thirteen books, including Psalms, Proverbs, and Job.

This triad of *Torah, Nevi'im,* and *Ketuvim* is referred to by the Hebrew acronym *Tanach,* fashioned from the first letter of each of the Hebrew names. When we speak of *The* Torah, we are speaking only of the first five books of the Bible.

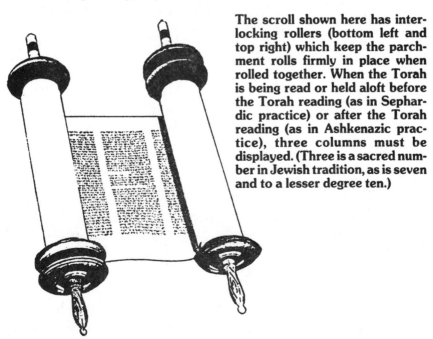

The scroll shown here has interlocking rollers (bottom left and top right) which keep the parchment rolls firmly in place when rolled together. When the Torah is being read or held aloft before the Torah reading (as in Sephardic practice) or after the Torah reading (as in Ashkenazic practice), three columns must be displayed. (Three is a sacred number in Jewish tradition, as is seven and to a lesser degree ten.)

THE THIRTY-NINE BOOKS OF THE BIBLE

THE TORAH	THE PROPHETS	THE HOLY WRITINGS
Genesis	Joshua	Psalms
Exodus	Judges	Proverbs
Leviticus	I Samuel	Job
Numbers	II Samuel	Song of Songs
Deuteronomy	I Kings	Ruth
	II Kings	Lamentations
	Isaiah	Ecclesiastes
	Jeremiah	Esther
	Ezekiel	Daniel
	Hosea	Ezra
	Joel	Nehemiah
	Amos	I Chronicles
	Obadiah	II Chronicles
	Jonah	
	Micah	
	Nahum	
	Habakkuk	
	Zephaniah	
	Haggai	
	Zechariah	
	Malachi	

How a Torah Scroll Is Prepared

The Torah Scroll *(Sefer Torah)* is written in black ink on sheets of parchment. An average sheet contains forty-two lines of text, although some contain as many as sixty. The height of the average Torah parchment ranges from eighteen to twenty-two inches. The sheets are sewn to one another with thread made from the dried veins of a kosher animal. Wooden rollers are attached to each end so that the scroll can be rolled from portion to portion without the parchment being unnecessarily handled.

Two typical columns from a handwritten Torah scroll used in the synagogue. Note that the text contains neither vowel points nor punctuation. The open spaces within the text are mandated by law, and if a scribe neglects to leave the proper spacing, the Torah may not be read in the synagogue.

Torah Processions

A Torah procession is held every time a Torah is removed

from the ark for a Sabbath or festival public reading. The person who leads the service—the cantor or a layman—carries the Torah around the synagogue, affording congregants an opportunity to acknowledge their love for the Torah by kissing its mantle.

A very special procession is held on Simchat Torah, when every congregant is given the opportunity to carry the Torah.

Holding and Transferring the Torah

When holding a Torah or carrying it in procession, one should always hold it in the right arm, over the right shoulder. When passing the Torah from one person to another, the scroll should be handed over so that it is received in the right arm. The right side is the favored side in Jewish tradition.

Synagogue Torah Readings

Portions of the Torah are read in the synagogue on every Sabbath, on major and minor holidays, and on Mondays and Thursdays. On many occasions an additional reading from the Prophets, known as the *haftara,* is chanted.

A quorum of ten adults *(minyan)* must be present when the Torah is read in public.

No Punctuation in the Torah Scroll

The Torah scroll from which a public Torah reading is conducted contains no punctuation, no vowel points, and no musical notes. The melody for each word must be studied in advance and committed to memory.

The prophetic portion *(haftara),* on the other hand, is read from a printed book that includes punctuation, vowel points, and musical notations. Different melodies are used for chanting the Torah and *haftara* readings.

Torah Cantillation

In printed Bibles, below and above the Hebrew words, musical notations, known in Hebrew as *te'amim* ("tastes, flavors") and in Yiddish as *trop,* can be found. Although there is only one system of notation, not all communities use the same melody for each of the *te'amim.* One will notice a sharp difference in the melodies used in Ashkenazic and Sephardic synagogues.

קַדְמָא מְנַח זַרְקָא מָנַח סְגוֹל מָנַח ׀ מָנַח רְבִיעִי מֻהְפַּךְ
פַּשְׁטָא זָקֵף קָטֹן זָקֵף־גָּדוֹל מֵרְכָא טִפְחָא מָנַח אֶתְנַחְתָּא
פָּזֵר תְּלִישָׁא־קְטַנָּה תְּלִישָׁא־גְרוֹלָה קַדְמָא וְאַזְלָא
אַזְלָא־גֵּרֶשׁ גֵּרְשַׁיִם דַּרְגָּא תְּבִיר יָתִיב פָּסִיק ׀ סוֹף־פָּסִיק
שַׁלְשֶׁלֶת קַרְנֵי־פָרָה מֵרְכָא־כְפוּלָה יָרֵחַ־בֶּן־יוֹמוֹ:

These are the names of the cantillation notes. The symbols
above and below the words are the notes themselves. These
symbols appear in printed copies of the Pentateuch and
the rest of the Bible, but not in handwritten Torah scrolls
read in the synagogue.

(Left) Over the centuries, beautifully-designed mantles
have been created to adorn the Torah scroll. This is in
keeping with advice of the Sages of the Talmud: "Have
among your cherished possessions a beautiful Scroll of the
Law copied by a talented scribe, written with fine ink and
quill, and wrapped in beautiful silk."

(Right) The *mappa,* used in many synagogues to cover the
Torah when it is not being read, is generally about twelve
by fourteen inches and is made of the same type of material
used for Torah mantles and ark covers.

TORAH ACCESSORIES

Primary Function of the Torah Mantle

Although a Torah cannot be defiled by touching it with bare hands, out of respect for the scroll's sanctity it has become traditional to keep it covered with a mantle when not being read.

Secondary Function of the Torah Mantle

The function of the mantle is not only to protect but also to beautify the scroll. The Talmud says that a Torah should be "wrapped in beautiful silk," but mantles fashioned out of velour or velvet are commonly used as well. White mantles are favored on holidays, particularly Rosh Hashana and Yom Kippur, and colored ones are used during the rest of the year.

To enhance a mantle's appearance, it is usually adorned with a variety of machine- or hand-embroidered designs, the most popular of which are the Ten Commandments and the Star of David.

Smaller Torah Covering

Out of respect for the Torah, whenever the Torah reading is interrupted for the recitation of a special prayer, the scroll is covered with its mantle or with a simple piece of lined material (called a *mappa*) specially made for this purpose.

The Torah Gartl

A rolled-up Torah is tied with a long band of material called

A Torah *gartl* is generally a length of material two or three inches wide and long enough to encircle a scroll two times. When tied, it holds together the rolls of parchment. Above is a modern binder (with elastic inside) attached to sterling silver buckles. In earlier centuries it was commonplace to convert the swaddling clothes used at a child's *brit* into a *gartl*, which was wrapped around the Torah designated to be read at the boy's Bar Mitzva.

a *gartl* in Yiddish. The function of the *gartl* is to encircle the Torah and keep it secure.

The Breastplate

Generally made of silver, a breastplate suspended from a chain is draped over the Torah mantle to further enhance the Torah scroll. The plate, usually 8 x 10 inches, is an imitation of the breastplate worn by the High Priest in biblical times (Exodus 28:13-30; 29:8-21).

On this traditional breastplate, one will notice the oval panel towards the bottom, in which there is space to engrave the name of a donor. The rectangular box above the panel contains small interchangeable plates engraved with the names of the various holidays. The plate bearing the name of the holiday being celebrated is placed in front so that it is clearly visible.

(Left) Sterling silver crowns, such as those pictured here, will be found adorning one or more Torah scrolls in the ark. Authorities consider the crown to be the most important Torah adornment, and they cite the statement in the Ethics of the Fathers (4:17) as proof: "There are three crowns: the crown of the Law [Torah], the crown of the Priestly office, and the crown of a good name."

(Right) Single crown adornments which fit over one of the two scroll finials are known to have been in use as far back as the tenth century. Some scholars believe that the bells attached to the single and double crowns are intended to call attention to the presence of the Torah when it is carried in procession. Other scholars assume that the purpose of the bells is to create noise which wards off evil spirts.

The Torah Crowns

The crown being a symbol of royalty, it is natural that our ancestors chose it as an adornment for the Torah, the holiest object in Jewish life. Sometimes one large silver crown is fitted over both finials (poles) of the Torah rollers, and sometimes smaller crowns are fitted over each of the two finials. The single crown is generally called a *keter Torah,* and the smaller ones are called *rimmonim* (singular, *rimmon*) or *atzay cha'yim* (singular, *etz cha'yim*).

The Torah Pointer

The Torah pointer, usually made of silver or wood, is used by the Torah reader to point to the words as he reads from the Torah scroll. Thus, he avoids touching the parchment with his bare hand. The Torah pointer is called a *yad* ("hand") in Hebrew because it is fashioned in the shape of a hand with an extended index finger.

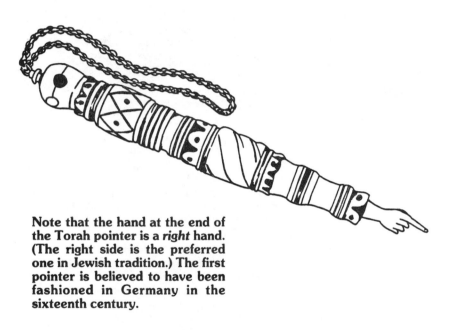

Note that the hand at the end of the Torah pointer is a *right* hand. (The right side is the preferred one in Jewish tradition.) The first pointer is believed to have been fashioned in Germany in the sixteenth century.

THE CALL TO THE TORAH

What Is an Aliya?

An *aliya* ("ascent") is a call to ascend the pulpit, approach the Torah, and recite the Torah blessings before a Torah portion is read and after it has been completed. A number of such Torah honors are awarded whenever an official Torah reading is conducted in public. The person awarded an *aliya* is called an *oleh* ("one who ascends").

Quorum Requirement

Before the Torah may be read officially in public, a quorum of ten adults *(minyan)* must be present. If a quorum cannot be gathered, the Torah may be read but *aliyot* (plural of *aliya*) may not be awarded.

Distribution of Torah Honors

When the Torah is read, depending on the holiday, three, four, five, six, or seven *aliyot* are awarded. On Sabbath mornings seven such honors are awarded, on Yom Kippur morning six, on festival mornings five, on Rosh Chodesh and on the Intermediate Days of Passover and Sukkot four. On Monday and Thursday mornings, on Saturday and Yom Kippur afternoons, and on Chanuka three *aliyot* are awarded.

Aliyot for Women

Orthodox congregations do not call women to the Torah, although in early talmudic times (100 B.C.E. to 200 C.E.) women were awarded *aliyot* and even read their own Torah portions. Today, Reform and many Conservative congregations follow the talmudic tradition of allowing women to receive *aliyot* and read from the Torah.

The Talmud makes it clear that a Torah scroll used in the synagogue cannot be made ritually unclean by anyone, including women during their menstrual period. In fact, Moses Maimonides (twelfth century) emphasized that anyone, even a non-Jew, may handle a Torah scroll.

Ashkenazic Aliya Awards

In Ashkenazic tradition a Priest *(Kohen)* always receives the first *aliya*. A Levite *(Levi)* always receives the second *aliya*. All other Jews, called Israelites *(Yisre'elim)*, are awarded the balance. The following persons among the Israelites are given preference:

- a groom on the Sabbath preceding his wedding
- a groom on the Sabbath following his wedding
- a Bar or Bat Mitzva

- the father of a newborn child
- a person observing a *Yahrzeit*
- a person obligated to recite the *Ha-gomel* prayer (see page 150)
- a mourner on the Sabbath after completing the *Shiva* period
- visiting dignitaries.

Sephardic Aliya Awards

Like Ashkenazim, Sephardim reserve the first three Torah honors for a *Kohen, Levi,* and *Yisrael,* in that order. But whereas Ashkenazim will not offer another *Kohen* or *Levi* any of the other prescribed *aliyot,* Sephardim sometimes call a *Kohen* or *Levi* for any *aliya* from the fourth onward.

Aliyot of Blood Relatives

Although not specifically prohibited by talmudic law, it has become traditional not to give consecutive *aliyot* to blood relatives. Thus, two brothers, or fathers and sons, are generally not called to the Torah successively.

Approaching the Pulpit

When honored with an *aliya,* one should approach the platform *(bima)* via the shortest route as a display of eagerness to accept the honor. When leaving the pulpit, one takes the longest route to indicate reluctance of taking leave of the Torah.

Standing During Aliyot

In Sephardic congregations, as a sign of respect, all family members rise and remain standing while a relative recites the first and second Torah blessings. In some congregations the family remains standing throughout the actual reading of the particular Torah portion.

Recalling the Oleh

To avoid embarrassing an individual, once a person has been

called up for an *aliya,* he may not be sent back to his seat in favor of another person.

RECITING THE BLESSINGS

Torah Blessings Chart

For the convenience of the individual being honored, and to avoid embarrassment to those less learned, a chart with the Torah blessings printed in large type, both in Hebrew and English transliteration, is kept on the reading table in full view of the honoree.

The First Torah Blessing

Before the recipient of an *aliya* pronounces the first Torah blessing, the Torah reader points to the word in the scroll where the reading will begin. The honoree then touches the spot with a fringe of his *talit* (women use the corner of a Bible or prayerbook), kisses the fringe (or book), and recites the first Torah blessing:

בָּרְכוּ אֶת יְיָ הַמְבֹרָךְ.

Barechu et Adonai Ha-mevorach.

Praised be God, the Blessed One.

[The congregation responds:]

בָּרוּךְ יְיָ הַמְבֹרָךְ לְעוֹלָם וָעֶד.

Baruch Adonai Ha-mevorach le-olam va'ed.

Praised be God, the Blessed One, forever and ever.

[The honoree repeats the response and then continues:]

בָּרוּךְ אַתָּה יְיָ, אֱלֹהֵינוּ מֶלֶךְ הָעוֹלָם, אֲשֶׁר בָּחַר בָּנוּ מִכָּל הָעַמִּים, וְנָתַן לָנוּ אֶת תּוֹרָתוֹ. בָּרוּךְ אַתָּה יְיָ, נוֹתֵן הַתּוֹרָה.

Baruch ata Adonai, Elohenu melech ha-olam, asher bachar banu mi-kol ha-amim, ve-natan lanu et Torato. Baruch ata, Adonai, noten ha-Torah.

Praised be Thou, O Lord our God, King of the universe, who has chosen us from among all peoples and given us the Torah. Praised be Thou, who gave us the Torah.

Different Wording

The wording used in Reconstructionist and many Sephardic services is slightly different. Instead of *asher bachar banu* ("who has chosen us"), Reconstructionists use the words *asher ker-vanu la-avodato* ("who has brought us closer to His service"). Sephardim preface the *Barechu* with the words *Adonai ima-chem* ("God be with you") addressed to the congregation, to which the congregation responds, *Yevarechecha Adonai* ("May God bless you").

The Second Torah Blessing

After the *baal koray* has concluded the Torah reading, the honoree touches the Torah once again and recites the concluding Torah blessing:

בָּרוּךְ אַתָּה יְיָ, אֱלֹהֵינוּ מֶלֶךְ הָעוֹלָם, אֲשֶׁר נָתַן לָנוּ תּוֹרַת אֱמֶת, וְחַיֵּי עוֹלָם נָטַע בְּתוֹכֵנוּ. בָּרוּךְ אַתָּה יְיָ, נוֹתֵן הַתּוֹרָה.

Baruch ata Adonai, Elohenu melech ha-olam, asher natan lanu Torat emet, ve-cha'yay olam nata be-tochenu. Baruch ata Adonai, noten ha-Torah.

Praised be Thou, O Lord our God, King of the universe, who has given us a Torah of truth and implanted within us eternal life. Praised be Thou, O Lord, who gave us the Torah.

Mi She-berach Prayer

In many synagogues the *Mi She-berach* prayer is pronounced by the sexton or Torah reader after the honoree has recited the second Torah blessing. The prayer opens with the words "May He who blessed [*Mi she-berach*] our fathers Abraham, Isaac, and Jacob send His blessings upon. . . ." At this point the honoree's name and his father's name are mentioned. However, when the blessing is in behalf of a sick person, the mother's name is used.

Synagogue Donations

When the *Mi She-berach* prayer is recited after an honoree has completed his *aliya,* it is customary in some Orthodox synagogues (particularly those that follow the Sephardic tradition) for the honoree to announce a donation. The most common donation is eighteen dollars. This amount has become popular because eighteen is the numerical equivalent of the Hebrew word *chai,* meaning "life" (the Hebrew letter *chet* equals eight and the letter *yod* equals ten). Some honorees donate thirty-six dollars, or two times *chai.*

In Sephardic congregations one also hears the sum of twenty-six dollars being announced, twenty-six being the numerical equivalent of *Yehova,* the Hebrew word for God. Sephardim occasionally donate one hundred and one dollars, which is derived from the numerical value of the Hebrew name Michael, the guardian angel mentioned in the Book of Daniel.

Saluting the Torah Honoree

After one who has been given an *aliya* leaves the pulpit to return to his seat, it is customary in Ashkenazic synagogues for congregants to say aloud, *Yishar kochacha,* sometimes colloquially pronounced *Yasher koiach,* meaning "May you grow in strength." Sephardim salute the honoree by waving the fringes of the *talit* toward him and/or by shouting *Chazak u-varuch,* "Be strong and be blessed."

Showering the Honoree With Candy

An old tradition still practiced in some synagogues is to shower bridegrooms, Bnai Mitzva, and other celebrants with candy or other sweets after they have recited the second Torah blessing. The gesture expresses the hope that a sweet future awaits them.

Maftir and Haftara

The person who receives the final *aliya*, which is referred to as *maftir*, usually recites the *haftara*. The *haftara*, a selection from the Prophets that is related in some way to the Torah portion of the day, is chanted after the Torah scroll has been prepared for its return to the ark.

In Ashkenazic congregations most Bar or Bat Mitzva celebrants chant the *haftara*. Generally, in Sephardic congregations the Bar Mitzva (Sephardim do not conduct the Bat Mitzva ceremony) is not awarded *maftir* and does not recite the *haftara*.

Raising the Torah

In Ashkenazic practice, after the reading of a Torah scroll has been completed, an honoree (called a *magbiha*, "one who raises") is called to the pulpit to first unroll the scroll so that three columns of script are visible and then to raise the Torah and hold the scroll aloft, displaying the script before the congregation. The congregation then calls out:

וְזֹאת הַתּוֹרָה אֲשֶׁר שָׂם מֹשֶׁה לִפְנֵי בְּנֵי יִשְׂרָאֵל,
עַל פִּי יְיָ בְּיַד מֹשֶׁה.

Ve-zot ha-Torah asher sam Moshe lifnay B'nay Yisrael, al pi Adonai be-yad Moshe.

This is the Torah that Moses set before the Children of Israel.

At this point the honoree, still holding the scroll aloft, takes the designated seat.

In most Sephardic congregations, the raising and display of the Torah scroll is done before the Torah reading begins. When the reading has been completed, it is removed from the table unceremoniously and prepared to be returned to the ark.

Dressing the Torah

In Ashkenazic congregations, after the *magbiha* is seated,

a second honoree (the *golel* [female: *golelet*], "one who rolls up") rolls the scroll closed, ties the Torah band (*gartl*) around it, covers it with the mantle, and adorns it with its silver ornaments. The scroll is now ready to be returned to the ark after the *haftara* has been recited.

What to Do
WHEN YOU RECEIVE AN ALIYA

A synagogue official will advise you in advance which *aliya* you are being awarded. When called to approach the Torah, the following Torah etiquette should be followed:

- Ascend the pulpit and stand in front of the Torah.

- When the *baal koray* points to the first word of the reading, take one of the fringes of your *talit,* touch the spot that has been pointed to, then bring the fringe to your lips and kiss it. A woman should use a Bible or prayerbook unless, as is sometimes the case, she is wearing a *talit.*

- Recite the Torah blessing. If you do not know it by heart, read it from the large card on the reading table. The words are printed in Hebrew and in transliteration.

- The *baal koray* will then read the Torah portion. When he is finished, he will (in most cases) point to the last word that was read aloud. Touch the *talit* fringe to that spot and then kiss the fringe.

- Recite the second blessing, then move to the right to make room for the next honoree.

- Wait there until the next *aliya* is over and the second blessing has been pronounced.
- Then shake hands with the officials on the pulpit and return to your seat.

8

The Sabbath

A DAY OF REST

Introduction

From the moment the Sabbath is ushered in on Friday evening with the lighting of candles to the moment it is ushered out by the flaming light of the *Havdala* candle, Jews direct their thoughts to the message of the Sabbath: God is the light of the world and the source of Creation. This is emphasized in the Friday night blessing over wine (the *Kiddush*) and in the liturgy of each of the three Sabbath services.

To the first-century Jewish philosopher Philo of Alexandria, "the Sabbath is a holy day set apart for the building up of the spiritual element in man." And the twelfth-century luminary Moses Maimonides pointed out that "the warnings against the desecration of the Sabbath are as numerous as those against worshipping idols . . . Anyone who does not observe the Sabbath denies God, Creator of the world."

The laws, customs, and ceremonies associated with the Sabbath were introduced to create an atmosphere that would heighten man's spirituality. As a holy day—that is, one set aside for religious contemplation—Jews distinguish it from the rest of the week by attending synagogue services, enjoying meals with family, devoting time to Torah study, and generally abstaining from business and other mundane activities.

The Sabbath has been called a day of delight. Isaiah (58:13-14) put it this way: "If you do not trample on the Sabbath by pursuing your [weekday] activity . . . If you call the Sabbath 'delight,' then you can seek the favor of the Lord."

In Jewish tradition, one of the ways to "seek the favor of the Lord" is to have compassion for one's fellow man. The Rabbis indicated how deeply they felt about this when deciding between the rulings of the School of Shammai and the School of Hillel on the propriety of visiting the sick on the Sabbath. The former felt that doing so would disturb the peace and enjoyment of the day of rest, while the latter felt that such visitations would enhance the healing process. The Rabbis sided with Hillel, indicating that man best expresses the essence of the Sabbath when he displays concern for his fellow man.

WELCOME TO THE SABBATH

Importance of the Sabbath

The Sabbath represents the climax of Creation. The Book of Genesis (2:1-3) relates that after creating the world in six days, God rested on the seventh. Jewish tradition teaches that we emulate God when we rest on the seventh day of each week, thus allowing body and soul to be refreshed and, in a sense, recreated.

Work and the Sabbath

Jewish law demands that, in order to honor the Sabbath, certain types of work be avoided. The Bible mentions only a few, including plowing and harvesting (Exodus 34:21) and kindling fire (Exodus 35:3). The Talmud elaborates on the concept of work, listing thirty-nine categories of prohibited activity.

These include writing, carrying, sewing, tearing, and cutting. Rabbinic authorities today are not all agreed on the degree to which these prohibitions must be observed.

The Sabbath and Yom Kippur

The Sabbath is the most important day in the Jewish calendar, even more so than Yom Kippur. Penalties for violation of the Sabbath are much more severe than those for violation of Yom Kippur.

Welcome to the Sabbath Queen

To usher in the Sabbath, sixteenth-century Kabbalists who lived in Safed, Palestine, introduced the song *Shalom Alechem,* meaning "Peace Be Unto You." These mystics would also go out into the fields, dressed in Sabbath clothes, and chant, "Come, let us welcome the Sabbath Queen."

Preparing for the Sabbath

To prepare themselves ritually for the Sabbath (as well as holidays), some Orthodox men today still follow the once common practice of immersing themselves in a *mikva.* See page 34 for more on the *mikva.*

CANDLELIGHTING

Origin of Candlelighting

It was common practice in earlier centuries to use candles for illumination. Not until the eighth or ninth century was a blessing prescribed for Friday night and holiday candlelighting in order to add a sense of spirituality to these sacred days.

Candlelighting Time

Candles are lighted at sundown, usually eighteen minutes before sunset and approximately forty minutes before nightfall.

They may be lighted earlier in the day and, if they are, the person lighting the candles must begin observing the Sabbath at that time.

Why Two Candles?

In referring to Sabbath observance in the Ten Commandments (Exodus 20:8 and Deuteronomy 5:12), two different terms are used. In Exodus the commandment reads "Remember the Sabbath Day," and in Deuteronomy the wording is "Observe the Sabbath Day." This led to the practice of lighting two Sabbath candles to remind us to remember the day and to observe its regulations.

Why More Than Two Sabbath Candles?

The Rabbis of the Talmud encouraged the lighting of more than two candles on the Sabbath, for they felt that light adds to the Sabbath joy. In some households a candle is lighted for every member of the family, including grandchildren and other close relatives. In some households, two-, three-, or five-branched candelabra are used.

Candlelighting by Singles

Single men and women who run their own households are obligated to light Sabbath and holiday candles.

Extending Candle Life

To extend the burning life of candles keep them in the refrigerator or freezer for an hour or two before using, especially in hot weather.

It is also advisable to cut straggly wicks short so that the candle wax will not melt prematurely or smoke.

When to Pronounce the Blessing

Usually, blessings are recited before an act is performed. However, Sabbath candlelighting takes place before the blessing is pronounced, since on the Sabbath, if one lights the candles after the blessing has been recited, she/he would in fact be violating the Sabbath, which begins when the blessing has been recited.

Why the Eyes Are Covered

Since the Sabbath candles are lighted before the blessing is recited, the eyes are covered with one's hands so as not to enjoy the light until after the blessing has been pronounced.

Candlelighting Blessings

After the candles have been kindled, both hands are brought up to cover the eyes so as to block out the light while the blessing is recited:

בָּרוּךְ אַתָּה יְיָ, אֱלֹהֵינוּ מֶלֶךְ הָעוֹלָם, אֲשֶׁר קִדְּשָׁנוּ בְּמִצְוֹתָיו, וְצִוָּנוּ לְהַדְלִיק נֵר שֶׁל שַׁבָּת.

Baruch ata Adonai, Elohenu melech ha-olam, asher kideshanu be-mitzvotav, ve-tzivanu le-hadlik ner shel Shabbat.

Praised be Thou, O Lord our God, King of the universe, who has sanctified us by His commandments and commanded us to kindle the Sabbath light.

Candlelighting for Holidays That Fall on a Sabbath

When a major holiday (Pesach, Shavuot, Rosh Hashana, Sukkot, and Shemini Atzeret) falls on a Sabbath, the words *v'shel yom tov*, "and for the festival," are added to the regular Sabbath candlelighting blessing:

בָּרוּךְ אַתָּה יְיָ, אֱלֹהֵינוּ מֶלֶךְ הָעוֹלָם, אֲשֶׁר קִדְּשָׁנוּ בְּמִצְוֹתָיו, וְצִוָּנוּ לְהַדְלִיק נֵר שֶׁל שַׁבָּת וְשֶׁל יוֹם טוֹב.

Baruch ata Adonai, Elohenu melech ha-olam, asher kideshanu be-mitzvotav, ve-tzivanu le-hadlik ner shel Shabbat v'shel yom tov.

Praised be Thou, O Lord our God, King of the universe, who has sanctified us by His commandments and commanded us to kindle the Sabbath and holiday lights.

On Yom Kippur a special blessing is recited. See page 268.

The She-hecheyanu

On the first two days of all major festivals (whether or not they fall on the Sabbath) the *She-hecheyanu* blessing is added to the candlelighting blessings. Note that Israelis and Reform Jews light candles only on the first day of festivals.

בָּרוּךְ אַתָּה יְיָ, אֱלֹהֵינוּ מֶלֶךְ הָעוֹלָם, שֶׁהֶחֱיָנוּ, וְקִיְּמָנוּ, וְהִגִּיעָנוּ לַזְּמַן הַזֶּה.

Baruch ata Adonai, Elohenu melech ha-olam, she-hecheyanu, ve-kiyemanu, ve-higiyanu la-zeman ha-zeh.

Praised be Thou, O Lord our God, King of the universe, who has kept us alive, and sustained us, and permitted us to enjoy this day.

SPECIAL SABBATH COOKING REGULATIONS

Cooking Prohibition

Since the Bible (Exodus 35:3) prohibits the kindling of a fire on the Sabbath, cooking of any kind is prohibited.

Warming Up Food on the Sabbath

In traditional homes a small flame is left burning on the stove to keep precooked food warm throughout the Sabbath. A sheet of tin, called a *blech* in Yiddish, or a piece of aluminum is placed over the burners to help distribute the heat.

Cooking on Festivals for the Sabbath

During a festival (Passover, Shavuot, Sukkot) it is permissible to cook only food that will be eaten during the festival. However, an exception is made when a festival falls on a Friday, since food must be prepared for the Sabbath.

To alert people that this leniency was instituted only for the sake of the Sabbath, an *Eruv Tavshilin* ceremony was created. *Eruv Tavshilin* means "mingling of cooked foods."

Eruv Tavshilin Procedure

The procedure involves cooking a dish or two—such as eggs, fish, or meat—for the Sabbath before the onset of the festival, keeping the thought in mind that the balance of the meal will be cooked on the festival. Together with a *challa*, the cooked food is set aside to be mingled with the foods that will be cooked on Friday for the Sabbath.

Eruv Tavshilin Blessing

On the day before the festival begins, food for the *eruv* ("mingling") is placed on a platter. It is raised and the following prayer is recited:

בָּרוּךְ אַתָּה יְיָ, אֱלֹהֵינוּ מֶלֶךְ הָעוֹלָם, אֲשֶׁר קִדְּשָׁנוּ בְּמִצְוֹתָיו, וְצִוָּנוּ עַל מִצְוַת עֵרוּב.

Baruch ata Adonai, Elohenu melech ha-olam, asher kideshanu be-mitzvotav, ve-tzivanu al mitzvat eruv.

Praised be Thou, O Lord our God, King of the universe, who has sanctified us by His commandments and commanded us concerning the law of *eruv*.

This is followed by the recitation in Aramaic of the following:

בְּדֵן עֵרוּבָא יְהֵא שְׁרֵא לָנָא לְמֵיפָא, וּלְבַשָׁלָא, וּלְאַטְמָנָא, וּלְאַדְלָקָא שְׁרָגָא, וּלְמֶעְבַּד כָּל צָרְכָּנָא, מִיּוֹמָא טָבָא לְשַׁבְּתָא.

B'den eruva yehay sh'ray lana le-mefa, u-le-vashala, u-le-atmana, u-le-adlaka sheraga, u-le-me-ebad kol tzorkana, mi-yoma tava le-Shabta.

Through the execution of this *eruv* may we be permitted to bake, cook, keep dishes warm, light Sabbath lights, and prepare during the festival all we need for the Sabbath.

THE SABBATH MEAL

White Sabbath Tablecloth

The Bible says that the twelve breads that were always on display in the ancient Temples of Jerusalem were laid out on a "pure table," and the white tablecloth traditionally used on the Sabbath is a reminder of that practice. White is a symbol of purity.

Wine for Kiddush

In ancient times wine was a popular beverage served with meals. To infuse the Sabbath meal with holiness, in the fifth-century B.C.E. the Men of the Great Assembly introduced the *Kiddush* prayer to be said over wine. *Kiddush* means "sanctification," and the prayer recalls the feat of Creation and Israel's emancipation from slavery. Thus, on the Sabbath the drinking of wine takes on special significance.

A great many styles of cups have been created over the centuries for use when the blessing over wine is recited on Sabbaths and holidays. On the left is a traditional style and on the right a more modern design. Most cups are fashioned from sterling silver. The Star of David and clusters of grapes are the most popular decorations engraved on or applied to *Kiddush* cups.

Making Kiddush Over Bread

If wine is unavailable, *Kiddush* may be recited over the *challa*. The *Ha-motzi* blessing is substituted for the wine blessing. (See page 146 for blessing.)

Kiddush Posture

The accepted posture when reciting *Kiddush* is a standing one, but there are many communities where *Kiddush* is recited while sitting. The Jews of the Balkan states and Greece stand for Friday night *Kiddush,* but sit for the *Kiddush* on Sabbath morning. Rabbi Moses Isserles, the Polish-born contributor to the *Code of Jewish Law,* says that it is acceptable to stand but preferable to sit.

The Kiddush

The first paragraph of this prayer, recited on Friday nights, is taken from the Book of Genesis, Chapter 2, verses 1-3.

וַיְהִי עֶרֶב, וַיְהִי־בְקֶר, יוֹם הַשִּׁשִּׁי.

וַיְכֻלּוּ הַשָּׁמַיִם וְהָאָרֶץ וְכָל־צְבָאָם. וַיְכַל אֱלֹהִים
בַּיּוֹם הַשְּׁבִיעִי מְלַאכְתּוֹ אֲשֶׁר עָשָׂה. וַיִּשְׁבֹּת בַּיּוֹם
הַשְּׁבִיעִי מִכָּל מְלַאכְתּוֹ אֲשֶׁר עָשָׂה. וַיְבָרֶךְ אֱלֹהִים
אֶת יוֹם הַשְּׁבִיעִי, וַיְקַדֵּשׁ אֹתוֹ, כִּי בוֹ שָׁבַת מִכָּל
מְלַאכְתּוֹ אֲשֶׁר בָּרָא אֱלֹהִים לַעֲשׂוֹת.

Va-yehi erev, va-yehi voker, Yom ha-shishi.
Va-yechulu ha-shama'yim ve-ha-aretz ve-chol tze-va'am. Va-yechal Elohim ba-yom ha-shevi'i melachto asher asa. Va-yishbot ba-yom ha-shevi'i mi-kol melachto asher asa. Va-ye-varech Elohim et yom ha-shevi'i, va-yekadesh oto, ki vo shavat mi-kol melachto asher bara Elohim la-asot.

And it was evening, and it was morning, the sixth day. And God completed the creation of the heaven and earth and all that they contained. And by the seventh day God finished His work and He rested. And God blessed the seventh day and hallowed it, because on that day He rested from all His work of Creation.

בָּרוּךְ אַתָּה יְיָ, אֱלֹהֵינוּ מֶלֶךְ הָעוֹלָם, בּוֹרֵא פְּרִי הַגָּפֶן.

Baruch ata Adonai, Elohenu melech ha-olam, boray peri ha-gafen.

Praised be Thou, O Lord our God, King of the universe, who created the fruit of the vine.

בָּרוּךְ אַתָּה יְיָ, אֱלֹהֵינוּ מֶלֶךְ הָעוֹלָם, אֲשֶׁר קִדְּשָׁנוּ בְּמִצְוֹתָיו וְרָצָה בָנוּ, וְשַׁבַּת קָדְשׁוֹ בְּאַהֲבָה וּבְרָצוֹן הִנְחִילָנוּ, זִכָּרוֹן לְמַעֲשֵׂה בְרֵאשִׁית. כִּי הוּא יוֹם תְּחִלָּה לְמִקְרָאֵי־קֹדֶשׁ, זֵכֶר לִיצִיאַת מִצְרָיִם. כִּי בָנוּ בָחַרְתָּ, וְאוֹתָנוּ קִדַּשְׁתָּ מִכָּל הָעַמִּים. וְשַׁבַּת קָדְשְׁךָ בְּאַהֲבָה וּבְרָצוֹן הִנְחַלְתָּנוּ. בָּרוּךְ אַתָּה יְיָ, מְקַדֵּשׁ הַשַּׁבָּת.

Baruch ata Adonai, Elohenu melech ha-olam, asher kideshanu be-mitzvotav ve-ratza vanu, ve-Shabbat kodsho be-ahava u-ve-ratzon hinchilanu, zikaron le-ma'asay ve-reshit. Ki hu yom techila le-mikra'ay kodesh, zecher li-yetziat Mitzra'yim. Ki vanu va-charta, ve-otanu kidashta mi-kol ha-amim. Ve-Shabbat kodshecha be-ahava u-ve-ratzon hinchaltanu. Baruch ata, Adonai, mekadesh ha-Shabbat.

Praised be Thou, O Lord our God, King of the universe, who has sanctified us and favored us through His commandments. Thou hast given us the holy Sabbath as our inheritance and as a reminder of the feat of Creation, for the Sabbath is the first of our sacred days recalling our liberation from Egypt. Thou hast chosen us and sanctified us above all peoples by bequeathing unto us Thy holy Sabbath as a cherished heritage. Praised be Thou, who has hallowed the Sabbath.

Kiddush on Chol Ha-moed

When one of the Intermediate Days (Chol Ha-moed) of Passover or Sukkot falls on a Sabbath, the regular Sabbath *Kiddush* is recited on Friday night (see page 201).

Challa for the Sabbath Table

Two unsliced *challot* (singular, *challa*) draped with a cloth cover are placed at the head of the Sabbath table. After the *Ha-motzi* blessing is recited (see page 146), the bread is cut or broken and distributed.

The Challa Cover

A decorative covering, often hand-embroidered, is placed over the Sabbath and holiday *challot* at mealtime. It is removed as soon as the blessing is recited.

Breaking the Challa

In some homes, after the head of the household pronounces the *Ha-motzi* blessing, he breaks off pieces of *challa* and gives one piece to each person at the table. This custom has its roots in the Talmud, where Rabbi Yochanan expressed the view that it is the duty of the host to break the bread.

Tossing the Challa

Passing objects from one person to another is considered bad luck in Jewish folklore, for it suggests passing trouble from one to another. Hence, the practice in some households is to toss bread onto each person's plate rather than hand it to the person directly. This custom is most common among Jews with kabbalistic leanings.

The Two Sabbath Challot

Two *challot* are placed on the Sabbath and holiday festival table, many commentators believe, to commemorate the double portion of manna that the Children of Israel enjoyed every Friday during their sojourn in the desert. But it is more likely that the breads symbolize the two rows of *challot* that were always kept on the altar in the Temple. Some families in the Moroccan community arrange twelve *challot* on the table for each Sabbath meal, a custom established in the sixteenth century by the Kabbalist Rabbi Isaac Luria, better known as the Ari.

Challa Sprinkled With Salt

"A man's table is like the altar," says the Talmud. In ancient times salt was sprinkled on all sacrifices. It has therefore become customary among traditional Jews to sprinkle salt on bread or *challa* before eating it.

Challa

3 envelopes dry yeast
½ cup sugar
1½ cups warm water (110 to 115 degrees F.)
½ cup vegetable oil
2 eggs
1 tablespoon salt
5 to 6 cups all-purpose flour
Egg wash (1 egg yolk mixed
    with 1 teaspoon water)

In a large bowl, dissolve the yeast and sugar in the warm water. Let stand until foamy, about 10 minutes. Beat in the oil, eggs, salt, and 2 cups of the flour. Beat in additional flour, one cup at a time, until the dough is too difficult to handle. Turn out onto a well-floured surface and knead for at least 10 minutes, until smooth and elastic, adding more flour as necessary.

Shape into a ball and transfer to a well-oiled bowl, turning to coat all sides. Cover with plastic wrap and let rise in a warm, draft-free place until doubled in bulk. Punch down, divide in half, then divide each half into 3 equal pieces (or more if you feel you can braid them together successfully). Roll out each of the pieces into a long rope shape. Braid together.

Place the braided *challa* on a greased baking sheet. Cover loosely with plastic wrap and let rise until doubled in bulk. Brush with the egg wash and bake in a preheated 375-degree F. oven until golden and hollow when tapped, about 30 minutes. Cool on wire racks. Makes 2 loaves.

Fish on Sabbath

In olden times fish was a delicacy that only the wealthy could afford. On Friday night, however, even the poorest Jewish family enjoyed a fish meal. Fish, the Sages say, was created on the fifth day, followed by man, who was created on the sixth day; and both were created to glorify the Sabbath—the seventh day.

Gefilte Fish

In the days when many Jews could not afford to buy a sufficient amount of fish to feed the whole family on the Sabbath, a solution to the problem was found. A small fish would be purchased and the flesh would be removed and ground up with other ingredients to extend it. The mixture was then stuffed into the skin of the fish and cooked. *Gefilte* means "filled" or "stuffed."

Sabbath Cholent

Cholent—a dish consisting of pieces of meat, beans, potatoes, and various other vegetables—was a favorite Sabbath dish in earlier times. After allowing it to cook for several hours before the Sabbath set in, the pot containing the stew was placed in a closed oven or on top of the stove, where it stayed warm until it was eaten at the Sabbath midday meal.

Tzimmes

A popular dish served on Sabbaths and holidays is called *tzimmes,* a casserole of vegetables or fruits sometimes combined with meat and other ingredients. Each locality prepares the dish in its own particular way. *Tzimmes* is a popular dish because it is easy to prepare and can be reheated repeatedly without ill effect.

Singing Songs at the Sabbath Table

In order to infuse the Sabbath with joy and spiritual meaning, the Kabbalists (mystics) of the sixteenth century, led by Rabbi Isaac Luria (known as the Ari) of Safed, introduced the custom of singing songs *(zemirot)* at the Sabbath table. The custom spread to all parts of the world.

CELEBRATING THE SABBATH
IN THE SYNAGOGUE

The Friday Night Service

With several variations and additions, the Friday night Sabbath service contains the same basic prayers as the weekday service. The *Barechu* (call to prayer), *Shema,* and *Amida* prayers are recited, and the service concludes with the *Alenu* and *Kaddish.* In addition, the Friday evening prayers include the introductory *Kabbalat Shabbat* ("Welcoming the Sabbath") service and the *Kiddush,* which is recited before the *Alenu.* These prayers are described on pages 172 and 201.

The structure of the *Amida* as it is recited on Friday night and at all Sabbath and holiday services differs from the weekday version in that it consists of only seven benedictions. The middle (fourth) blessing on Friday night comes at the end of a series of special Sabbath prayers that begin with the words *Ata kidashta* ("Thou has sanctified").

The Sabbath Morning Service

The basic prayers recited on weekday mornings are said on Saturday mornings as well. However, on Sabbath (and holiday) mornings the introductory *Shacharit* prayers include the *Nishmat* ("Soul [of all life shall bless Thy Name]"). When the New Moon or a festival coincides with the Sabbath, the *Shacharit* service ends with *Hallel.*

The Sabbath morning service includes a reading from the Torah. During the Torah reading, special events in the lives of the congregants are commemorated: babies are named, Bar and Bat Mitzva ceremonies are held, grooms are called to the Torah, and so on.

After the Torah is returned to the ark, the *Musaf* (additional) service, which consists primarily of the *Amida,* is held. The fourth blessing of the *Amida* begins with the words *Yismach Moshe* ("May Moses Rejoice"). This is often sung aloud by the congregants.

Prayer for the New Month

To bless the coming of a new Hebrew month (in Yiddish, *bentsh Rosh Chodesh*) a special prayer is pronounced before the Torah is returned to the ark on Sabbath morning. Introduced in the eighth century, this *Birkat Ha-chodesh* ("Blessing of the New Month") prayer consists merely of an announcement of the name of the new month and the day of the week on which it will commence. Ashkenazim later prefaced this declaration with a prayer beginning with the words *Yehi ratzon* ("May it be Thy will [to inaugurate this month for us in goodness and blessing . . .]").

Today Sephardim continue to follow the eighth-century formula for blessing the New Moon.

The Sabbath Afternoon Service

The Sabbath afternoon service *(Mincha)* consists basically of a recitation of Psalm 145 *(Ashray)*, the *Amida*, the *Alenu*, and the *Kaddish* for mourners. In addition, the *U-va Le-tziyon* ("May [a redeemer] Come to Zion") prayer follows the *Ashray*. The words of *U-va Le-Tziyon*, taken from the Book of Isaiah (59:20), were comforting to Jews whose lives were so often filled with uncertainty and who would once again have to face a hostile outside world when the Sabbath was over.

On Sabbath afternoon, the Torah is read immediately preceding the *Amida*. Only three Torah honors *(aliyot)* are awarded so as not to extend the service (in years past, this allowed sufficient time for preachers and teachers to deliver their discourses). During the Torah reading, Bar Mitzva and Bat Mitzva celebrations are sometimes held.

The (fourth) prayer of the Sabbath afternoon *Amida* is preceded by a series of special prayers beginning with the words *Ata Echad* ("Thou Art One [and Thy Name is One]").

A third Sabbath meal *(Se'uda Shelishit)* is served in the synagogue (or in the home) after the Sabbath *Mincha* service. See below.

The Oneg Shabbat

The idea of holding gatherings on Sabbath afternoon, at which time lectures are given, games played, and songs sung, was first suggested and instituted by Russian-born Chaim Nachman Bialik (1873-1934), the poet laureate of the Jewish people. He held the first *Oneg Shabbat* in his home in Tel Aviv after he settled there in 1924.

The name for the celebration was suggested to him by the verse in Isaiah (58:13), *"Ve-karata la-Shabbat oneg,"* "And you shall call the Sabbath a delight [*oneg*]." The name was later applied to the social hour that follows the late Friday evening service, which became the vogue in many Conservative and Reform synagogues in America.

The Third Sabbath Meal

According to tradition, three meals are to be enjoyed on the Sabbath. The first is eaten on Friday night; the second on Saturday at about noontime, after the morning service; and the third late in the afternoon, usually after the *Mincha* service.

The third and final repast of the Sabbath, called by many *Shalashudis* or *Shalosh Seudos,* is more accurately called *Seuda Shelishit* (literally, "the third meal").

The *Seuda Shelishit,* usually a very simple meal, consists of *challa,* herring or herring salad, plain cakes, and soda. It is common for a member of the congregation to sponsor the meal in commemoration of a marriage, a *Yahrzeit,* or some other occasion.

Ethics of the Fathers

On Sabbath afternoons, beginning with the Sabbath after Passover, it is traditional for congregants to study one chapter of the talmudic tractate Avot ("Fathers"), more popularly known as Ethics of the Fathers or Chapters of the Fathers (*Pirkay Avot*). This tractate, which contains incisive maxims of the early talmudic scholars *(Tana'im),* originally consisted of five chapters. Later, in post-talmudic times, when it became customary to read one chapter on each Sabbath afternoon from the end of Passover to Shavuot, a sixth chapter pertaining to Torah study and Revelation was added, and this sixth chapter was always read on the Saturday preceding Shavuot.

Subsequently the reading cycle was repeated so that the last reading would be held on the Sabbath before Rosh Hashana. This is the practice followed in most congregations today.

Among the popular teachings of the Ethics of the Fathers are:

- If I am not for myself, who will be for me? But if I am for myself only, what am I? And if not now, when?
- What is most essential is not study but practice.
- Make His will your will so that He will make your will His will.
- Do not separate yourself from the community.
- Do not judge your fellow man until you have been in his predicament.
- Do not say you will study when you have leisure; you may never enjoy leisure.
- It is not your duty to finish the work, but you are not free from starting it.
- Be submissive before a great person; be gentle toward the young; and receive all people in a cheerful manner.
- Everything is foreseen, yet freedom of choice is given us.
- Who is rich? He who is happy with his lot.
- Be the first to extend a greeting to your fellow man.

The Saturday Night Service

The Saturday night service (Maariv) differs only slightly from any weekday evening service. To distinguish this service from other Maariv services, after the Amida two special prayers are recited. One begins with the words Vi-yehi noam ("May the pleasantness [of my Lord]") and the second with Ve-ata kadosh ("And Thou art holy"). Both consist of numerous biblical quotations expressing the hope that even as we are engaged in a productive workweek, the spirit and holiness of the Sabbath will not be lost.

Before the Alenu is recited, a Havdala service is held to mark the end of the holy Sabbath and to distinguish it from the other six days of the week. See below for more about the concept of Havdala and the service conducted.

THE HAVDALA CEREMONY

Farewell to the Sabbath

The Sabbath ends with the *Havdala* ceremony. *Havdala* means "separation," separation of the holy Sabbath from the mundane workweek. The *Havdala* ceremony, originated by the Men of the Great Assembly 2,500 years ago, is conducted at the conclusion of the Sabbath and holidays once three stars have appeared in the sky, approximately eighteen minutes after sunset.

As part of *Havdala*, blessings over wine, spices, and the flame of a candle are recited. For the ceremony, the following items should be in readiness: wine, wine goblet, braided candle, matches, and a spicebox filled with spices.

The Wine of Havdala

A goblet of wine is filled to overflowing as a symbol of a full and prosperous week. The leader of the *Havdala* ceremony holds the goblet in his right hand and the spicebox in his left as he pronounces the blessing over wine.

Spices in Ancient Times

In ancient times, after a meal, aromatic spices were spread around an eating area to dissipate food odors. However, such activity was not permitted on the Sabbath. When spices were spread around for the first time after the Sabbath, a prayer was recited, adding a spiritual note to an ordinary practice.

Types of Spices

A variety of odoriferous products may be used as the *Havdala* spices. Bay leaves, cinnamon, and cloves are commonly used, as is allspice. All are readily available in food stores. In the Balkan countries and in Greece, Jews often use myrtle twigs. Sephardim in other countries have been known to use lemons.

The Spicebox

In the twelfth century it became customary to enclose the spices in special containers made of wood, pewter, or silver. Some of these are quite ornate and considered to be works of art. During the *Havdala* ceremony, the container, referred to as the *besomim* (spice) box, is passed around to each participant, who first recites the blessing over spices, then shakes the box to stir up the spices, and then sniffs them.

Before the twelfth century it was customary to recite the spice blessing over a myrtle branch placed in a special glass container. Later, a special container was designed to hold all types of odoriferous spices. Over the centuries, Jewish craftsmen created countless spicebox designs, and the style shown on the right, fashioned somewhat like a Gothic tower, became popular after the sixteenth century. The style pictured on the left is a contemporary design.

Scanning the Fingernails

After the leader and those assembled pronounce the blessing over the candlelight, all gaze at their fingernails to catch a glimpse of the reflected light. In ancient times, light was considered a safeguard against witches who would do harm during the coming week.

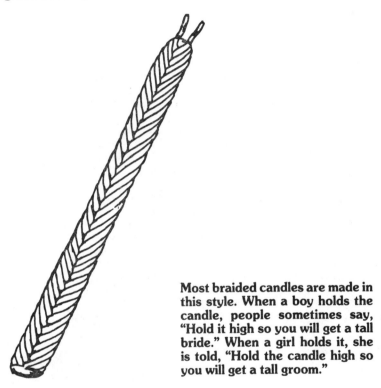

Most braided candles are made in this style. When a boy holds the candle, people sometimes say, "Hold it high so you will get a tall bride." When a girl holds it, she is told, "Hold the candle high so you will get a tall groom."

The Braided Candle

Originally two candles were used during the *Havdala* ceremony. Today a single multicolored braided candle with a double wick is used. It provides a torchlike flame that exudes warmth and charm for the closing moments of the Sabbath. Usually a young child holds the *Havdala* candle high in the air.

Concise Havdala Service

A braided candle is lighted and held by a child if one is present. The leader, raising a cup of wine, says:

כּוֹס יְשׁוּעוֹת אֶשָּׂא וּבְשֵׁם יְיָ אֶקְרָא.

הִנֵּה אֵל יְשׁוּעָתִי; אֶבְטַח וְלֹא אֶפְחָד. כִּי עָזִּי וְזִמְרָת יָהּ יְיָ, וַיְהִי לִי לִישׁוּעָה.

Kos yeshuot esa u-ve-shem Adonai ekra.

Hinay El yeshuati; evtach ve-lo efchad.

Ki azi ve-zimrat Ya Adonai, va-yehi li lishua.

I lift this cup of salvation and proclaim in the name of the Lord.

Behold! God is my salvation; I will trust in Him and will know no fear. The Lord is my strength and my song; He is the source of my deliverance.

בָּרוּךְ אַתָּה יְיָ, אֱלֹהֵינוּ מֶלֶךְ הָעוֹלָם, בּוֹרֵא פְּרִי הַגָּפֶן.

Baruch ata Adonai, Elohenu melech ha-olam, boray peri ha-gafen.

Praised art Thou, O Lord our God, King of the universe, who created the fruit of the vine.

The wine cup is set down and the spicebox is held aloft by the leader, who then pronounces the following blessing:

בָּרוּךְ אַתָּה יְיָ, אֱלֹהֵינוּ מֶלֶךְ הָעוֹלָם, בּוֹרֵא מִינֵי בְשָׂמִים.

Baruch ata Adonai, Elohenu melech ha-olam, boray minay vesamim.

Praised art Thou, O Lord our God, King of the universe, who has created many types of spices.

The spicebox is passed around, and all participants repeat the blessing and inhale the odor of the spices. Then, the candle that was kindled at the beginning of the ceremony is raised high, and the leader pronounces the following blessing:

בָּרוּךְ אַתָּה יְיָ, אֱלֹהֵינוּ מֶלֶךְ הָעוֹלָם, בּוֹרֵא מְאוֹרֵי הָאֵשׁ.

Baruch ata Adonai, Elohenu melech ha-olam, boray me'oray ha-esh.

Praised art Thou, O Lord our God, King of the universe, who has created the light of fire.

The leader cups his hands, holding his fingernails in a position that catches the reflection of the light. All present do likewise and repeat the blessing. Then, in unison, all recite or chant the joyous words spoken by the Jews when they were saved from the plot of Haman:

לַיְהוּדִים הָיְתָה אוֹרָה, וְשִׂמְחָה, וְשָׂשׂוֹן, וִיקָר.

La-Yehudim ha'yeta ora, ve-simcha, ve-sason, vi-yekar.

For the Jews there was light and joy; good cheer and restored dignity.

The leader continues with the final *Havdala* blessing:

בָּרוּךְ אַתָּה יְיָ, אֱלֹהֵינוּ מֶלֶךְ הָעוֹלָם, הַמַּבְדִּיל בֵּין קֹדֶשׁ לְחֹל, בֵּין אוֹר לְחֹשֶׁךְ, בֵּין יִשְׂרָאֵל לָעַמִּים, בֵּין יוֹם הַשְּׁבִיעִי לְשֵׁשֶׁת יְמֵי הַמַּעֲשֶׂה. בָּרוּךְ אַתָּה יְיָ, הַמַּבְדִּיל בֵּין קֹדֶשׁ לְחֹל.

Baruch ata Adonai, Elohenu melech ha-olam, ha-mavdil bayn kodesh le-chol, bayn or le-choshech, bayn Yisrael la-amim, bayn yom ha-shevi'i le-sheshet yemay ha-ma'aseh. Baruch ata, Adonai, ha-mavdil bayn kodesh le-chol.

Praised art Thou, O Lord our God, King of the universe, who created a distinction between the holy and the profane, between light and darkness, between Israel and the nations, between the seventh day and the rest of the week. Praised art Thou, O Lord, who made a distinction between the sacred and the profane.

The leader and children present taste the wine.

The *Havdala* ceremony may be concluded with the singing of some of the songs in the Appendix, particularly *Ani Ma'amin* and *Eliyahu Ha-navi*.

The Saturday Night Melaveh Malka Meal

After the Sabbath is over, many traditionalists partake of an extra meal, called the *Melaveh Malka*. The words *melaveh malka* mean "accompanying the queen." Partaking of this extra meal after the Sabbath is a way of bidding farewell to the Sabbath Queen.

According to legend, the *Melaveh Malka* custom originated with King David, who had asked God when he would die and was told it would happen on a Saturday. From that time on, when each Sabbath was over, David made a party to celebrate his survival. The nation-at-large rejoiced with him and adopted the practice of ushering out the Sabbath with a joyous meal.

9

THE SPRING HOLIDAYS I

PASSOVER

Introduction

Originally, Passover was two separate and distinct holidays: an agricultural holiday called Chag Ha-matzot ("Festival of Unleavened Bread") and a pastoral holiday called Chag Ha-pesach ("Festival of the Paschal Lamb"). These holidays developed independently in the springtime of the year, in the Hebrew month Nissan (March-April), and eventually the two were merged.

Since its inception Passover has basically been a family holiday. The Bible (Exodus 12) says: "On the tenth day of this month [Nissan] they [the Children of Israel] shall take to them every man a lamb, according to their father's houses, a lamb for a household . . . [to be] shared by members of the family." And to this day Passover is celebrated in the bosom of the home, although it is also marked by special holiday services conducted in the synagogue.

For the Jewish homemaker Passover is a time for cleaning the home thoroughly. Cupboards and closets are emptied and cleansed to make sure that no *chametz* (leaven) is present. This culminates in the formal *Bedikat Chametz* (searching out of leaven) and *Biur Chametz* (burning of leaven) ceremonies described in this chapter.

The highlight of the Passover holiday is the *Seder* service, during which the story of the Exodus of the Jews from Egypt is retold. The order (*seder* means "order") of the evening's events—that is, the sequence of prayers, narrative, activities, and songs—is indicated in a book known as the *Haggada* ("narrative").

PREPARING FOR THE HOLIDAY

The Scope of Passover

Passover, or Pesach as it is known in Hebrew, is the most celebrated of all Jewish holidays. Observed for seven days in Israel and generally as an eight-day holiday in the Diaspora, Passover commemorates the deliverance of the Children of Israel from bondage in Egypt after two hundred years of enslavement. The holiday is marked by the pageantry of the home Seder, festive synagogue services, the preparation and eating of special foods, and the striking absence of breads and many other foods eaten throughout the year.

In Israel, the first and seventh days of Passover are celebrated as full holidays. The five days in between, referred to as Intermediate Days (Chol Ha-moed), are celebrated as half-holidays. In the Diaspora, the first two and last two days of Passover are celebrated as full holidays, and the four Intermediate Days are celebrated as half-holidays. Work and travel are permitted on the Intermediate Days.

The Names of Passover

The original name for Passover is Chag Ha-pesach, meaning "Festival of the Paschal Lamb." With the advent of spring each year, the Hebrew nomads celebrated this pastoral festival by offering one of their flock as a sacrifice to the Lord.

When the Israelites settled down to work the land, in commemoration of the beginning of the grain harvest they celebrated an agricultural holiday known as Chag Ha-matzot, "Festival of the Unleavened Bread." The two holidays later merged and became associated with the Exodus from Egypt, an event which also occurred in the spring of the year, on the fifteenth of the Hebrew month Nissan.

Why Eight Days of Passover?

In biblical times the Passover festival was celebrated for seven days (as prescribed in Exodus 12:18, Exodus 13:7, and Deuteronomy 16:3). However, an extra day was added to the holiday when the Jews were exiled from Palestine by the Romans in the year 70 C.E. and uncertainty about the calendar arose.

With the Jewish communities widely dispersed, it was impossible for all to be reached and advised of precisely when the New Moon was sighted in Jerusalem. Consequently, one could not always be certain of the correct day on which to begin a holiday. To eliminate confusion, an extra day was added to Passover (and the other festivals) to make sure that all communities would be observing the festival on the correct day.

PROHIBITED AND PERMITTED FOODS

What Is Prohibited?

The Book of Exodus (13:7) specifically mandates that on Passover "no leaven shall be seen in all your borders." Accordingly, any food that has become sour (fermented), and by extension any utensil that has come in contact with such food, is prohibited during Passover. These forbidden foods and utensils are characterized in Hebrew as *chametz,* literally meaning "sour."

The Five Prohibited Grains

The following five grains and anything made from them are considered *chametz:* wheat, barley, spelt, rye, oats. The use of these grains during Passover is strictly prohibited except for the purpose of making *matza.* The *matza* exception was made only because the Bible mandates that *matza* be eaten during Passover, and in order to make *matza* one of these grains has to be used.

The Mandate to Eat Matza

The obligation to eat *matza* on Passover is stated several times in the Bible:

- Exodus 13:7 says, "Throughout the seven days [of Passover] unleavened bread shall be eaten."
- Exodus 12:18 says, "In the first month [Nissan], from the fourteenth day of the month at evening, you shall eat unleavened bread."

Dough That Doesn't Sour

After water is added to one of the grains for making *matza,* the dough is kneaded and shaped quickly, placed in the oven to bake, and then removed—all within eighteen minutes. Dough processed at this pace does not have time to ferment, and hence the *matza* is unleavened when taken from the oven.

MORE ABOUT MATZA

Poor Man's and Rich Man's Bread

Because *matza* is relatively inexpensive and quick to make, the Haggadah refers to it as "poor man's bread" or "bread of affliction" *(lechem oni).*

When other ingredients—most often wine, oil, honey, or eggs—are added to the flour and water normally used to make *matza,* the result is called "rich man's *matza*" *(matza ashira).* Sometimes referred to as "the bread of opulence," this type of *matza* may not be served at the Seder, at which only "poor man's *matza*" is served.

Guarded Matza

Those who are exceptionally careful in their observance of

the laws of Passover will eat only *matza shemura* ("guarded *matza*")—*matza* that has been carefully watched from the moment the grain is cut until it is baked as *matza*. This meticulous surveillance is to insure that no water or moisture comes into contact with the flour prior to making the dough, for moisture would start the process of fermentation.

Round Matzot

Originally, all *matzot* (plural of *matza*) were round. In 1875, in England, a *matza*-baking machine was invented that made square *matzot*—and with much greater speed. How *matza* is shaped plays no role in determining whether it is kosher for Passover.

Matza Perforations

Matza is perforated before baking to allow air to escape and thus retard fermentation. The perforations also prevent the dough from rising during baking.

The Novelty of Matza

Matza is not eaten on the day preceding Passover so that tasting the *matza* at the Seder will be a novelty. Thus, although *matza* may be eaten throughout the year, observant Jews abstain from doing so immediately before Passover.

PRE-PASSOVER CEREMONIES

Divesting Oneself of Chametz

Since the Bible (Exodus 13:7) mandates that a Jew may not possess *chametz* during Passover, a legal fiction was created to enable the homemaker to divest himself of such items for the duration of the holiday. All *chametz* is stored away in a closet and "sold" to a non-Jew for a token fee, thus temporarily transferring ownership. It is understood that the agreement is to be cancelled when Passover ends. All arrangements are made through a rabbi or a synagogue official who has been designated to serve as the individual's agent.

The Search for Chametz

Because it is forbidden that even a trace of leavened food remain in the house during Passover, a search called *Bedikat Chametz* is conducted by the master of the house on the evening of the fourteenth of Nissan, the night before the first Seder. The house has already been thoroughly cleaned by the homemaker, so this is a symbolic gesture.

The procedure involves placing a small piece of bread on the windowsills in each room of the house. The homemaker recites a prayer and then, with a wooden spoon and a feather in hand, proceeds by candlelight to "search" room after room, often followed by the children of the house. The homemaker brushes the bread pieces into the wooden spoon. When all rooms have been "searched" and it is certain that all the bread has been collected, the homemaker ties together the spoon, feather, and candle and sets the bundle aside to be burned the next morning.

The Search Blessing

Before the search begins, the homemaker recites:

בָּרוּךְ אַתָּה יְיָ, אֱלֹהֵינוּ מֶלֶךְ הָעוֹלָם, אֲשֶׁר קִדְּשָׁנוּ בְּמִצְוֹתָיו, וְצִוָּנוּ עַל בִּעוּר חָמֵץ.

Baruch ata Adonai, Elohenu melech ha-olam, asher kideshanu be-mitzvotav, ve-tzivanu al biur chametz.

Praised art Thou, O Lord our God, King of the universe, who has commanded us concerning the removal of *chametz*.

After the search, the *chametz* is wrapped up and set aside to be burned the next morning. The following declaration is made:

כָּל חֲמִירָא וַחֲמִיעָא דְּאִכָּא בִרְשׁוּתִי, דְּלָא חֲמִתֵּה וּדְלָא בִעַרְתֵּה וּדְלָא יְדַעְנָא לֵהּ, לִבָּטֵל וְלֶהֱוֵי הֶפְקֵר כְּעַפְרָא דְאַרְעָא.

Kol chamira va-chamia de-ika vi-reshuti, de-la chamitay u-de-la vi'artay u-de-la yedana lay, li-batel ve-le-hevay hefker ke-afra de-ara.

Any and all *chametz* that is still in my possession, that I have not seen and have not removed because I have no knowledge of it, let it be ownerless like the dust of the earth.

Burning the Chametz

The spoon with the crumbs, along with the candle and feather that were used the night before, are taken outside the home and burned. This ceremony of burning, which is held between nine and ten A.M., is called *Biur Chametz*.

While the *chametz* is burning, the following statement, similar to that uttered the previous night, is made:

כָּל חֲמִירָא וַחֲמִיעָא דְּאִכָּא בִרְשׁוּתִי, דַּחֲזִתֵּהּ וּדְלָא
חֲזִתֵּהּ דַּחֲמִתֵּהּ וּדְלָא חֲמִתֵּהּ, דְּבִעַרְתֵּהּ וּדְלָא
בִעַרְתֵּהּ, לִבָּטֵל וְלֶהֱוֵי הֶפְקֵר כְּעַפְרָא דְּאַרְעָא.

Kol chamira va-chamia de-ika vi-reshuti, da-chazitay u-de-la chazitay, da-chamitay u-de-la chamitay, de-viartay u-de-la viartay, li-batel ve-le-hevay hefker ke-afra de-ara.

Any *chametz* still in my possession, whether I have seen it or not, whether I have recognized it or not, whether I have removed it or not, let it be ownerless like the dust of the earth.

When Passover Begins on Saturday Night

When Passover begins on Saturday night, the search for *chametz* is done on Thursday night and the burning of the *chametz* is done on Friday morning.

Food for the Needy—Ma'ot Chitim

Ma'ot means "money," and *chitim* means "grain." According to an ancient custom, funds were solicited before Passover so that the poor would have the wherewithal to buy grain with which to make *matza* for the holiday. The practice of collecting funds for the needy on Passover is widely observed today in Jewish communities throughout the world.

Fast of the Firstborn

Among traditional Jews, on the day before Passover (that is, the fourteenth of Nissan) the firstborn son of a father or a mother fasts as an expression of thanks for the deliverance of the firstborn Israelites who were spared when the firstborn of the Egyptians were visited by the tenth plague. The fast, which begins at dawn, is referred to in Hebrew as Taanit Bechorim. If the fourteenth of Nissan falls on the Sabbath, the fast is observed on the preceding Thursday.

The Firstborn Siyyum

So that the firstborn, who are obligated to abstain from food and drink on the day before Passover, may be spared the inconvenience of fasting, the Rabbis introduced the idea of arranging for a *Siyyum* (literally, "completion") on that day. The study of a tractate of the Talmud is undertaken earlier in the year, to be completed on the day before Passover. The rabbi or anyone who has studied the tractate delivers a short discourse about Passover during the morning service, and this is followed by a festive repast. This meal, called *Se'udat Mitzva*, relieves all firstborn who participate from fasting for the balance of the day. (See page 12 for more on *Se'udat Mitzva*.)

Female Firstborn

It is customary in many communities, particularly among Sephardic and Conservative Jews, for women who are firstborn to be present at the *Siyyum* and to be involved in the study period and the festive repast, for they too were spared from the devastating tenth plague. In the several references to the plague in the Book of Exodus and the Book of Numbers, it is the firstborn in general who are singled out for elimination, not just the male firstborn.

KOSHERING POTS, PANS, DISHES, AND UTENSILS

The Fundamental Rule

Although a food may be kosher for use throughout the year, any product that is fermented or can cause fermentation (souring) is *chametz* and may not be consumed on Passover. Likewise, all pots, pans, dishes, and sundry eating and cooking utensils that have come in contact with *chametz* must be cleansed and purged (koshered) before they can be used for Passover. Items that cannot be purged must be set aside for the duration of the holiday and different utensils and dishes substituted.

Which Articles Can Be Koshered?

Generally speaking, to determine which pans, dishes, flatware, and other cooking and eating utensils can be made kosher for Passover, four factors must be considered:

First, *the material out of which the item is made.* If the material is porous (and therefore absorbent) and cannot withstand intense heat (to which it must be subjected to be made kosher—see below), the item will not be usable for Passover. Included in this category are pottery and earthenware. If the material is nonporous—such as metal flatware and glassware of all kinds—it can be successfully purged and thereby made kosher for Passover.

Second, *how the item is constructed.* Items that have seams or are assembled from more than one piece—such as flatware with wooden or plastic handles or pots with curled lips—may not be koshered for Passover. Conversely, one-piece items may be koshered.

Third, *the condition of the item.* Regardless of material or construction, any item that is chipped, cracked, or that has been mended is not eligible for koshering because food particles that would be difficult to purge may have penetrated it.

Fourth, *the temperature of the food to which the item was exposed.* Thus, for example, ordinary glass dishes onto which hot foods were placed during the course of the year cannot be koshered successfully for Passover (if the glass were exposed to high heat, it would crack). However, glassware used only as receptacles for cold foods can be made kosher for Passover.

Koshering Eligible Articles

The Talmud sets forth a basic principle that the homemaker should keep in mind when trying to decide the appropriate method to use in koshering a given item. The principle is: the method of purging follows the method of cooking. So, for example, if a particular pot had been used for boiling food during the year, that pot can be made kosher for Passover by immersing it in boiling water.

There are four methods by which an item can be made kosher for Passover:

1. immersion in boiling water
2. purging by fire
3. immersion in cold water
4. autoclaving

Koshering in Boiling Water

Traditionally, items to be made kosher by this process are immersed briefly in a large pot or other container filled with boiling water. However, the large container must itself first be koshered.

To do so, fill the container with rapidly boiling water (or bring the water to a boil over direct heat) until it overruns the rim and flows down the sides. Some people fill the container to below the rim and then add a stone or piece of metal that has been heated over a flame until red hot. This helps the water retain its heat and forces the water over the sides.

Items that are to be made kosher through immersion in the large container must first be thoroughly washed and scrubbed and then allowed to remain unused for twenty-four hours.

When the time for immersion has arrived, fill the large container with boiling water and drop in the items to be purged for Passover. After they have been immersed for a few seconds, remove them (with tongs) and rinse them under cold running water.

These items are now said to have been *kashered,* meaning that they are ready for Passover use.

Note: Items that are too large to be immersed may be made kosher by first scouring them, allowing them to remain unused for twenty-four hours, then running hot water over the exterior and interior surfaces, and finally by rinsing with cold water.

Purging by Fire

This method of koshering for Passover is used primarily for pots and pans, oven interiors, burners of a stove, and other items that have come into direct contact with fire. Generally this is done by exposing the surface of the item to intense heat.

For example, the interior of an oven is made kosher for Passover by turning up the heat to the highest point possible so as to effectively burn up all particles of food that may have clung to the oven surfaces. When cool, the oven is then thoroughly scoured and cleansed. Needless to say, self-cleaning ovens, which burn off encrusted food through an automatic process, make preparing for Passover that much easier.

Small metal items—pots, pans, utensils—that are encrusted with food can be koshered by exposing the articles to intense heat until they virtually glow. Some people use a blowtorch to accomplish this.

Koshering by Soaking

This procedure involves soaking articles in room-temperature water for three days, changing the water daily. Items koshered in this manner are those that would not survive exposure to intense heat and that have only been used to hold cold foods during the course of the year. Glassware, particularly drinking glasses, are koshered by soaking.

Koshering by Autoclaving

Autoclaving is a process of sterilizing (or cooking) by super-heated steam under pressure. Some authorities consider auto-claving a superior way of koshering utensils because cracks and crevices are purged more effectively than by boiling water. Other authorities do not approve of autoclaving as a method of koshering dishes and utensils because the *Code of Jewish Law* only specifies the use of water and fire as koshering agents.

Can Pyrex Be Koshered?

Pyrex is heat-resistant glass, and as such it can be immersed in boiling water with little danger of cracking. Therefore, most authorities agree, it can be made kosher for Passover.

Koshering Electrical Appliances

Since blenders, food processors, and other electrical appliances cannot be immersed in water, they cannot be koshered as a whole. However, if the parts are detachable—such as the beaters and bowls of an electric mixer—they can be koshered, and the entire appliance can be used for Passover.

Koshering Microwaves

Unlike an oven, a microwave need not be made kosher for Passover, since cooking is done by radiation and only the goods placed in it, not the oven surfaces, are affected by the heat. The interior is easily made kosher for Passover by a thorough cleaning. The Conservative rabbinate recommends boiling a glass of water in the microwave so as to steam-clean the interior.

Microwave ovens with a browning element cannot be koshered for Passover.

Koshering Refrigerators

Refrigerators with enameled interiors can be made kosher simply by washing the surfaces thoroughly. Since refrigerator interiors are always cold, *chametz* is not absorbed.

Koshering Dishwashers

Because extremely hot water is used in dishwashers, koshering the machines is not required. It is recommended, however, that before using a dishwasher for Passover, it be run through one or two cycles without dishes in it. Detergent should be used.

Aluminum Lining

In many households, heavy-duty aluminum foil is used to cover surfaces that constantly come in contact with *chametz* during the year. This includes stovetops, refrigerator shelves, and countertops. Foil is also used to line oven racks.

KOSHER FOR PASSOVER FOODS

Products Not Requiring Rabbinic Certification

In the past, many food items were prohibited for Passover use because they were processed by hand and the chance of *chametz* getting mixed in was a real problem. Today food products are prepared by sophisticated machinery, and there is little likelihood of that occurring. Hence, additive-free items such as sugar and honey; coffee and tea; fresh, dried, and frozen fruits and vegetables; and all kosher meats, fowl, and fish do not require special certification attesting to their fitness for Passover use. Many observant Jews, however, insist that all food items bear labels indicating that their manufacture has been supervised by a rabbinic authority.

Products Requiring Rabbinic Certification

All food items whose suitability for Passover is questionable must be certified by a rabbinic authority.

The Hebrew words *kasher le-Pesach* (כשר לפסח) or the English words "kosher for Passover," along with the symbol of the certifying rabbi or rabbinic group, will appear on the label of a product that has been certified. Sometimes the letter P will appear after the symbol, which indicates that the item is approved for Passover, as in the following instances: Ⓤₚ, Ⓚₚ. (On products approved for year-round use, the P stands for *pareve*.)

See page 108-109 for a list of certifying agencies and their symbols.

Sephardic vs. Ashkenazic Practice

On Passover, Sephardim generally permit the use of rice, corn, and leguminous plants such as peas and beans (*kitniyot* in Hebrew). Syrian Jews eat fresh peas and beans but not dried peas and beans. Moroccans eat fresh green beans but for the most part forbid the use of rice and dried beans. A particular Sephardic community often allowed particular foods to be used on Passover because the foods were diet staples and substitutes were not available.

Ashkenazim prohibit the consumption of rice and leguminous foods on Passover, primarily out of fear that if these items were ground up to make flour, the flour might be mistaken for one of the five biblical grains (wheat, barley, spelt, oats, rye) and would be used to bake *matza,* in violation of Jewish law (see page 218).

Alcoholic Beverages

Scotch, rye, bourbon, beer, or any alcoholic beverage made from one of the five biblical grains may not be consumed on Passover.

Matza Products

Ordinary flour may not be used during Passover except to make *matza. Matza,* however, can be used to make cakes, cookies, and other items. Thus, food manufacturers have made available *matza farfel,* which is simply *matza* that has been broken into small pieces; *matza meal,* which is *matza* that has been ground until granular; and *matza cake meal,* which is *matza* that has been ground until powdery.

Baking Soda and Baking Powder

Baking soda (sodium bicarbonate), which is an antacid as well as a leavening agent, is not a fermenting agent and hence is kosher for Passover use.

Baking powder, also a leavening agent but not a fermenting agent, is considered not kosher for Passover by Ashkenazim because it contains cornstarch. Use of corn on Passover is prohibited by Ashkenazic authorities but permitted by Sephardim.

Erba Food Products, Inc., of Brooklyn, New York, has produced a baking powder (made with potato starch) that is acceptable to Ashkenazim. The product is distributed under the brand name Haddar.

Adapting Recipes for Passover Use

Here are some suggestions for converting year-round recipes to Passover use:

- Instead of breadcrumbs, use *matza* meal.
- Instead of using flour as a thickener, use potato starch (use half the quantity of the flour called for) or egg yolk (one yolk being equivalent to one tablespoon of flour).
- If kosher for Passover baking powder is not available, instead of one teaspoon of baking powder use ¼ teaspoon of baking soda plus ½ teaspoon cream of tartar.

THE FAMILY SEDER

The Seder Celebration

The Seder is a family home service and meal. Depending upon the tradition one follows, it is held on the first and second nights of Passover or on the first night only to commemorate the release of the Children of Israel from Egyptian bondage.

Traditional Jews in the Diaspora generally conduct a Seder on the first and second nights of Passover. In Israel, however, all Jews celebrate a Seder only on the first night of Passover, since only the first and last days of Passover are full holidays. The five Intermediate Days are observed as half-holidays. Reform Jews and some Conservative Jews in the Diaspora follow the Israeli practice. The disparity in observance is related to uncertainty about the calendar (see page 218).

Candlelighting on Passover

Before the Seder, at the usual candlelighting time, and on the evenings of the last two days of the holiday, the homemaker lights the holiday candles and recites the regular holiday blessings (page 256). The blessings can be found in most Haggadot.

The *She-hecheyanu* blessing (page 198) is recited after the candlelighting blessing on the first two evenings of Passover, but not on the seventh and eighth evenings.

The Haggada

The Haggada is the prayerbook of the Seder. It details the procedures of the evening, recounts the dramatic story of the Exodus from Egypt, and includes selections from the Book of Psalms plus a variety of festive songs. The Haggada in its original form (which is different from ours today) was introduced about 2,500 years ago by the Members of the Great Assembly and has continued to evolve over the centuries.

Multiplicity of Haggadot

Since the first handmade Haggada appeared in the thirteenth century, more than 3,500 Haggadot (plural of Haggada) have been published in all parts of the world. Many lavishly illustrated editions have become collectors' items.

The Seder Kittel

The *kittel* is a festive robe worn on joyous occasions in ancient times. The Book of Leviticus (16:4) describes the white garment worn by the High Priest when he officiated in Temple days. Among Ashkenazim, during the Seder ceremony the leader often wears a white robe *(kittel),* a symbol that adds majesty to the proceedings. Sephardim do not wear a *kittel* at the Seder or on any other occasion.

Three Matzot

Three *matzot* are placed on the Seder table in front of the leader. Two of the three *matzot* represent the loaves of bread normally found on the Sabbath and festival dinner table. The third is added in honor of the special nature of the holiday. A popular interpretation is that the three *matzot* represent the three classes that comprise the Jewish community: Priests, Levites, and Israelites.

The Seder Tray

The Seder tray (or Seder plate), which is set on the table in front of the leader's place setting, has six compartments to hold the symbolic Passover foods. These are bitter herbs *(maror)*, a fruit-nut mixture resembling mortar *(charoset)*, roasted shankbone *(zero'a)*, a roasted egg *(baytza)*, a vegetable *(karpas)*, and a second vegetable that is more bitter than *karpas* *(chazeret)*.

Bitter Herbs

The head of a horseradish or a small amount of grated horseradish is displayed on the Seder plate. These bitter herbs, called *maror* in Hebrew, symbolize the bitter lives endured by the Israelites when they were enslaved in Egypt.

Two Servings of Maror

Maror is served twice during the Seder. The first time, it is mixed with *charoset* (see below) to cut the sharp taste. The second time, it is placed between two pieces of *matza* and is served as Hillel's Sandwich. This is how the great scholar Hillel served *maror* at his first-century B.C.E. Seder celebration.

Charoset

Charoset (also pronounced *charoses*) is one of the six symbolic foods on the Seder tray. This fruit-and-nut paste is a reminder of the mortar that the Israelite slaves were forced to make for their taskmasters. Although there are many *charoset* recipes, the most popular is a mixture of chopped apple, ground nuts, cinnamon, and a dash of wine for moisture. Aside from the symbolic amount of *charoset* placed on the Seder tray, a small amount is served to each participant together with the *maror* (bitter herbs) during the Seder.

Ashkenazic Charoset

This is the *charoset* with which most Americans are familiar.

6 large apples, peeled and cored
1 cup chopped walnuts, almonds, or pecans
1½ teaspoons ground cinnamon
3 teaspoons honey (optional)
⅓ cup sweet red wine

Coarsely grate the apples and add the nuts. Combine the remaining ingredients and mix well until the mixture has the consistency of rough paste. Chill. Makes about 3 cups.

Sephardic Charoset

Sephardim generally favor *charoset* featuring dried fruits, particularly dates. Here is one version.

4 medium-sized apples, peeled and cored
1 pound pitted dates
Cold water
2 cups chopped pecans or almonds
¼ cup white vinegar
½ cup sweet red wine

In a medium-sized saucepan place the apples and dates. Add cold water to cover, and cook over medium heat until the apples are tender and the water is just about evaporated. Pass the apples and dates through a grinder or food mill or process in a blender or food processor. Transfer to a bowl and stir in the chopped nuts, vinegar, and wine. If too thick, add wine or water until the desired consistency is reached. Makes about 3½ cups.

The Shankbone

Called *zero'a* in Hebrew, the shankbone is one of the symbolic foods placed on the Seder tray. It serves to remind us of the paschal lamb eaten on Passover by all families in Temple times. Customarily, a roasted beef bone or the roasted neck of a fowl is substituted for the shankbone.

Karpas

This Seder plate symbol is usually a green vegetable such as parsley, cucumber, or celery, selected because of the association of Passover with springtime and the rebirth and revival of nature. Many Jews of East European extraction use boiled potato. The modern-day custom of dipping *karpas* in salt water has its roots in the ancient practice of dipping a vegetable in salt water as an *hors d'oeuvre* before a meal.

Chazeret

On the Seder tray, the vegetable used as *chazeret* is, like the *maror*, symbolic of the bitter lot of the enslaved Israelites. Lettuce, watercress, radish, or any other vegetable that has a tendency to be or become bitter is used as *chazeret*.

The Roasted Egg

A hardboiled, unshelled, roasted or browned egg *(baytza)* is one of the symbols on the Seder tray. It serves as a reminder of the regular festival sacrifice brought in the days when the Temple stood in Jerusalem. In Hebrew the sacrifice is known as *Korban Chagiga* ("Holiday Offering").

Passover Eggs

Since a great many eggs are consumed during the week of Passover, one should be aware that there is no difference in quality between brown and white eggs, and brown eggs are very often sold at lower prices.

Storing Shelled Eggs

Hardboiled eggs that have been shelled and are being held for use at the Seder should be kept in the refrigerator in a covered container. Shelled eggs are porous and will absorb the odors of foods stored near them.

No-crack Eggs

A few drops of vinegar added to the water in which eggs are boiled will keep the shells from cracking and the whites from oozing out. Another crack-prevention method is to pierce a hole in the wider end of each egg before placing it in the water.

When an eggshell cracks during boiling, seal it immediately by adding a splash of vinegar to the boiling water.

Egg Dipped in Salt Water

Before the formal Seder meal, an *hors d'oeuvre* of sliced, diced, or whole hardboiled eggs is served. Each participant takes some egg on a spoon and dips it in salt water. The egg is a reminder of the holiday sacrifice brought in Temple times.

The Stolen Matza

At one point during the Seder the leader breaks off a piece of the middle *matza* that sits on the Seder tray and hides it in a napkin or bag. Children look for it, and if they are successful in finding it, the leader must ransom the *matza* by promising a gift.

The hidden *matza* is called *afikomon*, a Greek word meaning "dessert." It is the last of the foods eaten at the Seder meal, and a Seder cannot continue until each Seder participant has had a piece of this dessert.

Reclining at the Seder

In ancient Palestine, when the Temple was in existence, it was customary for all celebrants at a Seder to sit on the floor, propped up by pillows. When drinking each of the four cups of wine, they would lean to the left in the manner of free men, as they would while eating the meal.

Today, the leader of the Seder leans on a pillow placed next to him, symbolizing the emancipation of the Children of Israel and the Exodus from Egypt.

Four Cups of Wine

Traditionally, on Sabbaths and holidays two cups of wine are used at mealtime: one for *Kiddush* and one for the recitation of Grace After Meals. On Passover, a special holiday, two more cups are added, and all four cups are consumed during the course of the Seder. A popular interpretation suggests that the four cups of wine were instituted because the Book of Exodus records four different expressions used by God in connection with the release of the Israelites from bondage: I shall *bring forth,* I shall *deliver,* I shall *redeem,* and I shall *take out.*

The Fifth Cup

In some homes, a fifth cup is filled at the end of the Seder to acknowledge the redemption of Jews after the Holocaust and the establishment of the State of Israel.

Red Wine vs. White Wine

The Talmud considers red wine to be superior to white wine, and it is therefore preferred for Seder use.

White Wine and the Blood Libel

An old German tradition calls for the use of white wine during the Seder since red wine can be mistaken for blood. This practice has its roots in the oft-repeated, unfounded accusation that Jews used the blood of Christian children at the Seder.

Ten Drops of Wine

When the part of the Haggada that lists the ten plagues is read, participants at the Seder remove a drop of wine from their cups with a fingertip or a spoon. This is considered a way of expressing empathy with the Egyptians, who had to endure so much suffering because of misguided leaders.

The Cup of Elijah

At the conclusion of the Seder meal a special goblet, known as the Cup of Elijah, is filled with wine. In Jewish tradition Elijah the Prophet represents the person who will usher in the Messianic Age, a time when peace will prevail throughout the world. Elijah is a welcome guest at every Seder and, to demonstrate that fact, at a specific time during the Seder service the front door of the house is opened to bid him welcome.

See the Appendix, page 317, for a special song of welcome to Elijah.

Wine Stain Removal

Blot wine stains immediately with an absorbent cloth or paper napkin. If possible, place absorbent material under the stained area. Apply tap water to the area and continue blotting. If the stain persists, stretch the fabric over a bowl, apply salt, and pour hot water over it. Another remedy is to apply to the area a 50/50 solution of water and vinegar.

Kiddush for Passover

The *Kiddush* recited as part of the Seder is found in every Haggada. The *Kiddush* for the last day of Passover is, with a slight variation, the same as that recited on Shavuot and Sukkot. See page 245.

The Four Questions

To involve children in the proceedings of the evening, four questions were designed to be asked of the leader. Generally, the youngest child at the Seder asks the questions. If children are not present, anyone may recite them.

Introduction:

מַה־נִּשְׁתַּנָּה הַלַּיְלָה הַזֶּה מִכָּל־הַלֵּילוֹת?

Ma nishtana ha-laila ha-zeh mi-kol ha-lelot?

Why is this night different from all other nights? I have four questions to ask about this.

First Question:

שֶׁבְּכָל־הַלֵּילוֹת אָנוּ אוֹכְלִין חָמֵץ וּמַצָּה, הַלַּיְלָה
הַזֶּה כֻּלּוֹ מַצָּה?

She-be-chol ha-lelot anu ochlin chametz u-matza, ha-laila ha-zeh kulo matza?

Why is it that on all other nights during the year we eat either bread or *matza*, but on this night we eat only *matza*?

Second Question:

שֶׁבְּכָל־הַלֵּילוֹת אָנוּ אוֹכְלִין שְׁאָר יְרָקוֹת, הַלַּיְלָה
הַזֶּה מָרוֹר?

She-be-chol ha-lelot anu ochlin she-ar yerakot, ha-laila ha-zeh maror?

Why is it that on all other nights we eat all kinds of vegetables, but on this night we eat bitter herbs?

Third Question:

שֶׁבְּכָל־הַלֵּילוֹת אֵין אָנוּ מַטְבִּילִין אֲפִלּוּ פַּעַם אֶחָת,
הַלַּיְלָה הַזֶּה שְׁתֵּי פְעָמִים?

She-be-chol ha-lelot en anu matbilin afilu pa'am echat, ha-laila ha-zeh shetay fe'amim?

Why is it that on all other nights we do not dip even once, but on this night we dip twice?

Fourth Question:

שֶׁבְּכָל הַלֵּילוֹת אָנוּ אוֹכְלִין בֵּין יוֹשְׁבִין וּבֵין
מְסֻבִּין, הַלַּיְלָה הַזֶּה כֻּלָּנוּ מְסֻבִּין?

She-be-chol ha-lelot anu ochlin bayn yoshvin u-vayn mesubin, ha-laila ha-zeh kulanu mesubin?

Why is it that on all other nights we eat either sitting or reclining, but on this night we eat in a reclining position?

Leader:

Your questions are well stated, and they will be answered in the course of the Seder we celebrate tonight to commemorate the deliverance of our ancestors from ancient Egypt, the house of bondage.

SEDER CHECKLIST

The traditional homemaker should have the following in readiness for the Seder:

- candlesticks and candles
- a pillow against which the leader of the Seder can recline
- a Haggada for each participant
- wine goblets for the participants
- a wine goblet to serve as Elijah's Cup
- wine sufficient to fill each goblet four times and Elijah's Cup once
- a Seder tray with the six symbolic Passover foods described on pages 231 through 236
- *matza* to be served at the meal
- three unbroken *matzot* to be placed under the Seder tray, each separated by a cloth or napkin
- a cloth, napkin, or bag in which the leader can place the *afikomon*
- a cup and bowl for the washing of hands
- several dishes of salt water placed in easy reach of the participants
- a dish of vegetables to be distributed to the participants as *karpas:* parsley, cucumber, celery, radish, boiled potato, or the like
- a dish of grated horseradish for distribution to the participants as *maror*

- a dish of *charoset* for distribution to all participants
- shelled, hardboiled eggs to be distributed to all participants before the meal.

THE OMER PERIOD

The Omer

The Bible (Leviticus 23:99ff.) says that when the Children of Israel are settled in the Promised Land and grow their crops, the first sheaf (bundle) of the springtime harvest (the barley crop) shall be brought to the Priest as an offering. The grain was ground and sifted, and one *omer* (an ancient dry measure which equals about four liters) of this barley flour was mixed with oil and frankincense (spice) "to create a pleasing odor before the Lord." This sacrifice was brought only on the second day of Passover, the sixteenth day of Nissan.

Counting the Days After the Omer

Jews speak of "counting the *Omer*." What is being counted, in effect, are the forty-nine days between the second day of Passover and Shavuot.

The Bible (Leviticus 23:15-16) says, "And from the day on which you shall bring the sheaf offering . . . you shall count off seven weeks until the day after the seventh week [Shavuot]." The forty-nine-day period between Passover and Shavuot is referred to as the *Sefira* ("counting") period.

During the course of the *Sefira* period a special *Omer*-counting blessing is recited as part of the evening service. Those holding a second Seder count the first night of the *Omer* during the Seder service itself.

Salt and Sefira

Sephardic Jews with roots in Morocco often keep salt in their pockets during the *Sefira* period for two reasons: as a reminder to count each day and as a safeguard against evil spirits.

Lag B'Omer

According to a widely accepted tradition, the period between Passover and Shavuot is a time of national mourning because in the year 134 or 135 C.E. a dreadful plague decimated the ranks of the student body in the academy of Rabbi Akiba. The plague abated on the thirty-third day of the *Omer* count, and we call that day Lag B'Omer, meaning "thirty-three days into the *Omer*." Mourning is cancelled on that day, and celebrations and festivities are permitted. In Israel, schoolchildren go on outings on Lag B'Omer.

Weddings on Lag B'Omer

Among traditional Jews, weddings are banned on certain days of the seven-week period between Passover and Shavuot. Joyous days such as Lag B'Omer and Rosh Chodesh are exceptions. See page 46 for details.

END-OF-PASSOVER CUSTOMS

The Last Day of Passover

After the evening *(Maariv)* service on the last day of Passover, Sephardim conduct a variety of ceremonies unknown to Ashkenazim. Syrian Jews take stalks of wheat and pretend to beat each other with them to symbolize that the wheat *(chametz)* may now be eaten. Moroccan Jews celebrate the end of Passover with a *Maimuna* (or *Mimona),* a colorful, happy celebration during which a variety of sweet foods are served.

Post-Passover Challa

At the conclusion of the Passover holiday, Jews of the Soviet Ukraine often bake *challot* decorated with keys made from *challa* dough. These are representations of the key to the "gate of release" from Egyptian bondage.

10
THE SPRING HOLIDAYS II
SHAVUOT

Introduction

Shavuot (also pronounced Shavuos) is known by many names, including Chag Ha-shavuot ("Feast of Weeks"), Chag Ha-bikurim ("Festival of First Fruits"), and Chag Ha-katzir ("Harvest Festival"). Each of these names is related to the agricultural origins of the holiday, which was celebrated in late spring when the new wheat crop was harvested.

Since Shavuot falls on the fiftieth day after the beginning of Passover, the two holidays have become closely linked. The Talmud considers Shavuot a concluding holiday to Passover and even refers to it by the name Atzeret, meaning "conclusion."

Although the Bible does not associate Shavuot with the Revelation on Mount Sinai, the Talmud does. Scholars, following the biblical account, calculated that the date of the agricultural festival of Shavuot and that of the event at Mt. Sinai coincided. Therefore, it was natural that the one-time agricultural holiday would become a time for celebrating the Torah. In fact, in the Middle Ages it became customary for pious people to devote the entire night of Shavuot to the study of Torah.

At the end of the nineteenth century, Reform Judaism introduced the Confirmation ceremony into the Shavuot service. Today, in Reform, Conservative, and even some Orthodox congregations, this is a time when girls and boys, generally thirteen to sixteen years of age, confirm their allegiance to the Jewish way of life.

HISTORICAL BACKGROUND

A Pilgrim Festival

Shavuot, the Feast of Weeks (Chag Ha-shavuot in Hebrew), is so called because it is celebrated seven weeks and one day after the second day of Passover. Shavuot, along with Passover and Sukkot, is one of the three major Pilgrim Festivals in the Jewish calendar.

The pilgrims who came to Jerusalem on Shavuot in Temple times brought with them the first "fruits" of the wheat crop that was harvested at that time of year (May-June). Loaves of bread were made from the wheat, and two loaves were offered as a sacrifice on the altar.

Pentecost

Because Shavuot is celebrated on the fiftieth day after the advent of Passover, it has been called Pentecost, a Greek word meaning "fiftieth [day] after Passover." The Hebrew date is the sixth of Sivan.

A Two-day Diaspora Holiday

The Bible calls for the observance of Shavuot as a one-day holiday, but because notification that the New Moon had been sighted did not always reach the far-flung Diaspora communities on time, a second day was added to Shavuot (and the other major festivals) to avoid the possibility of celebrating the holiday on the wrong day. In Israel Shavuot is observed for only one day, a practice also followed by Reform and some Conservative Jews in the Diaspora.

Shavuot and Revelation

Although in biblical times Shavuot was an agricultural holiday, in talmudic times it became associated with the Revelation on Mount Sinai. The Rabbis noted that the agricultural holiday of Shavuot and the events that took place on Mount Sinai occurred in the same season of the year. Torah-study sessions were inaugurated, and Shavuot became a holiday on which to affirm one's loyalty to the Torah and the Jewish way of life.

Time of the Giving of the Torah

The third-century C.E. talmudic scholar Rabbi Eleazar was probably the first to refer to Shavuot as *Zeman Matan Tora-tenu,* "Time of the Giving of the Torah." He noted that on Shavuot it is important to rejoice with good wine and food in celebration of the Revelation on Mount Sinai.

Shavuot Study Period

The Zohar, written by the second-century mystic Rabbi Simon bar Yochai, says that it behooves a man to study Torah on the night that Israel received the Torah, and in the sixteenth century Solomon Alkabetz of Safed introduced the custom of preparing to celebrate Shavuot by staying up all night to study Torah. The tradition of studying in preparation for the holiday, known as *Tikkun Shavuot* ("preparing for Shavuot"), is still observed in synagogues in a variety of forms, but few people stay up for the entire night. One of the books used on this night, known as *Tikkun Layl Shavuot,* is an anthology of readings assembled from biblical, talmudic, and kabbalistic sources.

A Jerusalem Tradition

In Jerusalem today it is customary for those who have spent the night of Shavuot studying in the local synagogue or other places of assembly to go to the Western Wall at sunrise for the morning *(Shacharit)* prayers.

Candlelighting for Shavuot and Other Festivals

Candlelighting prayers are the same for all holidays except Yom Kippur. See page 256.

Kiddush for Shavuot and Other Festivals

The following is recited not only on Shavuot but also on Passover, Sukkot, and Shemini Atzeret.

[When the holiday falls on Friday night begin here:]

וַיְהִי עֶרֶב, וַיְהִי־בְקֶר, יוֹם הַשִּׁשִּׁי.

וַיְכֻלּוּ הַשָּׁמַיִם וְהָאָרֶץ וְכָל־צְבָאָם. וַיְכַל אֱלֹהִים
בַּיּוֹם הַשְּׁבִיעִי מְלַאכְתּוֹ אֲשֶׁר עָשָׂה. וַיִּשְׁבֹּת בַּיּוֹם
הַשְּׁבִיעִי מִכָּל מְלַאכְתּוֹ אֲשֶׁר עָשָׂה. וַיְבָרֶךְ אֱלֹהִים
אֶת יוֹם הַשְּׁבִיעִי, וַיְקַדֵּשׁ אֹתוֹ, כִּי בוֹ שָׁבַת מִכָּל
מְלַאכְתּוֹ אֲשֶׁר בָּרָא אֱלֹהִים לַעֲשׂוֹת.

[On weekdays begin here:]

בָּרוּךְ אַתָּה יְיָ, אֱלֹהֵינוּ מֶלֶךְ הָעוֹלָם, בּוֹרֵא פְּרִי
הַגָּפֶן.

[On Sabbath add words in parentheses:]

בָּרוּךְ אַתָּה יְיָ, אֱלֹהֵינוּ מֶלֶךְ הָעוֹלָם, אֲשֶׁר בָּחַר
בָּנוּ מִכָּל עָם, וְרוֹמְמָנוּ מִכָּל לָשׁוֹן, וְקִדְּשָׁנוּ
בְּמִצְוֹתָיו. וַתִּתֶּן לָנוּ יְיָ אֱלֹהֵינוּ בְּאַהֲבָה (שַׁבָּתוֹת
לִמְנוּחָה וּ) מוֹעֲדִים לְשִׂמְחָה, חַגִּים וּזְמַנִּים
לְשָׂשׂוֹן, אֶת יוֹם (הַשַּׁבָּת הַזֶּה וְאֶת יוֹם)

[On Shavuot say:]

חַג הַשָּׁבֻעוֹת הַזֶּה, זְמַן מַתַּן תּוֹרָתֵנוּ

[On Sukkot say:]

חַג הַסֻּכּוֹת הַזֶּה, זְמַן שִׂמְחָתֵנוּ

[On Shemini Atzeret (and Simchat Torah) say:]

הַשְּׁמִינִי חַג הָעֲצֶרֶת הַזֶּה, זְמַן שִׂמְחָתֵנוּ

[On Passover say:]

חַג הַמַצוֹת הַזֶה, זְמַן חֵרוּתֵנוּ

(בְּאַהֲבָה) מִקְרָא קֹדֶשׁ, זֵכֶר לִיצִיאַת מִצְרָיִם. כִּי
בָנוּ בָחַרְתָּ וְאוֹתָנוּ קִדַּשְׁתָּ מִכָּל הָעַמִּים, (וְשַׁבָּת)
וּמוֹעֲדֵי קָדְשֶׁךָ (בְּאַהֲבָה וּבְרָצוֹן) בְּשִׂמְחָה וּבְשָׂשׂוֹן
הִנְחַלְתָּנוּ. בָּרוּךְ אַתָּה יְיָ, מְקַדֵּשׁ (הַשַׁבָּת וְ)יִשְׂרָאֵל
וְהַזְמַנִּים.

[On Saturday night only add:]

בָּרוּךְ אַתָּה יְיָ, אֱלֹהֵינוּ מֶלֶךְ הָעוֹלָם, בּוֹרֵא מְאוֹרֵי
הָאֵשׁ.

בָּרוּךְ אַתָּה יְיָ, אֱלֹהֵינוּ מֶלֶךְ הָעוֹלָם, הַמַבְדִּיל בֵּין
קֹדֶשׁ לְחֹל, בֵּין אוֹר לְחֹשֶׁךְ, בֵּין יִשְׂרָאֵל לָעַמִּים,
בֵּין יוֹם הַשְׁבִיעִי לְשֵׁשֶׁת יְמֵי הַמַעֲשֶׂה; בֵּין קְדֻשַׁת
שַׁבָּת לִקְדֻשַׁת יוֹם טוֹב הִבְדַּלְתָּ, וְאֶת יוֹם הַשְׁבִיעִי
מִשֵׁשֶׁת יְמֵי הַמַעֲשֶׂה קִדַּשְׁתָּ; הִבְדַּלְתָּ וְקִדַּשְׁתָּ אֶת
עַמְּךָ יִשְׂרָאֵל בִּקְדֻשָׁתֶךָ.
בָּרוּךְ אַתָּה יְיָ, הַמַבְדִּיל בֵּין קֹדֶשׁ לְקֹדֶשׁ.

[Conclude with the *She-hecheyanu,* which is omitted on the
last two nights of Passover.]

בָּרוּךְ אַתָּה יְיָ, אֱלֹהֵינוּ מֶלֶךְ הָעוֹלָם, שֶׁהֶחֱיָנוּ,
וְקִיְּמָנוּ, וְהִגִּיעָנוּ לַזְמַן הַזֶה.

Transliteration of the Kiddush

[When the holiday falls on Friday night begin here:]

Va-yehi erev, va-yehi voker, Yom ha-shishi.
Va-yechulu ha-shama'yim ve-ha-aretz ve-chol tze-
va'am. Va-yechal Elohim ba-yom ha-shevi'i melachto
asher asa. Va-yishbot ba-yom ha-shevi'i mi-kol
melachto asher asa. Va-ye-varech Elohim et yom ha-
shevi'i, va-yekadesh oto, ki vo shavat mi-kol melachto
asher bara Elohim la-asot.

[On weekdays begin here:]

Baruch ata Adonai, Elohenu melech ha-olam, boray peri ha-gafen.

[On Sabbath add words in parentheses:]

Baruch ata Adonai, Elohenu melech ha-olam, asher bachar banu mi-kol am, ve-romemanu mi-kol lashon, ve-kideshanu be-mitzvotav. Va-titen lanu Adonai Elohenu be-ahava (shabbatot li-menucha u-) moadim le-simcha, chagim u-zemanim le-sason, et yom (ha-Shabbat ha-zeh ve-et yom)

[On Shavuot say:]

Chag Ha-shavuot ha-zeh, zeman matan Toratenu

[On Sukkot say:]

Chag Ha-sukkot ha-zeh, zeman simchatenu

[On Shemini Atzeret (and Simchat Torah) say:]

Shemini Chag Ha-atzeret ha-zeh, zeman simchatenu

[On Passover say:]

Chag Ha-matzot ha-zeh, zeman cherutenu

(be-ahava) mikra kodesh, zecher li-yetziat Mitzra'yim. Ki vanu vacharta ve-otanu kidashta mi-kol ha-amim, (ve-Shabbat) u-mo'aday kodshecha (be-ahava u-veratzon) be-simcha u-vesason hinchaltanu. Baruch ata, Adonai, mekadesh (ha-Shabbat ve-) Yisrael ve-ha-zemanim.

[On Saturday night only add:]

Baruch ata Adonai, Elohenu melech ha-olam, boray me-oray ha-esh.

Baruch ata Adonai, Elohenu melech ha-olam, ha-mavdil bayn kodesh le-chol, bayn or l'choshech, bayn Yisrael la-amim, bayn yom ha-shevi'i l'sheshet yemay ha-ma'aseh; bayn kedushat Shabbat li-kedushat Yom Tov hivdalta, ve-et yom ha-shevi'i mi-sheshet yemay ha-

ma'aseh kidashta; hivdalta ve-kidashta et amcha Yisrael bi-kedushatecha.

Baruch ata, Adonai, ha-mavdil bayn kodesh l'kodesh.

[Conclude with the *She-hecheyanu,* which is omitted on the last two nights of Passover.]

Baruch ata Adonai, Elohenu melech ha-olam, she-hecheyanu, ve-kiyemanu, ve-higiyanu la-zeman ha-zeh.

Translation of the Kiddush

[When the holiday falls on Friday night begin here:]

And it was evening, and it was morning, the sixth day. And God completed the creation of the heaven and earth and all that they contained. And by the seventh day God finished His work and He rested. And God blessed the seventh day and hallowed it, because on that day He rested from all His work of Creation.

[On weekdays begin here:]

Praised be Thou, O Lord our God, King of the universe, who created the fruit of the vine.

[On Sabbath add words in parentheses:]

Praised be Thou, O Lord our God, King of the universe, who has exalted us above all nations and sanctified us with Thy commandments. Thou, O Lord our God, hast graciously given us (Sabbaths for rest and) joyous, festive holidays, and hast given us in particular (this Sabbath and) this

[On Shavuot say:]

Festival of Weeks, the holiday of the giving of the Torah

[On Sukkot say:]

Festival of Tabernacles, the holiday of our rejoicing

[On Shemini Atzeret and Simchat Torah say:]

Festival of the Eighth Day of Assembly, the holiday of our rejoicing

[On Passover say:]

Festival of Unleavened Bread, the holiday of our redemption

[Continue here:]

a time of holy convocation in remembrance of the Exodus from Egypt. Thou hast selected us above all peoples and graciously bequeathed unto us Thy holy (Sabbath and) festivals in which to be joyful. Praised be Thou, O Lord our God, who hallows (the Sabbath,) Israel and the festivals.

[On Saturday night only add:]

Praised be Thou, O Lord our God, King of the universe, who created the light of fire.

Praised be Thou, O Lord our God, King of the universe, who distinguished between the holy and the profane, between light and darkness, between Israel and the nations, between the seventh day and the other days of the week. Thou hast distinguished between the holiness of the Sabbath and the holiness of festivals and hast hallowed the seventh day above the six working days. Thou hast distinguished and sanctified Thy people Israel with thy holiness.

Praised be Thou, O Lord our God, who differentiates between the greater holiness and the lesser holiness.

[Conclude with the She-hecheyanu, which is omitted on the last two nights of Passover.]

Praised be Thou, O Lord our God, King of the universe, who has kept us alive, and sustained us, and permitted us to enjoy this day.

Akdamut and Azharot

Akdamut, meaning "introduction," is an Aramaic poetic prayer (piyut) read on Shavuot as an introduction to the Torah reading of the day, which describes the events that transpired from the Exodus to the giving of the Torah on Mount Sinai. Only Ashkenazim recite Akdamut.

To honor the Torah on Shavuot, Sephardim recite a piyut entitled Azharot, which includes a listing of the 613 positive and negative commandments (mitzvot) of the Torah.

Book of Ruth

The Book of Ruth is read in the synagogue on Shavuot—the holiday of the giving of the Torah—because Ruth showed her loyalty to the Torah by accepting Judaism. In some synagogues it is read before the Torah reading; in others it is read before the afternoon *(Mincha)* service.

King David and Ruth

According to legend, King David was born and died on the same day, the sixth of Sivan, which is Shavuot. Ruth is a direct ancestor of David, and this is another reason, some say, for reading the Book of Ruth on Shavuot.

Shavuot and Confirmation

Confirmation of boys and girls began in Reform congregations in nineteenth-century Germany and subsequently spread to America, where it was introduced by Rabbi Isaac Mayer Wise. The ceremony is held on Shavuot, which marks the giving of the Torah to the Children of Israel on Mount Sinai. During the ceremony teenage boys and girls reaffirm their loyalty to Judaism. (See page 27 for more on the Confirmation ceremony.)

SHAVUOT FOODS

Challa With a Ladder

In keeping with an old tradition, some Jews who bake their own *challot* (plural of *challa*) decorate them with a ladder made from dough in commemoration of the ascent of Moses to Mount Sinai to receive the Torah. Some Jews shape their Shavuot *challot* in the form of a mountain.

Dairy Foods on Shavuot

It is traditional to serve dairy foods and honey on Shavuot because the phrase "honey and milk under thy lips," found in the Song of Songs (4:11), implies that the words of the Torah energize our spirits as honey and milk do our bodies.

Matza on Shavuot

Jews from Morocco save *matzot* from Passover and on Shavuot crumble them into small pieces, pour a honey-milk mixture over them, and serve the dish as a holiday meal appetizer.

Cheese Blintzes and Kreplach

Two cheese blintzes, representing the two tablets of the Ten Commandments received by Moses on Mount Sinai, are traditionally eaten on Shavuot. Triangular cheese-filled *kreplach* are also a favorite Shavuot delicacy. The triangle shape represents the three parts of the Bible: Torah, Prophets, and Holy Writings.

Borekes

Borekes, cheese-filled pastries, are a favorite Sephardic Shavuot treat, particularly among Jews of Turkish origin.

Baked Cheese Blintzes

Serve these hearty baked *blintzes* with sour cream, applesauce, fresh fruit, or preserves.

Cheese Filling:
> 1 pound creamed cottage cheese
> 1 egg (graded large), beaten
> 3 ounces cream cheese, softened
> 1 teaspoon sugar
> Salt and freshly ground pepper to taste

In a bowl, mix all ingredients throughly. The filling is now ready to use.

Blintz Blanket:
> 3 eggs
> 3 tablespoons cornstarch
> 9 tablespoons water
> ¼ pound unsalted butter or margarine plus 2
> tablespoons for frying

In a mixing bowl, combine the eggs, cornstarch, and water. Beat the mixture thoroughly. Let rest for 20 minutes. Cover a working space with cheesecloth or wax paper to lay out the *blintz* blankets for cooling.

Lightly grease a skillet with butter or margarine. Place the skillet over a low heat and pour in 2 tablespoons' worth of the mixture, just enough to thinly coat the pan. As soon as the blanket is lightly cooked on one side, remove it from the pan and set to cool. Repeat the process until you have used up the batter, lightly regreasing the pan before cooking each blanket.

Preheat the oven to 350 degrees F. Place about 2 tablespoons' worth of the cheese filling on each *blintz* blanket. Fold the top and bottom of each, then the sides, around the filling, shaping rectangular packages.

In a lightly-greased baking pan large enough to accommodate the *blintzes*, place the *blintzes* flap side down. Melt the remaining butter or margarine and pour it over the *blintzes*, covering thoroughly. Bake for approximately 60 minutes, until golden brown. Serves 4.

Baked Cheese Loaf

This easy-to-prepare loaf is a nice substitute for cheese *blintzes*. Chopped walnuts add a pleasant accent.

> **2 eggs (graded large)**
> **½ teaspoon vanilla extract**
> **1 pound farmer cheese**
> **¼ cup sugar**
> **Dash of freshly ground pepper**
> **½ cup seedless raisins**
> **Cinnamon (optional)**

In a medium-sized bowl, beat the eggs with the vanilla extract. Blend in the cheese, sugar, pepper, and raisins. Taste and add more sugar if needed.

Preheat the oven to 350 degrees F. Grease a 3 x 7-inch loaf pan and pour in the cheese mixture. Sprinkle the top with cinnamon if desired. Bake in a preheated oven for 30 minutes. Serve hot or cold with sour cream and blueberries, strawberries, or raspberries. Serves 4.

11

THE FALL HOLIDAYS I

ROSH HASHANA AND YOM KIPPUR

Introduction

The fall holidays begin during the month of September, on the first day of the Hebrew month Tishri. The first ten days of this holiday period—from Rosh Hashana through Yom Kippur—are called the Days of Awe. In the special prayers recited during these days, God is revered and celebrated as Creator and Master of the universe, and we are called upon to examine ourselves and consider the state of our spiritual lives.

Although the Ten Days of Awe officially commence on the first day of Tishri, this period of introspection in fact begins one month earlier, on the first of Elul. During Elul, special prayers are added to the liturgy, and the *shofar* is sounded in the synagogue each day as part of the morning service to remind us that the most awesome holidays in the Jewish calendar are approaching.

The focus of Rosh Hashana is the synagogue service, which features the sounding of the *shofar,* as prescribed in the Bible. The Rosh Hashana liturgy contains dozens of poems composed over the last two millenia, many of which are recited only during the High Holidays to distinctive melodies. Rosh Hashana is also a holiday of distinctive foods: the pomegranate, the many

253

seeds of which represent the hope for a productive year; honey-laden treats which symbolize the hope for sweet days ahead; and bread loaves (*challot*) in various symbolic shapes and designs.

Yom Kippur is a solemn day of prayer and fasting, beginning with the Kol Nidre service and ending with the sounding of the *shofar* twenty-five hours later. In traditional synagogues, many Jews wear white gowns (*kittels*) as a symbol of purity. and avoid wearing leather shoes, which are a sign of luxurious living. During the recitation of the Yom Kippur prayers, the attention of each Jew focuses on his relationship with God and his fellow man.

PREPARING FOR ROSH HASHANA

Days of Awe

In Jewish tradition, the holiest period of the year begins with Rosh Hashana, celebrated on the first day of the Hebrew month Tishri (which falls some time during the month of September), and concludes with Yom Kippur, on the tenth of Tishri. This ten-day period of prayer and introspection is known as the "Days of Awe" or the "Ten Days of Repentance." The Hebrew term is *Aseret Yemay Teshuva.*

The Month of Elul

According to Judaism, preparation for the High Holy Day period begins on the first day of Elul, one month before Rosh Hashana. In most synagogues, throughout the month the *shofar* is blown during the weekday morning service and special prayers (such as Psalm 27) are recited. In many Sephardic congregations, special *Selichot* (penitential) prayers are added to the liturgy.

Midnight Selichot Prayers

Special *Selichot* prayers are recited in the synagogue on the Saturday night preceding Rosh Hashana. The custom arose because the psalmist declared, "At midnight I will rise to thank Thee [God]" (Psalms 119:62). If Rosh Hashana falls early in the week (Tuesday or earlier), the Saturday night *Selichot* are recited one week earlier.

In recent years, many congregations have been holding the Saturday night *Selichot* service an hour or two before midnight. A study period precedes the prayer service.

Grave Visitations

According to tradition, during the High Holy Day period a Heavenly Tribunal judges the fate of every person. Many people believe that their departed loved ones can intercede and effect a favorable decision for them, and for this reason they visit cemeteries where their parents and other relatives are buried. During these visitations, which take place throughout the month of Elul (August-September) up until Yom Kippur, memorial prayers are recited.

ROSH HASHANA IN THE JEWISH CALENDAR

Two-day Holiday

Jews the world over celebrate Rosh Hashana for two days despite the fact that the Bible describes it as only a one-day holiday. The Rabbis of the Talmud found it necessary to make this calendar adjustment because Rosh Hashana is the only holiday celebrated on the first day of the month (the first day of Tishri), and the announcement could not be made until witnesses appeared to testify to the fact that they had seen the New Moon. Since witnesses were often delayed, Rosh Hashana was made a two-day holiday so that Jews could be sure that they were observing the holiday on the proper day.

Most Reform congregations celebrate Rosh Hashana as a

one-day holiday, preferring to follow biblical law rather than the later rabbinic innovation.

Rosh Hashana as the New Year

Although the Bible speaks of Nissan (the month in which Passover falls) as the first month of the year, we celebrate the New Year in Tishri, the seventh month in the Jewish calendar. In ancient Palestine this was the month when the final harvest of the previous year had been completed and a new annual cycle was about to begin.

The traditional Rosh Hashana greeting is *Le-shana tova tikatev* (plural, *tikatevu*), "May you be inscribed [in the Book of Life] for a good year."

Lo Adu Rosh

The first day of Rosh Hashana can never fall on a Sunday, Wednesday, or Friday. A good way to remember these days is to memorize the phrase *Lo Adu Rosh,* which means that Rosh Hashana *(Rosh)* cannot *(Lo)* fall on A-D-U. In Hebrew script the letters are *alef, dalet,* and *vav,* the letter *alef* having the numerical value of one, *dalet* being the equivalent of four, and *vav* representing six. In this case, the reference is to the first, fourth, and sixth days of the week (Sunday, Wednesday, and Friday).

CANDLELIGHTING AND KIDDUSH

Candlelighting Blessings for Rosh Hashana and Other Holidays

The following candlelighting blessings are recited on all holidays except Yom Kippur. See page 268.

בָּרוּךְ אַתָּה יְיָ, אֱלֹהֵינוּ מֶלֶךְ הָעוֹלָם, אֲשֶׁר קִדְּשָׁנוּ בְּמִצְוֹתָיו וְצִוָּנוּ לְהַדְלִיק נֵר שֶׁל (שַׁבָּת וְשֶׁל) יוֹם טוֹב.

Baruch ata Adonai, Elohenu melech ha-olam, asher kideshanu be-mitzvotav, ve-tzivanu le-hadlik ner (shel Shabbat v'shel) yom tov.

Praised be Thou, O Lord our God, King of the universe, who has sanctified us by His commandments and commanded us to kindle (the Sabbath and the) holiday lights.

[Recite on both nights of Rosh Hashana:]

בָּרוּךְ אַתָּה יְיָ, אֱלֹהֵינוּ מֶלֶךְ הָעוֹלָם, שֶׁהֶחֱיָנוּ,
וְקִיְּמָנוּ, וְהִגִּיעָנוּ לַזְּמַן הַזֶּה.

Baruch ata Adonai, Elohenu melech ha-olam, she-hecheyanu, ve-kiyemanu, ve-higiyanu la-zeman ha-zeh.

Praised be Thou, O Lord our God, King of the universe, who has given us life, and sustained us, and permitted us to reach and enjoy this moment.

Kiddush for Rosh Hashana

The prayer over wine is recited on the first two evenings of Rosh Hashana.

[On Friday night begin here:]

וַיְהִי עֶרֶב, וַיְהִי־בֹקֶר, יוֹם הַשִּׁשִּׁי.
וַיְכֻלּוּ הַשָּׁמַיִם וְהָאָרֶץ וְכָל־צְבָאָם. וַיְכַל אֱלֹהִים
בַּיּוֹם הַשְּׁבִיעִי מְלַאכְתּוֹ אֲשֶׁר עָשָׂה. וַיִּשְׁבֹּת בַּיּוֹם
הַשְּׁבִיעִי מִכָּל מְלַאכְתּוֹ אֲשֶׁר עָשָׂה. וַיְבָרֶךְ אֱלֹהִים
אֶת יוֹם הַשְּׁבִיעִי, וַיְקַדֵּשׁ אֹתוֹ, כִּי בוֹ שָׁבַת מִכָּל
מְלַאכְתּוֹ אֲשֶׁר בָּרָא אֱלֹהִים לַעֲשׂוֹת.

Va-yehi erev, va-yehi voker, Yom ha-shishi.
Va-yechulu ha-shama'yim ve-ha-aretz ve-chol tze-va'am. Va-yechal Elohim ba-yom ha-shevi'i melachto asher asa. Va-yishbot ba-yom ha-shevi'i mi-kol melachto asher asa. Va-ye-varech Elohim et yom ha-shevi'i, va-yekadesh oto, ki vo shavat mi-kol melachto asher bara Elohim la-asot.

And it was evening, and it was morning, the sixth day.

And God completed the creation of the heaven and earth and all that they contained. And by the seventh day God finished His work and He rested. And God blessed the seventh day and hallowed it, because on that day He rested from all His work of Creation.

[On weekdays begin here. On Friday night continue here and add the words in parentheses:]

בָּרוּךְ אַתָּה יְיָ, אֱלֹהֵינוּ מֶלֶךְ הָעוֹלָם, בּוֹרֵא פְּרִי הַגָּפֶן.

Baruch ata Adonai, Elohenu melech ha-olam, boray peri ha-gafen.

Praised be Thou, O Lord our God, King of the universe, who created the fruit of the vine.

בָּרוּךְ אַתָּה יְיָ, אֱלֹהֵינוּ מֶלֶךְ הָעוֹלָם, אֲשֶׁר בָּחַר־ בָּנוּ מִכָּל־עָם וְרוֹמְמָנוּ מִכָּל־לָשׁוֹן וְקִדְּשָׁנוּ בְּמִצְוֹתָיו. וַתִּתֶּן־לָנוּ יְיָ אֱלֹהֵינוּ בְּאַהֲבָה אֶת (יוֹם הַשַּׁבָּת הַזֶּה וְאֶת) יוֹם הַזִּכָּרוֹן הַזֶּה, יוֹם (זִכְרוֹן) תְּרוּעָה (בְּאַהֲבָה) מִקְרָא קֹדֶשׁ זֵכֶר לִיצִיאַת מִצְרָיִם. כִּי בָנוּ בָחַרְתָּ וְאוֹתָנוּ קִדַּשְׁתָּ מִכָּל־ הָעַמִּים. וּדְבָרְךָ אֱמֶת וְקַיָּם לָעַד. בָּרוּךְ אַתָּה יְיָ, מֶלֶךְ עַל כָּל־הָאָרֶץ, מְקַדֵּשׁ (הַשַּׁבָּת וְ) יִשְׂרָאֵל וְיוֹם הַזִּכָּרוֹן.

Baruch ata Adonai, Elohenu melech ha-olam, asher bachar banu mi-kol am ve-romemanu mi-kol la-shon v'kideshanu be-mitzvotav. Va-titen lanu Adonai Elohenu be-ahava et (yom ha-Shabbat ha-zeh v'et) yom ha-zikaron ha-zeh, yom (zichron) terua (be-ahava) mikra kodesh zecher li-yetziat Mitzra'yim. Ki vanu vacharta ve-otanu kidashta mi-kol ha-amim. U-deva-recha emet ve-ka'yam la-ad. Baruch ata, Adonai, me-lech al kol ha-aretz me-kadesh (ha-Shabbat ve-) Yisrael ve-yom ha-zikaron.

Praised be Thou, O Lord our God, King of the universe, who has exalted us above all nations and sanctified us with Thy commandments. Thou, O Lord, hast gracious-ly given us (this Sabbath day and) this Day of Remem-brance as a day for (remembering the) blowing (of) the *shofar* and as a day for remembering the exodus from Egypt. Thou hast chosen and sanctified us above all peoples. Thy promise is true and everlasting. Praised be Thou, O Lord, King of all the earth, who hast sanctified (the Sabbath,) Israel and the Day of Remembrance.

[On Saturday night add the following *Havdala* selection:]

בָּרוּךְ אַתָּה יְיָ, אֱלֹהֵינוּ מֶלֶךְ הָעוֹלָם, בּוֹרֵא מְאוֹרֵי הָאֵשׁ.

בָּרוּךְ אַתָּה יְיָ, אֱלֹהֵינוּ מֶלֶךְ הָעוֹלָם, הַמַּבְדִּיל בֵּין קֹדֶשׁ לְחֹל, בֵּין אוֹר לְחֹשֶׁךְ, בֵּין יִשְׂרָאֵל לָעַמִּים, בֵּין יוֹם הַשְּׁבִיעִי לְשֵׁשֶׁת יְמֵי הַמַּעֲשֶׂה. בֵּין קְדֻשַּׁת שַׁבָּת לִקְדֻשַּׁת יוֹם טוֹב הִבְדַּלְתָּ. וְאֶת־יוֹם הַשְּׁבִיעִי מִשֵּׁשֶׁת יְמֵי הַמַּעֲשֶׂה קִדַּשְׁתָּ. הִבְדַּלְתָּ וְקִדַּשְׁתָּ אֶת־ עַמְּךָ יִשְׂרָאֵל בִּקְדֻשָּׁתֶךָ. בָּרוּךְ אַתָּה יְיָ, הַמַּבְדִּיל בֵּין קֹדֶשׁ לְקֹדֶשׁ.

Baruch ata Adonai, Elohenu melech ha-olam, boray me'oray ha-esh.

Baruch ata Adonai, Elohenu melech ha-olam, ha-mavdil bayn kodesh le-chol, bayn or le-choshech, bayn Yisrael la-amim, bayn yom ha-shevi'i le-sheshet yemay hama'aseh. Bayn kedushat Shabbat li-kedushat yom tov hivdalta, ve-et yom ha-shevi'i mi-sheshet yemay hama'aseh kidashta. Hivdalta ve-kidashta et amcha Yisrael bi-kedushatecha. Baruch ata, Adonai, ha-mavdil bayn kodesh le-kodesh.

Praised be Thou, O Lord our God, King of the universe, who has created the light of fire.

Praised be Thou, O Lord our God, King of the universe, who created a distinction between the holy and the profane, between light and darkness, between Israel and the nations, between the seventh day and the rest of the week. Thou hast made a distinction between the holiness of the Sabbath and the holiness of the festival, and hast hallowed the seventh day above the six working days. Thou hast distinguished and sanctified Thy people Israel with Thy holiness.

Praised be Thou, O Lord, who made a distinction between the sacred and the profane.

בָּרוּךְ אַתָּה יְיָ, אֱלֹהֵינוּ מֶלֶךְ הָעוֹלָם, שֶׁהֶחֱיָנוּ,
וְקִיְמָנוּ, וְהִגִּיעָנוּ לַזְּמַן הַזֶּה.

Baruch ata Adonai, Elohenu melech ha-olam, she-hecheyanu, ve-kiyemanu, ve-higiyanu la-zeman ha-zeh.

Praised be Thou, O Lord our God, King of the universe, who has given us life, and sustained us, and permitted us to reach and enjoy this moment.

The High Holiday Color

White, the symbol of purity in Jewish tradition, is the color of the High Holidays as well as other holidays. The idea stems from the prophet Isaiah, who wrote (1:18): "Though your sins be as [red as] scarlet [hence, real and uncontestable], they shall be as white as snow [after repentance]." This accounts for the Ashkenazic tradition of men wearing a white *kittel* (robe) on Rosh Hashana and Yom Kippur and at the Passover Seder, and also for the custom of changing Torah scroll mantles and ark curtains to white on all holidays.

Some Sephardim, such as Moroccans, dress in white clothing on Yom Kippur, but they do not wear a *kittel*. In some communities only the rabbi and *chazan* (cantor) wear white on Rosh Hashana and Yom Kippur.

High Holiday Liturgy

Prayers recited in the synagogue during the High Holidays are contained in a special prayerbook called the *Machzor* (literally, "cycle [of prayers]"). See Chapter Seven, In the Synagogue, for more about the *Machzor* and for a discussion of the distinctive prayers that apply to these holidays.

Aliyot on Rosh Hashana

At traditional services, five *aliyot* are awarded on each of the two days of Rosh Hashana, unless the holiday falls on a Sabbath, in which case seven *aliyot* are distributed.

THE SHOFAR

Shofar Origin

In ancient times, the *shofar* was always sounded to herald the arrival of a new month. The Book of Psalms (81:4) reminds us of this custom when it says: "Blow the horn [*shofar*] on the New Moon, on the full moon for our feast day."

The first day of the seventh month of the year (Tishri) is significant because it marks the beginning of the new year. In the Torah (Leviticus 23:24), God commands Moses as follows:

> Speak to the Israelite people and say: In the seventh month, on the first day of the month, you shall observe complete rest. It is to be a sacred occasion commemorated with loud blasts [of the *shofar*].

The Ram's Horn

The horn of the ram is most commonly used as the *shofar* on Rosh Hashana because it is identified with the intended sacrifice of Isaac by Abraham, an event which according to tradition occurred on Rosh Hashana. At the last moment before Abraham was to sacrifice Isaac, he found a ram caught in a thicket and used it as a substitute sacrifice.

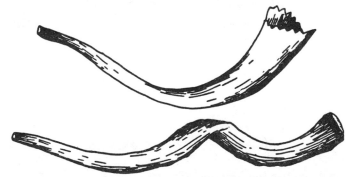

A *shofar* may be made from the horn of a ram, mountain goat, antelope, or gazelle. The horns of these animals are basically hollow and are therefore suitable for use as a musical instrument.

The *shofar* shown on top is the type used in most congregations. The longer, curved one below is the style traditionally favored by Yemenite Jews.

Horns of Cows

The horn of a kosher animal other than a ram may be used as a *shofar* provided that the horn is naturally hollow. However, the cowhorn was rejected by the Rabbis of the Talmud because the cow is associated with the sin of the Israelites who worshipped the Golden Calf in the desert.

The Shofar Blasts

The three types of *shofar* blast sounded on Rosh Hashana are called *tekia, shevarim,* and *terua. Tekia* is one long blast; *shevarim* is a series of three undulating short blasts; and *terua* is a series of nine staccato blasts. Depending on the congregation, the number of blasts sounded in the course of the morning service ranges from thirty-six to one hundred.

Shofar on the Sabbath

In Temple times, the *shofar* was sounded on the Sabbath. However, after the destruction of the Temple the Rabbis ruled that a person may not blow the *shofar* on the Sabbath because it might result in his carrying the *shofar* in public on the Sabbath, which would be a violation of rabbinic law. Today, in Orthodox and Conservative synagogues the *shofar* is never sounded on the Sabbath, whereas in Reform congregations, which for the most part observe Rosh Hashana for only one day, the *shofar* is sounded on the Sabbath.

ROSH HASHANA FOODS

Round Challot for Rosh Hashana

To symbolize the hope that the New Year will bring with it a well-rounded, complete life undisturbed by tragedy, round *challot* (plural of *challa*) are used on Rosh Hashana.

Bird-shaped Challot

As an expression of hope that their prayers will be carried to heaven on the wings of a bird, some Jews, particularly those with origins in the Russian Ukraine, shape their *challot* to resemble a bird or adorn them with birdlike decorations made from dough.

Fish Head

It is customary among some Jews to serve the head of a fish on Rosh Hashana in the hope that those present will attain a role of leadership in the coming year—that is, "be a head, not a tail."

New Fruit for Rosh Hashana

It is traditional on Rosh Hashana to serve seasonal fruit not previously eaten that year. Among the fruits frequently served are pomegranates, apples, figs, and grapes. The tasting of new produce offers the opportunity to pronounce the *She-hecheyanu* prayer, which expresses thanks for having reached this particular moment in health and in peace. (See page 198 for the *She-hecheyanu* prayer.)

The Pomegranate

A favorite fruit in biblical times, the pomegranate became identified with fertility and prosperity because of the many hundreds of seeds contained in it. Since it is hoped that Rosh Hashana will usher in a happy and productive year, the pomegranate is widely served as a holiday food.

The Healing Power of Apples

The apple, a popular food in Jewish tradition, is noted for its healing power as well as its sweetness. The historian Josephus tells us that whenever King Herod (73-4 B.C.E.) felt faint, he would eat an apple. In talmudic times apples were often sent as gifts to sick people. On Rosh Hashana the apple is served with honey or dipped in honey to symbolize the expectation of "a good, sweet New Year."

Figs on Rosh Hashana

In ancient Palestine figs ripened in late August and were in great abundance just before Rosh Hashana. Because of their sweet taste, it was natural for figs (like honey and apples) to become a popular food for a holiday on which everyone wishes his neighbor "a happy and sweet New Year."

Bees and Honey

The Talmud considered honey, a favorite Rosh Hashana food, to be one of "seven healing substances." Interestingly, although the bee is not listed in the Bible as kosher, the honey that it stores in its body is considered kosher.

It is traditional on Rosh Hashana to eat *challa* that has been dipped in honey.

Using Honey for Sugar

To convert a year-round cake or cookie recipe to a High Holiday specialty, try substituting honey for the sugar. Use ½ cup honey for every cup of sugar called for. As a rule, reduce the liquid in the recipe by ¼ cup for every cup of honey, and bake at a temperature 25 degrees F. lower than that called for in the recipe.

Tayglach

This favorite holiday confection consists of dough pieces that are boiled in a honey syrup until golden brown. The sticky, crunchy *tayglach* ("dough pieces" in Yiddish) are sometimes garnished with chopped nuts or candied fruit.

Lekach

Honey cake is called *lekach* in Yiddish, a word taken from the Hebrew meaning "portion." Eating honey cake as a pre-service, morning snack symbolizes the hope that one will be blessed with a "goodly portion" in the year ahead.

New Year Honey Cake

3 cups unsifted all-purpose flour
2 teaspoons sifted baking powder
1 teaspoon baking soda
1 teaspoon salt
1 teaspoon cinnamon
1 teaspoon freshly grated nutmeg
4 eggs (graded large)
1¼ cups sugar
¾ cup vegetable oil
1 cup honey
1 cup strong brewed coffee
1 teaspoon vanilla extract
2 tablespoons sliced almonds (optional)

Preheat the oven to 350 degrees F. Grease well and lightly flour one 9-cup bundt pan and one 8½ x 4½ x 2½-inch loaf pan.

Sift together the flour, baking powder, baking soda, salt, nutmeg, and cinnamon. Set aside.

In a large mixing bowl, beat together the eggs and sugar until creamy. Add the oil and beat well. Add the honey and continue beating until well combined.

Alternately add the sifted dry ingredients and the coffee to the egg mixture. Add the vanilla and mix until blended.

Pour the batter into the prepared pans and sprinkle the almonds across the top if desired. Bake at 350 degrees F. for 10 minutes, then reduce the heat to 325 degrees and bake for about 50 minutes, until a toothpick inserted in the center comes out dry.

Let cool for 10 minutes, then remove from the pans. Transfer to wire racks and continue to cool. Makes about 18 generous portions.

Rosh Hashana Carrots

Sweetened carrots are served on Rosh Hashana because the Yiddish word for carrots is *meiren* (or *meren*), meaning "to increase." *Meiren,* prepared with honey in a variety of ways, carry the hope that a sweet year, one in which good fortune will increase, lies ahead.

Carrots sliced crosswise resemble coins, and when sweetened with honey, they make a favorite Rosh Hashana dish. The coins are a symbol of prosperity.

Chassidim Serve Beets

Chassidim serve beet roots or beet leaves on Rosh Hashana because the Hebrew for beet is *selek,* and *selek* is the root of a key word used in the phrase "May we rid ourselves [*sheyistalku*] of our enemies."

The Tashlich Ceremony

On the afternoon of the first day of Rosh Hashana many Jews visit a body of living (moving) water into which they empty their pockets of crumbs to symbolize that they are "casting their sins into the depths of the sea" (Micah 7:19). If the first day of Rosh Hashana is a Sabbath, the ceremony is postponed to Sunday.

YOM KIPPUR

A Day of Atonement

The Ten Days of Penitence begin on the first day of Rosh Hashana and extend through Yom Kippur. In Jewish tradition, during this period God passes judgment over every individual, with final judgment rendered on Yom Kippur, a day devoted to prayer, fasting, and atonement for one's sins.

Preparing for Yom Kippur

A practice primarily observed by some Orthodox Jews is known as *kaparot* (also pronounced *kapores*), a traditional way of atoning for sins one has committed during the previous year. On the day before Yom Kippur, one waves a live fowl over his or her head (a male waves a rooster, a female waves a hen) three times and recites the prayer below. The chicken is then taken to a *shochet* for slaughtering.

When money is used instead of a fowl, the money is waved over the head, and the words indicated in brackets are substituted. Thus, it is believed, one's sins are transferred to the money.

זֶה חֲלִיפָתִי, זֶה תְּמוּרָתִי, זֶה כַּפָּרָתִי. זֶה הַתַּרְנְגוֹל*
יֵלֵךְ לְמִיתָה (זֶה הַכֶּסֶף יֵלֵךְ לִצְדָקָה) וַאֲנִי אֶכָּנֵס
וְאֵלֵךְ לְחַיִּים טוֹבִים אֲרוּכִים וּלְשָׁלוֹם.

Zeh chalifati, zeh temurati, zeh kaparati. Zeh ha-tarn'gol** yelech l'mita [zeh ha-kesef yelech li-tzedaka] va-ani ekanes v'elech l'cha'yim tovim aruchim u-l'shalom.

This is my substitute, this is my vicarious offering, this is my atonement. This rooster*** will go to his death [this money shall go to charity] and I will enter a good long life in peace.

The Yom Kippur Fast

Beginning at sunset on the evening of the tenth of the Hebrew month Tishri (generally falling in late September or early October) and ending approximately twenty-five hours later at nightfall, Jews the world over observe complete abstention from food and drink.

The requirement to fast on Yom Kippur stems from the Bible (Numbers 29:7), which says that on the tenth day of the seventh month [Tishri] one is to "afflict one's soul," which the Rabbis of the Talmud took to mean that one should refrain from eating food.

The Pre-fast Meal

On the afternoon before the Yom Kippur fast begins, Jews traditionally have a full meal to fortify themselves for the difficult day to follow. The meal generally consists of foods eaten at

---

*Women substitute תַּרְנְגוֹלֶת.
**Women substitute *tarn'golet.*
***Women substitute "hen."

Sabbath or holiday meals, but the salt content is kept to a minimum. Most families conclude the pre-fast meal at least one hour before leaving for the synagogue for the *Kol Nidre* service.

Favorite Pre-fast Dish

Kreplach, triangular-shaped dumplings commonly filled with chopped meat and chopped onions, are often served as part of the Yom Kippur pre-fast meal. The chopped ingredients are reminders of the flogging (chopping) to which Jews once subjected themselves as atonement for their sins.

Who Fasts on Yom Kippur?

All adult Jews are required to fast. Boys younger than thirteen and girls younger than twelve are not obligated to fast on Yom Kippur, but they may do so. Persons too ill to fast are exempted if so ordered by a doctor.

Fasting for New Mothers

According to Jewish law, a new mother is *forbidden* to fast for the first three days after having given birth. For the next four days she is not *required* to fast, but may do so if she wishes.

Candlelighting for Yom Kippur

Before leaving home for the *Kol Nidre* service, recite the following:

בָּרוּךְ אַתָּה יְיָ, אֱלֹהֵינוּ מֶלֶךְ הָעוֹלָם, אֲשֶׁר קִדְּשָׁנוּ בְּמִצְוֹתָיו וְצִוָּנוּ לְהַדְלִיק נֵר שֶׁל (שַׁבָּת וְשֶׁל) יוֹם הַכִּפּוּרִים.

Baruch ata Adonai, Elohenu melech ha-olam, asher kideshanu be-mitzvotav, ve-tzivanu le-hadlik ner shel (Shabbat v'shel) Yom Ka-kippurim.

Praised be Thou, O Lord our God, King of the universe, Who has sanctified us with His commandments and commanded us to kindle the (Sabbath lights and the) lights of Yom Kippur.

[Continue with *She-hechayanu*. See page 257.]

Liturgy of Yom Kippur

The liturgy of Yom Kippur consists of five separate services: *Kol Nidre* (the evening service); *Shacharit (the early morning service); Musaf* (the second, or additional service, which ends at midday); *Mincha* (the afternoon service); and *Ne'ila* (the final service). See Chapter Seven, In the Synagogue, for a discussion of some of the specific prayers recited on Yom Kippur.

The Kol Nidre Service

The Yom Kippur evening service is called *Kol Nidre* because the first prayer recited is *Kol Nidre,* which literally means "all vows." This plea for nullification of vows made innocently or under duress is chanted three times by the cantor.

Kol Nidre Recited Early

The *Kol Nidre* service begins before sunset, before the holiday begins officially. This arrangement was made because the annulment of vows, which is the essence of the *Kol Nidre* prayer is a legal procedure, and such proceedings may not be conducted on a Sabbath or holiday.

Talit on Kol Nidre

The only occasion during the year that a *talit* is worn after dark by a congregant is Yom Kippur eve at the *Kol Nidre* service. Though prayershawls are not customarily permitted to be worn at night, in this case they are permitted because the prayershawl is actually donned before dark.

SYNAGOGUE RITES AND RITUALS

Sneakers on Yom Kippur

Because the Bible calls Yom Kippur "the day of affliction," many traditional Jews wear sneakers or soft slippers throughout the day, rather than leather shoes which are considered a luxury.

Breastbeating

As a symbol of penitence, it is customary to beat the left breast (over the heart) while pronouncing the *Al Chet* and the *Ashamnu* prayers, the two Confessions of sins recited at the various services on Yom Kippur. (See pages 165 and 167 for more about these prayers.)

Yizkor on Yom Kippur

The *Yizkor* service, during which close relatives are memorialized, is usually conducted after the Torah reading, before the *Musaf* service begins. Sephardim do not generally conduct a *Yizkor* service. In Reform congregations, the memorial service is recited in the afternoon, before the closing *(Ne'ila)* service.

Aliyot on Yom Kippur

Traditionally, at the morning service on Yom Kippur six *aliyot* are awarded, unless the holiday falls on a Sabbath, in which case seven Torah honors are distributed. In the afternoon, at the *Mincha* service, three *aliyot* are awarded. The third honoree is awarded with *Maftir Yona*, which is so designated because after the Torah reading the honoree chants the Book of Jonah as the *haftara*.

Ne'ila

Ne'ila, meaning "closing of the [Temple] gates," is the last of the five Yom Kippur services. It represents the closing of the gates of heaven, toward which the prayers of the day have been directed.

Since the ark is kept open throughout *Ne'ila*, many people follow the tradition of standing for the duration of the one and one-half to two-hour service.

The Last Shofar Blast

The last *shofar* blast of the Rosh Hashana–Yom Kippur period, sounded after the *Ne'ila* service, marks the end of Yom Kippur and the Days of Awe. (Many congregations today sound the *shofar* after the *Maariv* service has been completed.) The blast consists of one long, extended sound *(tekia gedola)*, after which the congregation cries out in unison: "Next year in Jerusalem!"

BREAKING THE FAST

Break-the-fast Meal

For the break-the-fast meal after Yom Kippur many families serve herring or another salty fish. The purpose is to induce thirst and encourage everyone to drink a lot of water, thus restoring fluids lost during the fast.

Chopped Herring

Herring, chopped or whole, is a traditional break-the-fast dish. By using a jar of prepared herring one can avoid the soaking, skinning, and boning. The dish can be prepared quickly in the following manner.

1 jar (12 ounces) herring in wine sauce
1 matzo
1 small onion, finely diced
1 medium-sized apple, peeled, cored, and cubed
2 hard-cooked eggs
1 tablespoon sugar (more or less, to taste)

Into a small bowl, drain the wine sauce from the jar of herring. Crush the matzo into it to absorb the liquid. Chop fine the herring, the onions from the jar, the diced fresh onion, and the apple. Add the soaked matzo and hard-cooked eggs. Continue to chop until thoroughly blended. Sweeten with the sugar. Yields a little more than 1 pound.

12

THE FALL HOLIDAYS II

SUKKOT, SHEMINI ATZERET, SIMCHAT TORAH

Introduction

During the Sukkot holiday, the Bible (Leviticus 23:42-43) says, "You shall live in booths [*sukkot*] seven days in order that future generations may know that I made the Israelite people live in booths when I brought them out of the land of Egypt." Today, this festival commemorating the forty-year trek of the Israelites through the desert to the Promised Land is celebrated as a seven-day holiday in Israel and the Diaspora.

Shemini Atzeret and Simchat Torah are often erroneously assumed to be part of the Sukkot holiday. Actually, they are individual holidays. In Israel today, Shemini Atzeret is observed as a one-day holiday that follows Sukkot; in the Diaspora Shemini Atzeret is celebrated for two days. In Israel, Simchat Torah is observed as part of Shemini Atzeret. In the Diaspora,

Simchat Torah is the second day of the two-day Shemini Atzeret celebration.

This chapter describes the important rituals, laws, and practices connected with Sukkot, Shemini Atzeret, and Simchat Torah. The most prominent of these are the building of the *sukka* and the arrangement of the *lulav* bouquet.

SUKKOT: HISTORICAL BACKGROUND

A Pilgrim Festival

Like Pesach (Passover) and Shavuot (Pentecost), Sukkot (Tabernacles) is one of the three Pilgrim Festivals. On these holidays, Jews from all over Palestine and nearby countries would come to Jerusalem by foot to visit the Temple and offer sacrifices. These Jews were known as *olay regel,* "those who came by foot." Hence, the three festivals came to be known as the *Shalosh Regalim,* "the three foot [pilgrim] festivals" (Exodus 23:14).

Sukkot in the Bible

Sukkot, popularly known as the Festival of Booths (Chag Ha-sukkot), is described in the Bible as a seven-day holiday that begins on the fifteenth day of Tishri, five days after Yom Kippur. It usually falls in late September or early October.

Sukkot in Israel

In Israel, as dictated by the Bible, Sukkot is observed for seven days. The first day only is a full holiday, on which one must abstain from work. The next five days are Intermediate Days (Chol Hamoed), which are considered half-holidays. The seventh and last day of Sukkot is Hoshana Rabba, also a half-holiday.

Sukkot in the Diaspora

In the Diaspora, as in Israel, Sukkot is a seven-day holiday. However, in the Diaspora the first two days of Sukkot are observed as full holidays and the remaining five days as half-holidays.

Reform congregations follow the Israeli practice.

The Yom Kippur/Sukkot Link

An ancient Jewish belief considers the first day of Sukkot to be the day on which a person begins accumulating sins for the next year. To offset this, and to start the new year with a positive religious act (mitzva), one begins to construct a sukka immediately after Yom Kippur is over.

Sukkot and Agriculture

Like Passover, Sukkot was originally purely an agricultural festival. In the Bible (Exodus 23:16) it is called "the Festival of Ingathering, when you gather in the yield of your field." The pilgrims who visited Jerusalem to celebrate the holiday brought with them some of their first fall crops and gave them to the Priests (Kohanim). A portion was offered as a sacrifice on the altar, and the balance was kept for use by the priestly families.

THE SUKKA STRUCTURE

The Sukka

The sukka is a temporary dwelling, a booth, in which one eats (and in some cases sleeps) throughout the seven-day holiday. It is a reminder of the booths in which the Israelites lived during their forty-year trek through the desert after the Exodus from Egypt.

Tabernacles

"Tabernacles," the English name for Sukkot, is derived from the Latin word tabernaculum, meaning "hut, temporary dwelling."

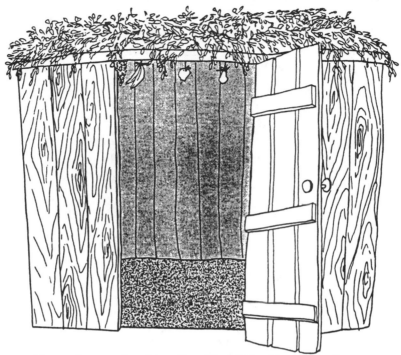

Many Jews take literally the biblical commandment (Leviticus 23:42), "You shall live in booths." They interpret the word "live" to mean that one must eat and sleep in the *sukka* for the duration of the Sukkot holiday. To accentuate the fact that the Rabbis considered "living" in a *sukka* more important than actually constructing one, a blessing is recited when one enters the structure, not when one builds it.

Sukka Construction

To simulate the loosely constructed, temporary dwellings of the Israelites in the desert, today's *sukkot* are made of loosely assembled walls made from wood panels or canvas, which are supported by wood or metal posts. The interior is decorated with fruits, vegetables, and artistic hangings of various kinds. Easy-to-assemble prefabricated *sukkot* are available from religious goods dealers.

Sukka Covering

The roof of the *sukka* usually consists of branches, shrubs, cornstalks, straw, or slats of wood. To be a valid *sukka,* the covering must be sufficiently dense that there will be more shade than sunlight inside the structure during the day, and yet not so dense that the stars will not be visible at night. The Hebrew name for the *sukka* covering is *sechach,* which literally means "covering."

Mezuza on a Sukka

A *sukka* is only a temporary dwelling and therefore a *mezuza* need not be affixed to its entrance.

Sukka Blessing

After reciting the *Kiddush* or the *Ha-motzi* prayer (page 146) in the *sukka,* the following is said:

בָּרוּךְ אַתָּה יְיָ, אֱלֹהֵינוּ מֶלֶךְ הָעוֹלָם, אֲשֶׁר קִדְּשָׁנוּ בְּמִצְוֹתָיו, וְצִוָּנוּ לֵשֵׁב בַּסֻּכָּה.

Baruch ata Adonai, Elohenu melech ha-olam, asher kideshanu be-mitzvotav, ve-tzivanu leshev ba-sukka.

Praised be Thou, O Lord our God, King of the universe, who has sanctified us with His commandments and commanded us to dwell in a tabernacle.

Candlelighting and Kiddush for Sukkot

The candlelighting blessings for Sukkot can be found on pages 256 and 257. See page 245 for the standard *Kiddush* for festivals. Recite the line appropriate for the Sukkot festival.

SUKKOT SYMBOLS

The Four Species

Aside from the *sukka* itself, four plant species are primary symbols of the holiday. These are the citron *(etrog),* palm branch *(lulav),* myrtle *(hadas),* and willow *(arava).* That these four species be taken together in hand and blessed on the holiday of Sukkot is prescribed in the Bible (Leviticus 23:40). The citron is always held in the left hand, whereas the other three symbols are held in the right hand (see below).

The Etrog

The Bible calls for "taking [on Sukkot] the fruit of a goodly tree." The type of fruit or the kind of tree is not specified, but the Rabbis interpreted this to mean the *etrog* (citron) tree and its fruit.

Etrog Most Important

The *etrog* is considered the most important of the four species, and it is therefore held in the left hand and is pressed close to the body, near the heart. The other three species are tied together and held in the right hand.

How an Etrog Grows

Not having been involved in agriculture, most authorities, including the authors of the *Code of Jewish Law,* have been unaware that the *etrog* grows with the fragile protuberance *(pittom)* facing downward. The thick stem *(ikutz)* is attached to the tree.

Positioning the Etrog

Before reciting the blessing over the *etrog* and *lulav* (see page 280), the citron, held in the left hand, is positioned so that the *pittom* (protuberance) faces upward. This is the opposite of the position in which the citron actually grows on the tree. After the blessing has been recited, the *etrog* is turned around and is held and carried with the *pittom* facing downward, the position in which the fruit grows naturally.

Broken Pittom

If the protuberance of the *etrog* is broken, the *etrog* is not considered kosher, and a blessing may not be recited over it.

The Pittom-less Etrog

Some *etrogim* (plural of *etrog*) grow without protuberances.

These *pittom*-less *etrogim* come from Algeria, Greece, Israel, and other Mediterranean countries. They are considered kosher.

Biting the Pittom

Eve convinced Adam to eat from the Tree of Knowledge, which God had planted in the Garden of Eden. In violation of God's warning (Genesis 2:3), they both ate the forbidden fruit.

Some Rabbis theorized that the forbidden fruit was a fig; others said it was an apple. But Rabbi Abba of Acco said: "It was the *etrog* [citron] tree [from which Adam and Eve ate]" (Genesis Rabba 15:7).

In Frankfort, Germany, in the twelfth and thirteenth centuries, it was common practice for a pregnant woman to bite off the *pittom* of the *etrog* after its last use on Hoshana Rabba, but she did not eat the fruit itself. Thus, she demonstrated that unlike Eve she obeyed God's commandment not to eat the forbidden fruit. As a reward, it was thought, she would enjoy painless and successful childbirth. Others thought that the reward would be a male child.

Storing the Etrog

If you purchase an *etrog* well in advance of the Sukkot holiday, store it in the produce bin of the refrigerator. Place a paper towel under the fruit to absorb excess moisture.

Etrog Jam

Since citrons grow on trees, and since in Jewish tradition Tu Bi-shevat, the fifteenth day of the Hebrew month Shevat, is celebrated as the festival of trees, a custom developed to make jam from the *etrogim* used on Sukkot and to save it for consumption on Tu Bi-shevat.

The Lulav

The Bible calls for "taking [on Sukkot] branches of date [palms]," which is the *lulav*.

The Myrtles

The Bible calls for "taking [on Sukkot] boughs of thick trees," which is interpreted by the Rabbis to refer to the myrtle, or *hadasim* (singular, *hadas*) as they are called in Hebrew. Three myrtles are used in the *lulav* bouquet.

The Willows

The Bible calls for "taking [on Sukkot] willows of the brook," known in Hebrew as *aravot* (singular, *arava*). Two willows are used in the *lulav* bouquet.

How to Assemble a Lulav Bouquet

When you purchase a *lulav* from your religious goods dealer, a holder made from palm leaves and having two pockets will be provided. Slide the holder over the *lulav,* and secure it using palm leaf strands pulled from the *lulav*. Insert three myrtles in the right side pocket and two willows in the left pocket. The solid, uncleffed spine of the *lulav* should face you as you do this. Additional strands can be tied around the *lulav* to prevent the leaves from spreading too far apart.

The *Iulav* bouquet is held in the right hand and the *etrog* in the left hand when the blessing is recited. Paradoxically, although we usually speak of *bentching etrog* (blessing *etrog*), the blessing actually mentions only the *lulav* (see page 280) because the *lulav* is the largest of the four species.

BLESSING AND PARADING THE FOUR SPECIES

Blessing the Etrog and Lulav

Each morning of the Sukkot holiday, at home or in the synagogue, the palm branch together with two willows and three myrtle branches are taken up in the right hand and the citron (etrog) is held in the left hand. The following blessing is then recited:

בָּרוּךְ אַתָּה יְיָ, אֱלֹהֵינוּ מֶלֶךְ הָעוֹלָם, אֲשֶׁר קִדְּשָׁנוּ בְּמִצְוֹתָיו, וְצִוָּנוּ עַל־נְטִילַת לוּלָב.

Baruch ata Adonai, Elohenu melech ha-olam, asher kideshanu be-mitzvotav, ve-tzivanu al netilat lulav.

Praised be Thou, O Lord our God, King of the universe, who has sanctified us by His commandments and commanded us to take up [wave] the *lulav*.

[On the first day of the holiday add:]

בָּרוּךְ אַתָּה יְיָ, אֱלֹהֵינוּ מֶלֶךְ הָעוֹלָם, שֶׁהֶחֱיָנוּ, וְקִיְּמָנוּ, וְהִגִּיעָנוּ לַזְּמַן הַזֶּה.

Baruch ata Adonai, Elohenu melech ha-olam, she-hecheyanu, ve-kiyemanu, ve-higianu la-zeman ha-zeh.

Praised be Thou, O Lord our God, King of the universe, for having kept us alive, and sustained us, and enabled us to reach and enjoy this day.

Waving the Lulav

After the *etrog/lulav* blessing is recited, the *lulav* is waved and/or shaken. It is also waved during the morning service when selections of the *Hallel* prayers are recited.

The act of waving, common in Temple times when sacrifices were brought on the altar, was generally considered helpful in bringing the offerer closer to God. Talmudic authorities of a more mystical bent believed that the act of waving wards off evil spirits.

Lulav-waving Procedure

While holding the *etrog* in the left hand (with the *pittom* facing downward) and the *lulav* bouquet next to it in the right hand, the *lulav* is pointed in six different directions and waved each time. (Some people wave only once, and some three times.)

Moving in a clockwise fashion, first point the palm branch straight ahead, then to the right, then (over the shoulder) to the back, then to the left. Next bring the *etrog* and *lulav* to the front, rest both briefly against the chest, then, holding them upright, raise them up toward the heavens and then lower them toward the ground. This ritual symbolizes that God's presence is everywhere.

Lulav Tradition

Some Jews follow the practice of saving their *lulavim* until the next Passover, at which time they use them to sweep up the breadcrumbs during the search for leaven ceremony and to start the fire when burning the leaven the following morning. (See pages 221 through 222 for a description of the *Bedikat Chametz* and *Biur Chametz* ceremonies.)

Procession With the Four Species

Throughout the Sukkot holiday, after the morning *(Shacharit)* service in Sephardic congregations and after the additional *(Musaf)* service in Ashkenazic congregations, congregants parade around the synagogue holding aloft their *etrog* and *lulav* bouquets as the cantor chants a prayer with the Hebrew refrain *hosha na,* meaning "O [God], please save us [in our exile and from those who would despoil and desecrate the site of the holy Temple]."

HOSHANA RABBA

Last Day of Sukkot

The last day of the seven-day Sukkot holiday is called Hoshana Rabba, meaning "Great Hosanna." A half-holiday equal in importance to the Intermediate Days of Sukkot, Hoshana Rabba marks the end of the long holiday period that begins with Rosh Hashana.

Synagogue Procession

On Hoshana Rabba, the last day on which the *lulav* and *etrog* are used, congregants parade their *etrogim* and *lulavim* around the synagogue seven times. The Talmud describes this Hoshana Rabba ritual, which originated in Temple times:

> Every day [of the first six days of the festival] they went around the altar once, saying, "We beseech Thee, O Lord, please save us; we beseech Thee, O Lord, to make us prosper [Psalms 118:25]." But on that [seventh] day they went around the altar seven times.

Beating Willows

At the morning service on Hoshana Rabba, after congregants holding the *etrog* and *lulav* have paraded around the pulpit (or entire synagogue) seven times (one for each day of the Sukkot holiday), each congregant takes a bunch of (usually from five to seven) willows and beats it against the back of a pew or on the floor, until some or all of the leaves have fallen off. The custom is linked to the old Yom Kippur practice of Jews submitting themselves to flogging as a sign of penitence, as Muslims do even today. In Jewish tradition Hoshana Rabba represents the day on which man has one final opportunity to plead for the annulment of any evil decree proclaimed against him on Yom Kippur.

Hoshana Rabba in Sephardic Practice

Many Sephardim, including Syrians, Moroccans, and those from Greece and the Balkans, observe Hoshana Rabba as a "Minor Yom Kippur." The men stay awake all night studying various Books of the Bible, focusing in particular on the Book of Psalms. In some congregations, the *shofar* is sounded at various intervals during the night; in others, the *Shacharit* service concludes with a series of *shofar* blasts.

Kreplach for Hoshana Rabba

Because willows are beaten on Hoshana Rabba, it has become customary to serve *kreplach* on this holiday. *Kreplach,* which are dumplings filled with chopped (beaten) meat, onions, and other ingredients, are also part of the food fare served at the pre-fast Yom Kippur meal.

SHEMINI ATZERET

The Holiday After Sukkot

The observance of Shemini Atzeret is mandated in the Bible (Leviticus 23:26): "On the eighth day [after the seven days of Sukkot] you shall hold a holy convocation; you shall do no work on it." Shemini Atzeret is a separate holiday. It is not the eighth day of Sukkot.

Yizkor on Shemini Atzeret

Shemini Atzeret is one of the four holidays on which *Yizkor,* the memorial prayer for the dead, is said aloud. *Yizkor* is recited on this holiday, rather than on Sukkot, because the Rabbis of the Talmud considered Shemini Atzeret to be the last day of Sukkot, although we know it to be a totally independent holiday.

Most Sephardic and Reform congregations do not conduct a *Yizkor* service on Shemini Atzeret.

Candlelighting and Kiddush for Shemini Atzeret

The candlelighting blessings for Shemini Atzeret can be found on pages 256 and 257. See page 245 for the standard *Kiddush* for festivals. Recite the line appropriate for Shemini Atzeret.

SIMCHAT TORAH

Simchat Torah

Simchat Torah means "Rejoicing in [or with] the Law [the Torah]." Like Shemini Atzeret, it is not connected with Sukkot. It is an independent holiday created in postbiblical times to celebrate the completion of the annual reading of the entire Torah.

Parade of the Torot

Simchat Torah is celebrated with much merriment in synagogues. All persons, including children, are called to the Torah for an *aliya* (Torah honor). The last part of the Book of Deuteronomy, followed immediately by the first part of the Book of Genesis, is read from two different Torot to express the never-ending cycle of Torah reading. Before the Torah is read, all the Torah scrolls are taken from the ark and are carried in joyful procession (called *Hakafot* in Hebrew) seven times around the synagogue. Worshippers take turns carrying the Torah scrolls. Children carrying flags generally follow the adults in procession.

Aliyot for Everyone

In the synagogue on Simchat Torah morning, everyone present, including children, is called upon to recite the Torah blessings, either individually or in groups. In larger congregations, small groups hold separate Torah readings in separate rooms so as to allow everyone to receive an individual *aliya*.

Simchat Torah in Israel

In Israel, Simchat Torah is not celebrated as a separate holiday. It is combined with the observance of Shemini Atzeret, as is the custom among Reform Jews.

Candlelighting and Kiddush for Simchat Torah

The candlelighting blessings for Simchat Torah can be found on pages 256 and 257. See page 245 for the standard *Kiddush* for festivals. Recite the line appropriate for Simchat Torah.

Revelry on Simchat Torah

As on Purim, on Simchat Torah it is acceptable to lose oneself in revelry in the synagogue. Congregants often consume liberal amounts of wine or liquor and then let themselves go, singing and dancing and merrymaking. There is a Yiddish folksaying that expresses the traditional attitude toward such behavior:

Kumt Simchat Torah, zeinen alle shikurim nichter.

"On Simchat Torah all drunkards are considered sober."

Chatan Torah and Chatan Bereshit

Two distinctive Torah honors are awarded on Simchat Torah. The recipient of the first honor is called the *Chatan Torah,* the "Bridegroom of the Torah," and for him the final portion of the Book of Deuteronomy is read. The person awarded the second honor is called the *Chatan Bereshit,* the "Bridegroom of Genesis," and for him the first portion of the Book of Genesis is read from a different Torah.

13
CHANUKA, PURIM, AND OTHER MINOR HOLIDAYS

Introduction

Rosh Hashana, Yom Kippur, Sukkot, Shemini Atzeret, Simchat Torah, Passover, and Shavuot are considered *major* holidays in Jewish tradition. What makes them so is that they are all mandated in the Torah, the first five books of the Bible. All of the major holidays are observed as rest days, with the same prohibitions against work as apply to the Sabbath applying to them.

In addition to the major holidays, the Jewish calendar includes a number of *minor* ones. Aside from the more popular Chanuka and Purim, the minor holidays include Tisha B'Av, a day of mourning for the destruction of the two Temples; Tu Bi-shevat, celebrated as the New Year for trees; and the more recently introduced Yom Ha-atzma'ut (Israel Independence Day) and Yom Ha-sho'ah (Holocaust Day).

Other than Purim, the story of which is recounted in the Book of Esther, none of the minor holidays is biblically mandated. Each is celebrated by the observance of distinctive rituals and ceremonies and by the inclusion in the prayer service of special readings.

CHANUKA HISTORY

The Story of Chanuka

Alexander the Great, the Greek king who ruled over Syria, Egypt, and Palestine in the fourth century B.C.E., was a friend of the Jews. But when Alexander died in 320 B.C.E., his kingdom was divided among several generals, and one of them, Seleucus, took control of Syria and Palestine. He and subsequent rulers imposed the Greek (Hellenistic) way of life, including its many heathen practices, upon the local inhabitants.

In 165 B.C.E., led by the Hasmonean family of Mattathias the Priest and his eldest son, Judah (called "the Maccabee"), the Jews succeeded in evicting the Syrian-Greeks from Palestine. Religious freedom was restored, and the Temple in Jerusalem, which the Syrian-Greek king Antiochus IV had converted into a pagan shrine, was cleansed, restored, and rededicated. The word *chanuka* means "dedication."

Source of the Chanuka Story

The story of the victory of the Jews over the Syrian-Greeks is not found in the Bible. It is recounted in the Book of Maccabees, one of the fourteen books of the Apocrypha.

The Miracle of the Oil

According to the Talmud, after the Temple had been cleansed and the Priests were ready to rekindle the seven-branched Temple *menora* (candelabrum), they could find only one jug of undesecrated oil, enough to keep the *menora* burning for one day. Miraculously, the oil kept burning for eight days.

This account is not found in the Book of Maccabees, but it is the generally accepted reason for the observance of Chanuka for eight days.

Chanuka Date

Since talmudic times, the victory of the Hasmoneans over the Syrian-Greeks has been observed as an eight-day holiday. On the evening of the twenty-fifth day of Kislev and on the seven days thereafter—a total of eight days—Chanuka candles are lighted and special blessings and hymns are recited. The holiday usually falls during the month of December.

The Word "Maccabee"

The heroes of Chanuka are called Maccabees. According to one theory *maccabee* is a Hebrew acronym formed from the first letter of each of the four words in the phrase *Mi kamocha ba-elim Adonai,* "Who among the mighty is like thee, O God?" This was the battle cry of the Hasmoneans.

A second theory suggests that *maccabee,* the Hebrew word "hammer," was a loving way of referring to Judah, the strong, fearless leader of the Hasmoneans.

CHANUKA LIGHTS

Chanuka Menora

Whereas the candelabrum used in the Temple was seven-branched, the *menora* designated to celebrate the Chanuka holiday has nine branches, each of which holds a cup into which oil or a candle is placed. Eight of the branches represent the eight days of the holiday; the ninth is for the *shamash.*

Function of the Shamash

Just as one of the lights of the seven-branched *menora* in the Jerusalem Temple was used to kindle the other six, so the ninth light of the Chanuka *menora* is used to kindle the other eight. The ninth light is the *shamash,* the "servant." Since its function is only to serve the others, it is not reckoned as one of the official *menora* lights.

Variety of Menorot

Menorot (plural of *menora*) are made of all types of material, including brass, copper, wood, ceramic, and sterling silver. Some are made to accommodate candles, some oil, and some both. *Menorot* with oil cups have removable pierced lids through which wicks are inserted. Olive oil is generally used.

Oil *menorot* are kindled in the same manner as candle *menorot,* and either a candle or a portable oil cup with a wick in it serves as the *shamash.*

Electric Menorot

Electric *menorot* are popularly used as decorative pieces. Traditionally, a candle or oil *menora* is used for the recitation of the candlelighting blessings, but where it is unsafe to do so, such as in hospitals and homes for the elderly, blessings may be recited over an electric *menora.*

Who Lights the Candles?

The head of the household—man or woman—may light the Chanuka candles and recite the blessings. In recent times, it has become common for parents to purchase small *menorot* (plural of *menora*) for use by children so that they too can light the Chanuka candles.

Procedure for
LIGHTING THE CHANUKA MENORA

For eight nights, beginning with the twenty-fifth day of the Hebrew month Kislev, candles are lighted in a Chanuka *menora* (candelabrum) as soon after nightfall as possible. (Some people use oil instead of candles.) On Friday nights, the regular Sabbath candles are lighted after the Chanuka lighting ceremony has been completed.

The eight cups that hold the Chanuka candles are arranged in a row, one for each night of the holiday. Every *menora* has one additional cup, a ninth cup, which is located in the center or to one side and is usually slightly elevated. This cup is for the *shamash.* The *shamash* is the first candle to be lighted each night (without a blessing), and from its flame all the other candles are lighted.

There are many styles of Chanuka *menorot*. In most, as above, the *shamash* candle is in the center, although in some styles the *shamash* holder is on the left side, recessed slightly. Over the centuries, *chanukiot* (singular, *chanukia*; Hebrew for Chanuka candelabrum) have been made in a wide range of materials, including brass, tin, silver, wood, and clay. Some are very simple, some quite ornate. Some are made for burning oil, some for candles, and some for both.

This is the procedure to follow when lighting the candles:

- On the first night of Chanuka place one candle in the *shamash* cup and one candle in the cup to your extreme right as you face the *menora*.

   On the second night of Chanuka insert a candle in the *shamash* cup. Then, place one candle in the first cup to the extreme right (as you did the night before) and take one more candle from the box of forty-four and insert it in the cup to the left of the first candle.

   On each subsequent night add one candle to the cup to the left of those used the previous night.

- On the first night of Chanuka, light the *shamash* candle with a match and, holding the candle aloft, recite the three blessings below. Then light the lone candle with the flame of the *shamash*.

   On the second and subsequent nights of the holiday, recite the first two blessings below. (The third blessing—the She-hecheyanu—is recited on the first night only.) Then, with the flame of the shamash candle, light the other candles from left to right (the newest addition is always lighted first).

* After the menora has been kindled, in traditional homes it is placed on a windowsill facing the street to serve as a reminder of all of the miraculous victories that saved the Jewish nation in the days of the Maccabees. In some households the candelabrum is placed on the windowsill and lighted there.

* The candlelighting ceremony is followed by the chanting or recitation of Ha-nerot Halalu and Ma'oz Tzur (see below). Then, refreshments are served, gifts distributed, and games played.

CHANUKA MENORA BLESSINGS

First blessing:

בָּרוּךְ אַתָּה יְיָ, אֱלֹהֵינוּ מֶלֶךְ הָעוֹלָם, אֲשֶׁר קִדְּשָׁנוּ בְּמִצְוֹתָיו, וְצִוָּנוּ לְהַדְלִיק נֵר שֶׁל חֲנֻכָּה.

Baruch ata Adonai, Elohenu melech ha-olam, asher kideshanu be-mitzvotav, ve-tzivanu le-hadlik ner shel Chanuka.

Praised be Thou, O Lord our God, King of the universe, who has sanctified us through His commandments and commanded us to kindle the Chanuka lights.

Second blessing:

בָּרוּךְ אַתָּה יְיָ, אֱלֹהֵינוּ מֶלֶךְ הָעוֹלָם, שֶׁעָשָׂה נִסִּים לַאֲבוֹתֵינוּ בַּיָּמִים הָהֵם בַּזְּמַן הַזֶּה.

Baruch ata Adonai, Elohenu melech ha-olam, she-asa nisim la-avotenu, ba-yamim ha-hem ba-zeman ha-zeh.

Praised be Thou, O Lord our God, King of the universe, who wrought miracles for our ancestors, in those days, at this time [of year].

Third blessing (recited on the first night only):

בָּרוּךְ אַתָּה יְיָ, אֱלֹהֵינוּ מֶלֶךְ הָעוֹלָם, שֶׁהֶחֱיָנוּ,
וְקִיְּמָנוּ, וְהִגִּיעָנוּ לַזְּמַן הַזֶּה.

Baruch ata Adonai, Elohenu melech ha-olam, she-hecheyanu, ve-kiyemanu, ve-higiyanu la-zeman ha-zeh.

Praised be Thou, O Lord our God, King of the universe, who has kept us alive, and sustained us, and enabled us to reach and enjoy this day.

Ha-nerot Halalu

After the blessings have been recited, all join in chanting or reciting *Ha-nerot Halalu* ("These Lights"):

הַנֵּרוֹת הַלָּלוּ אֲנַחְנוּ מַדְלִיקִין, עַל הַנִּסִּים, וְעַל
הַנִּפְלָאוֹת, וְעַל הַתְּשׁוּעוֹת, וְעַל הַמִּלְחָמוֹת,
שֶׁעָשִׂיתָ לַאֲבוֹתֵינוּ בַּיָּמִים הָהֵם בַּזְּמַן הַזֶּה, עַל יְדֵי
כֹּהֲנֶיךָ הַקְּדוֹשִׁים. וְכָל שְׁמֹנַת יְמֵי חֲנֻכָּה הַנֵּרוֹת
הַלָּלוּ קֹדֶשׁ הֵם, וְאֵין לָנוּ רְשׁוּת לְהִשְׁתַּמֵּשׁ בָּהֶם,
אֶלָּא לִרְאוֹתָם בִּלְבָד.

Ha-nerot halalu anachnu madlikin, al ha-nisim, ve-al ha-niflaot, ve-al ha-teshuot, ve-al ha-milchamot, she-asita la-avotenu ba-yamim ha-hem ba-zeman ha-zeh al yeday Kohanecha ha-kedoshim. Ve-chol shemonat yemay Chanuka ha-nerot halalu kodesh hem, ve-en lanu reshut l'hishtamesh ba-hem, ela lirotam bi-levad.

We light these candles to commemorate the miraculous happenings and unbelievable victories experienced by our ancestors in ancient times during this very season of the year. We kindle these holy lights for the eight days of Chanuka, and we use them to remind us, as we gaze on their flickering flames, that we must give thanks to God for having delivered a mighty army into the hands of a small band and for having delivered an arrogant and wicked tyrant to those who believe in the pursuit of the moral law.

Ma'oz Tzur

The famous hymn *Ma'oz Tzur* ("Rock of Ages") is sung after the candles are lighted. Its lyrics were composed in the Middle Ages by a poet whose first name was Mordechai, but the melody, which is of later vintage, was adopted from a German folksong popular in the fifteenth century. The hymn recalls the various exiles endured by the Jewish people and how, through the grace of God, they were saved. See page 320 for music and lyrics.

FAVORITE FOODS

Potato Latkes and Doughnuts

Potato *latkes* (pancakes) are a favorite Chanuka food among Jews throughout the world, but in Israel doughnuts are equally popular. What the two have in common is oil. Both, being deep-fried, are symbolic of the cruse of oil which miraculously burned for eight days.

Potato Latkes

3 cups grated or coarsely shredded potatoes
1 medium-sized onion, grated or finely minced
2 eggs
1 generous tablespoon flour
1½ teaspoons salt
Freshly ground pepper to taste
Oil for frying

In a medium-sized bowl, combine all the ingredients. Mix well. In a large heavy skillet, heat about one-quarter inch of oil. Drop potato mixture into the hot oil, one heaping tablespoonful at a time. Flatten the pancakes slightly, but do not allow them to touch. Fry slowly, turning once to brown both sides. Drain on paper towels. Serve piping hot with sour cream or applesauce. Serves 4 or 5.

Cheese Delicacies

Cheese is generally associated with Shavuot, but it is also linked to Chanuka. Its origin has been traced to the Book of Judith in the Apocrypha. According to legend, Judith, a member of the Hasmonean family, fed cheese to the general of Nebuchadnezzar's army which was poised to destroy Israel. The cheese made the general thirsty, and to quench his thirst he drank large amounts of wine. The general became drunk and Judith beheaded him, thus ensuring a Jewish victory.

Goose on Chanuka

In earlier centuries it was common practice to use the fat of fowl to prepare holiday delicacies. Because goose is so fatty a bird, it became traditional to serve goose on Chanuka and to render its fat, some of which was set aside for use on Passover.

GIFTS AND GAMES

Chanuka Gifts

Among Jews, gift-giving was primarily associated with Purim. In Eastern Europe a tradition developed for families to assemble on the fifth night of Chanuka, at which time Chanuka *gelt* ("money") was distributed to the children. In more recent times, because of the proximity of Chanuka to Christmas, when Christian children are showered with gifts, Jewish parents began giving other gifts in addition to Chanuka *gelt*. In some families a gift is given each night after the *menora*-lighting ceremony.

The Draydel

A *draydel* (in Hebrew, *sevivon*) is a four-sided top with one Hebrew letter on each side. Prior to the establishment of the State of Israel (1948) the letters found on all *draydels* were *nun, gimmel, hay,* and *shin.* These stood for the Hebrew words *nes gadol haya sham,* meaning "a great miracle happened there

Draydels are made of all types of materials, including lead, wood, plastic, and porcelain. Some are fashioned with four wings, and some are solid, as above.

[in ancient Palestine]." In Israel today, *draydels* contain the letters *nun, gimmel, hay, pay,* standing for *nes gadol haya po,* meaning "a great miracle happened here [in modern Israel]."

Playing Draydel

Draydel, a Yiddish word derived from the German *drehen,* means "to turn." The game is played by literally turning (spinning) the *draydel* top and waiting to see which letter will show face up when the *draydel* stops spinning and falls.

There are a variety of ways to play the game, but generally each participant places a coin or piece of candy (or some other item) in the "pot" to start the game. Each player spins in turn. If the *draydel* comes up with a *nun,* everyone adds to the pot; if it comes up with a *shin* or a *pay,* only the spinner adds to the pot; if it comes up with a *hay,* the spinner takes half; if it comes up with a *gimmel,* the spinner is the winner and takes all.

Card-playing

Card-playing on Chanuka is a tradition that began in the Middle Ages among older *yeshiva* students. At Chanuka time a respite from study was permitted, and students expressed the joy of the holiday by involving themselves in an open game of chance. The tradition continues to this day.

PURIM: FEAST OF LOTS

A Minor Holiday

As with Chanuka, Purim is not mentioned in the Five Books of Moses and, therefore, it is considered a minor holiday. Work prohibitions associated with major holidays do not apply to minor ones.

The Story of Purim

The story of Purim, recorded in the Book of Esther, centers about the plot of Haman, prime minister of King Ahasueros of Persia, to massacre the Jews of the country. Haman's plans were frustrated by "Mordecai the Jew" (as Haman referred to him) and his cousin Esther who, after winning a beauty contest, became the wife of King Ahasueros. Instead of the Jews being eliminated, Haman and his ten sons were hanged on the gallows that Haman had prepared for Mordecai's hanging.

Cousin, Not Uncle

The Book of Esther describes the support Esther received from Mordecai. Mordecai was Esther's cousin, not her uncle as many people mistakenly believe.

The Name Purim

Purim, the plural form of the Persian word *pur,* means "lots." According to the Book of Esther, Haman ordered that lots be drawn to determine the day on which his plot to annihilate the Jews should be carried out. The lottery was held, and the date selected was the thirteenth day of the Hebrew month Adar.

The Fast of Esther

In ancient Persia, protocol demanded that consent be received before anyone—even the queen—called on the king. Defying this order, Queen Esther appeared before the king without permission in order to plead for her people. Before undertaking her hazardous mission, Esther asked that all Jews support her by fasting on that day. Her effort was successful, and since then the thirteenth of Adar—the date of Esther's appearance before the king—has been observed as a fast day. In leap years the fast takes place in Adar II. The Fast of Esther is called Taanit Esther in Hebrew.

Purim in Jerusalem

Purim falls on the fourteenth of Adar, and Jews the world over celebrate Purim on that day. However, since Shushan, the capital of Persia, was a walled city, inhabitants of all cities known to be walled since the time of Joshua observe Purim one day later, on the fifteenth of Adar.

Inhabitants of Jerusalem, a walled city, read the Megilla (see below) and celebrate Purim on the fifteenth of Adar, while the rest of Israel observes the holiday on the fourteenth. The fifteenth day of Adar is called Shushan Purim.

Leap Years

In leap years (which occur seven times in every nineteen years), the Jewish calendar contains one extra month, Adar II. In leap years Purim is always celebrated on the fourteenth day of Adar II.

READING THE MEGILLA

The Megilla

The Book of Esther, which contains ten chapters, is part of the Hagiographa or Holy Writings (*Ketuvim* in Hebrew), the third part of the Bible. In Hebrew the book is called Megillat Esther (Scroll of Esther). *Megilla* is the Hebrew word for a scroll of any kind, but when one speaks of *The* Megilla, one means specifically the Scroll of Esther.

The Megilla read in the synagogue on Purim evening and morning is handwritten on parchment. Some Megillot are decorated with artistic renderings and are housed in ornate containers fashioned from brass, copper, or silver.

Reading the Megilla

The Megilla is read aloud in the synagogue at the evening and the morning service of the fourteenth of Adar. Everyone—men, women, and children—is mandated to listen to the reading.

בְּעֵינֵי הַמֶּלֶךְ וַיַּעַשׂ כֵּן אִישׁ יְהוּדִי הָיָה בְּשׁוּשַׁן
הַבִּירָה וּשְׁמוֹ מָרְדֳּכַי בֶּן יָאִיר בֶּן שִׁמְעִי בֶּן קִישׁ אִישׁ יְמִינִי אֲשֶׁר
הָגְלָה מִירוּשָׁלַיִם עִם הַגֹּלָה אֲשֶׁר הָגְלְתָה עִם יְכָנְיָה מֶלֶךְ
יְהוּדָה אֲשֶׁר הֶגְלָה נְבוּכַדְנֶצַּר מֶלֶךְ בָּבֶל וַיְהִי אֹמֵן אֶת
הֲדַסָּה הִיא אֶסְתֵּר בַּת דֹּדוֹ כִּי אֵין לָהּ אָב וָאֵם וְהַנַּעֲרָה
יְפַת תֹּאַר וְטוֹבַת מַרְאֶה וּבְמוֹת אָבִיהָ וְאִמָּהּ לְקָחָהּ מָרְדֳּכַי
לוֹ לְבַת וַיְהִי כְּהִשָּׁמַע דְּבַר הַמֶּלֶךְ וְדָתוֹ וּבְהִקָּבֵץ נְעָרוֹת
רַבּוֹת אֶל שׁוּשַׁן הַבִּירָה אֶל יַד הֵגַי וַתִּלָּקַח אֶסְתֵּר
אֶל בֵּית הַמֶּלֶךְ אֶל יַד הֵגַי שֹׁמֵר הַנָּשִׁים וַיִּיטַב הַנַּעֲרָה

The above selection, from Chapter 2 of the Book Esther, is an example of beautifully executed Hebrew calligraphy. The first word of the fifth line mentions (for the first and only time) the Hebrew name of Esther, which is Hadassah. Esther is the heroine's Persian name.

Booing Haman

Whenever Haman's name is mentioned during the reading

of the Megilla, congregants boo, hiss, clap, stamp their feet, or make noise of some kind. The most popular noisemaker is the *grogger*.

FOOD AND DRINK

Sending Eatables to Friends

Because Esther was successful in turning days of doom into days of gladness, it was mandated (Esther 9:22) that on Purim Jews show their joy and thankfulness by sending gifts to one another and to the poor in their midst. This custom became known as *mishloach manot* (*shalach-mones* in the vernacular), which literally means "sending portions." Today, it is traditional on Purim to send at least two eatables or other gifts to friends and to donate charity to the poor.

The Se'uda

On the afternoon of Purim it is customary for families to assemble and enjoy a festive meal called the *Purim Se'uda* or *Se'udat Purim*. Traditionally the meal was marked by a great deal of levity and drinking. The Talmud says: "On Purim a person should ply himself [with wine] until he can no longer recognize the difference [*ad d'lo yada*] between the words "cursed be Haman" and the words "blessed be Mordecai."

The Purim Challa

The braided *challa* served at the *Purim Se'uda* is made of long strands of dough. These represent the long ropes that were set up by Haman to execute Mordecai but which in the end were used to hang Haman and his ten sons.

Sweet-and-Sour Dishes

Among Chassidic Jews and others, sweet-and-sour dishes are prepared for the Purim meal to represent the dual aspects of the holiday: initial sadness and ultimate joy.

Classic Purim Pastry

The most popular of all Purim delicacies is the *hamantasch,* a German word meaning "Haman's pocket." This triangular-shaped pastry is filled with fruit, cheese, or poppyseeds (*mohn*). The pastry is so named, some say, because Haman stuffed his pockets with bribe money. The triangle shape is said to have been chosen as a reminder of the type of hat worn by Haman.

Hamantaschen (plural) are also called *oznay Haman* ("ears of Haman") because it was once the practice to cut off the ears of criminals before hanging them, and Haman was eventually hanged.

Hamantaschen

This perennial Purim favorite features a cookie dough and a prune filling. Feel free to substitute the filling of your choice.

Dough:
- **3 cups unsifted all-purpose flour**
- **3 eggs (graded large)**
- **3 teaspoons baking powder**
- **½ cup oil**
- **¾ cup sugar**
- **Pinch of salt**
- **1 teaspoon vanilla extract**
- **Grated rind of 1 lemon**

Sift the flour, baking powder, and salt into a large bowl. In another bowl, beat the eggs with the sugar and oil. Add the vanilla and grated rind.

Combine the dry mixture with the egg mixture. Mix well until the dough forms a ball. Transfer the dough to a floured surface and knead for about 2 minutes, until smooth.

Divide the dough into thirds, flatten, wrap in plastic wrap, and refrigerate for about an hour. Prepare the filling.

Filling:
> **1 pound pitted prunes, ground fine**
> **½ cup chopped walnuts**
> **¼ cup honey**
> **Grated rind of 1 lemon**
> **1 tablespoon lemon juice**

Combine all the ingredients and the filling is ready to use.

Preheat the oven to 350 degrees F. When the dough has been chilled, turn out one packet of dough onto a floured surface and roll it out to ⅛-inch thickness. With a cookie cutter or a glass, cut the dough into 3-inch circles.

Place a teaspoon of filling in the center of each round, then bring up the sides to form triangles. Pinch together the corners to seal. Transfer to lightly greased baking sheets and brush with egg wash (one teaspoon water mixed with one egg yolk) if desired. Repeat the process with the remaining packets of dough.

Bake the *hamantaschen* for 25 to 30 minutes, until lightly browned. Do not overbake. Transfer to racks to cool. Makes 56 or more.

Masquerading

Influenced by the Roman carnival, at the close of the fifteenth century Italian Jews introduced masquerading into the Purim celebration.

Although the Bible prohibits men from wearing women's garments (Deuteronomy 22:5), the Rabbis made an exception for Purim to increase the hilarity of the day. Masquerading is a prominent feature of the Adloyada Purim Carnival held annually in Tel Aviv (see page 299 for the origin of the name). Holding a Purim ball or party at which participants dress in costume is commonplace today.

OTHER MINOR HOLIDAYS

Rosh Chodesh—New Moon

In ancient times Rosh Chodesh—the celebration of the appearance of the new moon—was regarded as an important holiday. It was marked by the cessation of work, the offering of special sacrifices in the Temple, the blowing of the *shofar* in the sanctuary, and rejoicing in festive style in the home. Today Rosh Chodesh is a minor holiday marked only by the recitation of special prayers (such as the *Hallel*) normally recited on major holidays.

Yom Ha-sho'ah—Holocaust Day

The twenty-seventh day of the Hebrew month Nissan is commemorated as Holocaust Day (Yom Ha-sho'ah in Hebrew), a day of remembrance for the six million Jews who were victims of Nazi atrocities during World War II. On this day, special ceremonies are held at the Yad Va-shem memorial in Jerusalem and in many synagogues and places of memorial throughout the world.

In Israel, on the morning of Holocaust Day, sirens are sounded and all pedestrian and vehicular traffic comes to a halt. People exit their cars and stand in silence. Radio and television broadcasts are suspended. No human sound is heard throughout the country for two full minutes. All places of entertainment are closed for the day.

Yom Ha-zikaron—Day of Remembrance

In Israel, on the fourth of Iyyar, the day preceding Independence Day (Yom Ha-atzma'ut), a Day of Remembrance (Yom Ha-zikaron) is observed to honor those who made the supreme sacrifice during the 1948 War of Liberation. Vehicular and other movement ceases throughout the country for one minute beginning at eleven o'clock in the morning.

Yom Ha-atzma'ut—Independence Day

Yom Ha-atzma'ut, Independence Day, is celebrated in Israel

and by Jews everywhere on the fifth of Iyyar. It was on this date in the Hebrew calendar (corresponding to May 14, 1948) that Israel achieved statehood and became an independent nation for the first time since the year 70 C.E. In Israel, Yom Ha-atzma'ut is observed as a national and religious holiday. Parades are held in all major cities, and special prayers (including *Hallel*) are recited in synagogues.

If the fifth of Iyyar falls on a Friday or Saturday, the Independence Day celebration is held on the previous Thursday.

Although Yom Ha-atzma'ut falls during the *Sefira* period, the Orthodox rabbinate permits weddings to be held on that day.

Lag B'Omer

Lag B'Omer, the thirty-third day of the counting of the *Omer*, is observed on the eighteenth of Iyyar. See page 46 for a full explanation of this joyous minor holiday on which weddings are permitted.

Yom Yerushala'yim—Jerusalem Day

In Israel, the twenty-eighth day of Iyyar is celebrated as Jerusalem Unification Day, a holiday instituted to commemorate the recapture of East Jerusalem from the Jordanians on June 7, 1967, during the Six Day War. The city was unified for the first time in twenty years.

Although Yom Yerushala'yim falls during the *Sefira* period, the Orthodox rabbinate permits weddings to be held on that day.

Fast of the Seventeenth of Tammuz

The seventeenth day of the Hebrew month Tammuz (Shiva Asar B'Tammuz) marks the day in the year 586 B.C.E. when the walls of Jerusalem were breached by Nebuchadnezzar, king of Babylonia. Three weeks later, on Tisha B'Av, the first Temple was destroyed. Traditional Jews observe this day (usually falling in July) as a fast day. The fasting begins at dawn and ends at nightfall.

The Three Weeks

In the three weeks between the seventeenth of Tammuz and the ninth of Av (usually falling in July) the Babylonians laid siege to Jerusalem and destroyed the Temple. During this period, which became a time of mourning in the Jewish calendar year, weddings and other joyous celebrations are forbidden by Orthodox Jews.

The Nine Days

For traditional Jews, the first nine days of the Hebrew month of Av (which fall in July) constitute a period of intense mourning, for it was during this time that the First Temple was destroyed and the exile of Jews to Babylonia began. Weddings are not held, meat is not eaten, and wine is not consumed. Only on the Sabbath are the food prohibitions relaxed.

Tisha B'Av

The most important minor fast day in the Jewish calendar is Tisha B'Av, the ninth day of the month Av (Ab). On that day in the year 586 B.C.E. the Babylonians, led by King Nebuchadnezzar, besieged the Temple in Jerusalem and burned it to the ground. And on that same day 656 years later (70 C.E.) the Second Temple was destroyed by the Romans. Like Yom Kippur, fasting on Tisha B'Av begins on the evening of the night before the day itself and ends at nightfall twenty-five hours later. Tisha B'Av generally falls in July.

Fast of the Tenth of Tevet

On the tenth day of the month Tevet (Asara B'Tevet) a fast is observed in commemoration of the day on which the Babylonians began the siege of Jerusalem, the first of a series of events that led to the destruction of the city and the Temple. The fast, which usually falls in either December or January, begins at dawn and ends at nightfall.

Tu Bi-shevat

Chamisha Asar Bi-shevat, which means literally "the fifteenth [day] of [the month] Shevat," is also known as Tu Bi-shevat.

The word "tu" is spelled *tet vav*, letters which, when added together, have the numerical value of fifteen, *tet* being equal to nine and *vav* to six.

Chamisha Asar Bi-shevat is a midwinter holiday dating back to talmudic times. Honoring the first flowering of the trees after a long winter lull, this day is referred to in the Talmud as the New Year for Trees. Today, it is celebrated primarily in Israel by the planting of trees by children.

The eating of *bokser* (carob) on Tu Bi-shevat has long been a holiday custom. In Israel, in addition to *bokser*, dates, figs, and other fruits of Israel are eaten. Many Chassidim celebrate the holiday by eating fifteen different kinds of fruit.

Carob Brownies

Health-food faddists will particularly enjoy these nutrition-packed brownies.

½ cup honey
⅓ cup vegetable oil
2 tablespoons lecithin granules
2 eggs, beaten
1½ cups whole wheat pastry flour
¼ cup soy flour
¼ cup wheat germ
½ cup carob powder
½ teaspoon cinnamon
⅓ cup chopped walnuts
1 teaspoon vanilla extract

Preheat the oven to 350 degrees F. In a large bowl, beat together the honey, oil, and lecithin granules. Beat in the eggs. In a separate bowl mix together the flours and wheat germ. Gradually stir the flour mixture, the carob, and the cinnamon into the honey mixture. Then stir in the nuts and the vanilla. Turn the mixture into a greased 8-inch baking pan. Bake in the preheated oven for 25 minutes. Remove from the oven to a wire rack. Cut while still warm. Makes sixteen 2-inch brownies.

The Fast of Gedaliah

The third day of Tishri—the day after Rosh Hashana—is a fast day which commemorates the murder of Gedaliah four years after the Jews had been exiled to Babylonia in 586 B.C.E. After the dispersion, Nebuchadnezzar, king of Babylonia, had allowed a small Jewish community to remain in Palestine, and a gentle, peace-loving man named Gedaliah was appointed governor. When Gedaliah was assassinated by radical fellow Jews, the king expelled the remaining Jews.

Appendices

HA-TIKVA
(The Hope)

The Jewish national anthem.

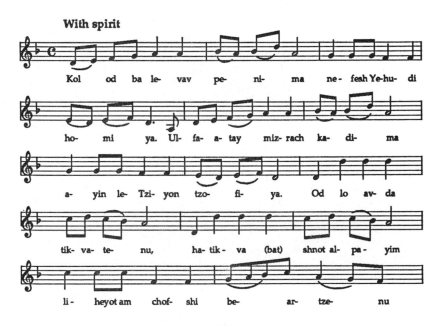

Kol od ba le- vav pe- ni- ma ne- fesh Ye-hu- di ho- mi ya. Ul- fa- a- tay miz- rach ka- di- ma a- yin le- Tzi- yon tzo- fi- ya. Od lo av- da tik- va- te- nu, ha- tik- va (bat) shnot al- pa- yim li- heyot am chof- shi be- ar- tze- nu

e- retz Tzi- yon vi- Y'ru-sha-la- yim. Li'- heyot am chof- shi

be- ar- tze- nu e- retz Tzi- yon vi- Y'ru-sha- la- yim.

Kol od ba-levav penima,
    nefesh Yehudi homiya.
Ulfa-atay mizrach kadima,
    a'yin l'Tziyon tzofiya.
Od lo avda tikvatenu,
    ha-tikva (bat) shnot alpa'yim
    li'heyot am chofshi be-artzenu
    eretz Tziyon vi-Y'rushalayim.

כָּל עוֹד בַּלֵּבָב פְּנִימָה,
נֶפֶשׁ יְהוּדִי הוֹמִיָה.
וּלְפַאֲתֵי מִזְרָח קָדִימָה,
עַיִן לְצִיּוֹן צוֹפִיָה.
עוֹד לֹא אָבְדָה תִּקְוָתֵנוּ,
הַתִּקְוָה בַּת שְׁנוֹת אַלְפַּיִם
לִהְיוֹת עַם חָפְשִׁי בְּאַרְצֵנוּ
אֶרֶץ צִיּוֹן וִירוּשָׁלָיִם.

HEVENU SHALOM ALECHEM
(We Bring You Greetings of Peace)

With spirit

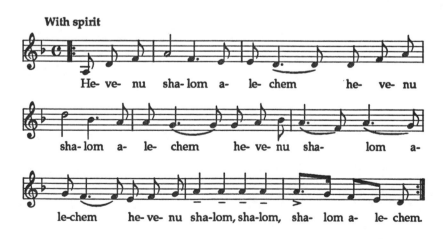

He- ve- nu sha-lom a- le- chem he- ve- nu

sha-lom a- le- chem he- ve- nu sha- lom a-

le-chem he- ve- nu sha-lom, sha-lom, sha- lom a- le- chem.

Hevenu shalom alechem.

הֲבֵאנוּ שָׁלוֹם עֲלֵיכֶם.

AM YISRAEL CHAI!
(The People of Israel Lives!)

Am Yisrael chai!
Am Yisrael chai!
Ad b'li dai,
Am Yisrael chai!

עַם יִשְׂרָאֵל חַי!
עַם יִשְׂרָאֵל חַי!
עַד בְּלִי דַי,
עַם יִשְׂרָאֵל חַי!

HAVA NAGILA
(Come Let Us Rejoice)

A very popular tune, often sung as celebrants dance the *hora*.

With spirit

Ha- va na-gi- la ha- va na-gi- la

ha- va na-gi- la ve- nis- me-cha ve- nis- me- cha

ha- va ne-ra-ne- na ha- va ne-ra-ne- na ha-va ne- ra- ne- na

ve- nis- me- cha u- ru u- ru a- chim

u-ru a- chim b'- lev sa-me-ach u-ru a- chim b'- lev sa-me-ach

u--ru a- chim u-ru a- chim b'- lev sa- me- ach.

Hava nagila ve-nismecha,
Hava neranena ve-nismecha,
Uru achim b'lev same'ach.

הָבָה נָגִילָה וְנִשְׂמְחָה,
הָבָה נְרַנְּנָה וְנִשְׂמְחָה,
עוּרוּ אַחִים בְּלֵב שָׂמֵחַ.

ATZAY ZETIM OMDIM

(Olive Trees Are Standing)

A Tu Bi-shevat song celebrating the olive tree,
which is found in abundance in Israel.
This is often sung as a round.

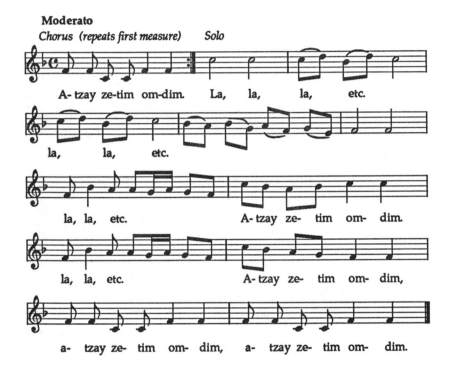

Atzay zetim omdim.
La, la, la...

עֲצֵי זֵיתִים עוֹמְדִים.
לַ, לַ, לַ...

CHAD GADYA
(One Only Kid)

A Passover folktale about the fate of one only kid.

Chad gadya, chad gadya.	.חַד גַּדְיָא, חַד גַּדְיָא
De-zabin aba bitray zuzay,	.דְּזַבִּן אַבָּא בִּתְרֵי זוּזֵי
chad gadya, chad gadya.	.חַד גַּדְיָא, חַד גַּדְיָא
Ve-ata shunra ve-achal le-gadya	.וְאָתָא שׁוּנְרָא. וְאָכַל לְגַדְיָא
de-zabin aba bitray zuzay,	.דְּזַבִּן אַבָּא בִּתְרֵי זוּזֵי
chad gadya, chad gadya.	.חַד גַּדְיָא, חַד גַּדְיָא
Ve-ata chalba ve-nashach le-shunra,	.וְאָתָא כַלְבָּא. וְנָשַׁךְ לְשׁוּנְרָא
de-achal le-gadya	
de-zabin aba bitray zuzay,	.דְּאָכַל לְגַדְיָא. דְּזַבִּן אַבָּא בִּתְרֵי זוּזֵי
chad gadya, chad gadya.	.חַד גַּדְיָא, חַד גַּדְיָא

(There are a total of ten verses to this song. Consult a Haggadah for the lyrics to the remaining verses.)

CHAG PURIM

(The Purim Holiday)

A tune celebrating Purim as a fun holiday marked by singing, dancing, and merrymaking.

Joyously

1. Chag Pu- rim, chag Pu- rim, chag ga- dol hu la- Yehu- dim.
2. Chag Pu- rim, chag Pu- rim, zeh el zeh shol- chim ma- not.

Ma- se- chot, ra'a- sha- nim, z'mi- rot, ri- ku- dim.
Mach-ma-dim, mam- ta- kim, tu- fi- nim, mig- danot.

Refrain:

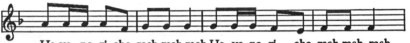

Ha-va na- ri- sha, rash,rash,rash.Ha- va na- ri- sha, rash,rash, rash.

Ha-va na- ri- sha, rash,rash, rash, ba- ra- a- sha- nim.

1. Chag Purim, chag Purim, chag gadol hu la-Yehudim.
   Masechot, ra' ashanim, z'mirot, rikudim. (Refrain)

2. Chag Purim, chag Purim, zeh el zeh sholchim manot.
   Machmadim, mamtakim, tufinim, migdanot. (Refrain)

Refrain:

Hava narisha, rash, rash, rash.
Hava narisha, rash, rash, rash.
Hava narisha, rash, rash, rash ba-ra'ashanim.

1. חַג פּוּרִים, חַג פּוּרִים, חַג גָּדוֹל הוּא לַיְהוּדִים.
מַסֵּכוֹת, רַעֲשָׁנִים, זְמִירוֹת, רְקוּדִים.

2. חַג פּוּרִים, חַג פּוּרִים, זֶה אֶל זֶה שׁוֹלְחִים מָנוֹת.
מַחֲמַדִּים, מַמְתַּקִּים, תּוּפִינִים, מִגְדָּנוֹת.

הָבָה נַרְעִישָׁה, רַשׁ, רַשׁ, רַשׁ, בָּרַעֲשָׁנִים.

CHANUKA

Tops spinning and candles burning add merriment to the holiday.

Lively

Cha- nu- ka,   Cha- nu- ka,   chag ya- fe kol kach.

Or cha- viv   mi- sa- viv,   gil l'- ye- led rach.

Cha- nu- ka,   Cha- nu- ka,   se- vi- von sov, sov.

Sov, sov, sov,   sov, sov, sov,   ma na- im va- tov.

Chanuka, Chanuka, chag yafe kol kach.
Or chaviv mi-saviv, gil l'yeled rach.
Chanuka, Chanuka, sevivon, sov, sov.
Sov..... ma na'im va tov.

חֲנֻכָּה, חֲנֻכָּה, חַג יָפֶה כָּל כָּךְ.
אוֹר חָבִיב מִסָּבִיב, גִּיל לְיֶלֶד רַךְ.

חֲנֻכָּה, חֲנֻכָּה, סְבִיבוֹן סֹב סֹב.
סֹב, סֹב, סֹב, סֹב, סֹב, סֹב,
מַה נָּעִים וָטוֹב.

DAYENU

(It Would Have Been Enough)

A popular Seder prayer expressing thanks for all the good things that have happened.

1. Ilu hotzianu mi-Mitzrayim,
   Hotzianu mi-Mitzrayim.
   Dayenu. (Refrain)

.1 אִילוּ הוֹצִיאָנוּ מִמִּצְרַיִם,
הוֹצִיאָנוּ מִמִּצְרַיִם. דַּיֵּנוּ.

2. Ilu natan lanu et ha-Shabat.
   Dayenu. (Refrain)

.2 אִילוּ נָתַן לָנוּ אֶת הַשַּׁבָּת.
דַּיֵּנוּ.

3. Ilu natan lanu et ha-Torah.
   Dayenu. (Refrain)

.3 אִילוּ נָתַן לָנוּ אֶת הַשַּׁבָּת.
דַּיֵּנוּ.

Refrain: Dayenu.

ELIYAHU HA-NAVI

(Elijah the Prophet)

A Passover favorite expressing the hope that the
prophet Elijah will appear soon.

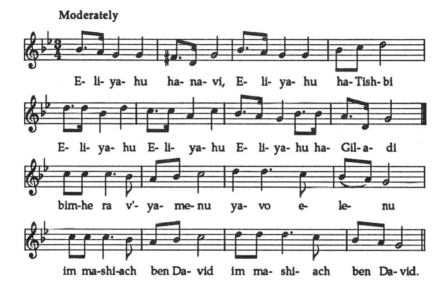

Eliyahu ha-navi,
Eliyahu ha-Tishbi,
Eliyahu ha-Giladi.
Bi-mhera v'ya-me-nu
    yavo elenu,
Im mashiach ben David.

אֵלִיָּהוּ הַנָּבִיא,
אֵלִיָּהוּ הַתִּשְׁבִּי,
אֵלִיָּהוּ הַגִּלְעָדִי.

בִּמְהֵרָה בְיָמֵינוּ,
יָבֹא אֵלֵינוּ,
עִם מָשִׁיחַ בֶּן דָּוִד.

HA-MAVDIL
(The Separation)

This farewell song to the Sabbath expresses the hope that
the sins of the past week have been forgiven and
that the new week will be a good one.

Ha-mav-dil bayn ko-desh,- bayn ko-desh l'- chol, cha-to-
te-nu hu yim-chol, zar-e-nu v'chas-pe-nu yar-beh ka-
chol v'cha-ko-cha-vim ba-lai- la. *Refrain:* Sha-vu-a
tov, sha-vu-a tov, sha-vu-a tov, sha-vu-a
tov, sha-vu-a tov, sha-vu-a
tov, sha-vu-a tov, sha-vu-a tov.

Ha-mavdil bayn kodesh l'chol,
chatatenu hu yimchol,
zarenu v'chaspenu yarbeh ka-chol
v'cha-kochavim ba-laila.

Refrain: Shavua tov...

הַמַּבְדִּיל בֵּין קֹדֶשׁ לְחוֹל,
חַטֹּאתֵינוּ הוּא יִמְחוֹל,
זַרְעֵנוּ וְכַסְפֵּנוּ יַרְבֶּה כַּחוֹל
וְכַכּוֹכָבִים בַּלַּיְלָה.
שָׁבוּעַ טוֹב ...

HINAY MA TOV
(How Good It Is)

This folk song, often sung as a round, expresses the sentiment
that it is extraordinarily good and pleasant
for brethren to dwell together in unity.

Lively

Hi- nay ma tov u- ma na- im
she- vet a- chim gam ya- chad.
Hi- nay ma tov
u- ma na- im
she- vet a- chim
she- vet a- chim gam ya- chad.

D. C.

Hinay ma tov u-ma na'im
Shevet achim gam yachad.

הִנֵּה מַה טּוֹב וּמַה נָּעִים
שֶׁבֶת אַחִים גַּם יָחַד.

MA'OZ TZUR
(Rock of Ages)

A popular Chanukah song that expresses
thanksgiving for victory over the enemy.

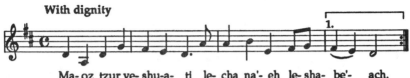

Ma- oz tzur ye- shu-a- ti le- cha na'- eh le- sha- be'- ach.
Ti- kon bet te- fi- la- ti ve- sham to- da ne-za

be- ach l'- et ta- chin mat- be- ach mi-tzar ham-na-be- ach

az eg- mor be- shir miz-mor cha- nu-kat ha-miz-be- ach be- ach.

Ma'oz tzur yeshuati lecha na'eh le-shabe'ach.
Tikon bet tefilati ve-sham toda ne-zabe'ach.
L'et tachin matbe'ach mitzar ha-menabe'ach.
Az egmor be-shir mizmor, chanukat ha-mizbe'ach.

מָעוֹז צוּר יְשׁוּעָתִי לְךָ נָאֶה לְשַׁבֵּחַ,
תִּכּוֹן בֵּית תְּפִלָּתִי וְשָׁם תּוֹדָה נְזַבֵּחַ.
לְעֵת תָּכִין מַטְבֵּחַ מִצָּר הַמְנַבֵּחַ,
אָז אֶגְמֹר בְּשִׁיר מִזְמוֹר, חֲנֻכַּת הַמִּזְבֵּחַ.

MY DRAYDL

A favorite Chanukah song describing the
little *draydl* (top) children love to spin.

I have a little draydl, I made it out of clay.
And when it's dry and ready, then draydl I shall play.
O draydl, draydl, draydl. I made it out of clay.
O draydl, draydl, draydl. Now draydl I shall play.

SHALOM ALECHEM

(Peace Unto You)

A song of welcome to the angels of peace, who have been sent by the King of Kings to usher in the Sabbath.

Slowly

Sha- lom a- le- chem mal- a- chay ha-sha- ret
Tzet- chem le- sha- lom mal- a- chay ha-sha- lom

mal-a- chay el- yon, mi- me- lech
mal-a- chay el- yon, mi- me- lech

mal- chay ha-me-la- chim, Ha-ka- dosh Ba- ruch Hu.
mal- chay ha-me-la- chim, Ha-ka- dosh Ba- ruch Hu.
Fine

Bo- a- chem le- sha- lom ma- a- chay ha- sha- lom

mal- a- chay el- yon, mi- me-lech mal- chay ha-me-la-chim

Ha-ka- dosh Ba- ruch Hu. Bo- a- chem le-sha- lom

mal- a- chay ha-sha- lom mal-a-chay el- yon, mi- me-lech

mal- chay ha-me-la-chim　Ha-ka-　dosh Ba-　ruch Hu.

D. C. al Fine

Shalom alechem malachay ha-sharet malachay elyon,
   mi-melech malchay ha-melachim, Ha-kadosh Baruch Hu.
Bo'achem le-shalom malachay ha-shalom malachay elyon,
   mi-melech malchay ha-melachim, Ha-kadosh Baruch Hu.
Barchuni le-shalom malachay ha-shalom malachay elyon,
   mi-melech malchay ha-melachim, Ha-kadosh Baruch Hu.
Tzetchem le-shalom malachay ha-shalom malachay elyon,
   mi-melech malchay ha-melachim, Ha-kadosh Baruch Hu.

שָׁלוֹם עֲלֵיכֶם מַלְאֲכֵי הַשָּׁרֵת מַלְאֲכֵי עֶלְיוֹן,
מִמֶּלֶךְ מַלְכֵי הַמְּלָכִים, הַקָּדוֹשׁ בָּרוּךְ הוּא.

בּוֹאֲכֶם לְשָׁלוֹם מַלְאֲכֵי הַשָּׁלוֹם מַלְאֲכֵי עֶלְיוֹן,
מִמֶּלֶךְ מַלְכֵי הַמְּלָכִים, הַקָּדוֹשׁ בָּרוּךְ הוּא.

בָּרְכוּנִי לְשָׁלוֹם מַלְאֲכֵי הַשָּׁלוֹם מַלְאֲכֵי עֶלְיוֹן,
מִמֶּלֶךְ מַלְכֵי הַמְּלָכִים, הַקָּדוֹשׁ בָּרוּךְ הוּא.

צֵאתְכֶם לְשָׁלוֹם מַלְאֲכֵי הַשָּׁלוֹם מַלְאֲכֵי עֶלְיוֹן,
מִמֶּלֶךְ מַלְכֵי הַמְּלָכִים, הַקָּדוֹשׁ בָּרוּךְ הוּא.

SIMAN TOV
(A Good Omen)

May good fortune be our lot and the lot of all Israel.

Joyfully

Si- man tov u- ma-zal tov v'- Si-man tov u- ma- zal tov,

Si- man tov u- ma-zal tov v'- Si-man tov u- ma- zal tov,

Si- man tov u- ma-zal tov v'- Si-man tov u- ma- zal tov

y'- hay la- nu nu

y'- hay la- nu y'- hay la- nu u- l'- chol Yis- ra-

el el y'- he la-nu y'-

he la- nu u- l'- chol Yis- ra- el. el.

Siman tov u-mazal tov,
y'hay lanu u-l'chol Yisrael.

סִימָן טוֹב וּמַזָּל טוֹב,
יְהֵא לָנוּ וּלְכָל יִשְׂרָאֵל.

YISRAEL VE-ORAITA
(Israel and the Torah)

A Shavuot melody celebrating the bond between Israel and the Torah.

Yisrael, Yisrael ve-oraita chad hu.
Torah ora, Torah ora, haleluyah.

יִשְׂרָאֵל, יִשְׂרָאֵל וְאוֹרַיְתָא חַד הוּא.
תּוֹרָה אוֹרָה, תּוֹרָה אוֹרָה, הַלְלוּיָה.

APPENDIX II

Rabbinic and Synagogue Organizations

Central Conference of American
    Rabbis
192 Lexington Avenue
New York, NY 10016
Telephone: (212) 684-4990

Chicago Rabbinical Council
3525 W. Peterson Avenue
Chicago, IL 60659
Telephone: (773) 588-1600

Commission on Jewish
    Chaplaincy
15 East 26th Street
New York, NY 10011
Telephone: (212) 532-4949

Council of Young Israel Rabbis
3 West 16th Street
New York, NY 10011
Telephone: (212) 929-1525

New York Board of Rabbis
10 East 73rd Street
New York, NY 10021
Telephone: (212) 879-8415

Rabbinical Alliance of America
3 West 16th Street
New York, NY 10010
Telephone: (212) 242-6420

Rabbinical Assembly
3080 Broadway
New York, NY 10027
Telephone: (212) 678-8060

Rabbinical Association of Greater
    Miami
4200 Biscayne Boulevard
Miami, FL 33137
Telephone: (305) 576-4000

Rabbinical Council of America
305 Seventh Avenue
New York, NY 10001
Telephone: (212) 807-7888

Rabbinical Council of
    Massachusetts
(Vaad Harabonim)
177 Tremont Street
Boston, MA 02111
Telephone: (617) 426-2139

Union of American Hebrew
   Congregations
838 Fifth Avenue
New York, NY 10021
Telephone: (212) 249-0100

Union of Orthodox Jewish
   Congregations
838 Fifth Avenue
New York, NY 10021
Telephone: (212) 563-4000

Union of Orthodox Rabbis of the
   United States and Canada
235 East Broadway
New York, NY 10002
Telephone: (212) 964-6337

United Synagogue of America
155 Fifth Avenue
New York, NY 10010
Telephone: (212) 260-8450

Vaas Hoeir of St. Louis
#4 Millstone Campus
St. Louis, MO 63146
Telephone: (314) 569-2770

Vaad Rabonei Haschuna
788 Eastern Parkway
Brooklyn, NY 11238
Telephone: (718) 604-8827

APPENDIX III

Selected Books for the Home Library

The following books deal with various aspects of the subject matter covered in this volume. Judaica shops and bookstores in larger metropolitan areas carry most of these titles.

Biblical and Postbiblical Literature

Chumash and Rashi, by A. M. Silverman and M. Rosenbaum (Philipp Feldheim). A five-volume Hebrew-English edition of the Pentateuch, with Rashi's commentary presented in Hebrew and in English translation.

Midrash Rabbah, edited by H. Freedman and M. Simon (Soncino Press). Contains, in English translation only, the homiletical, ethical, and moral interpretation of Scripture as expounded by the Rabbis of the Talmud. Includes popular folklore, parables, anecdotes, and the wit and wisdom of the Sages.

The Mishna, edited by Philip Blackman (Soncino Press). The Mishna, the first part of the Talmud, is the product of scholars who lived prior to 220 C.E. This edition contains the Hebrew text, an English translation, plus commentary.

The Mishnah, Herbert Danby, translator (Oxford University Press). A complete English-language edition, with an introduction and notes explaining the text.

Pentateuch & Haftorahs, edited by J. H. Hertz (Soncino Press). A one-volume Pentateuch popularly used in synagogues. Contains the Hebrew and English text plus commentary provided by the former Chief Rabbi of the British Commonwealth.

The Soncino Books of the Bible, edited by A. Cohen (Soncino Press). A fourteen-volume set with Hebrew text, English translation, and a lucid commentary by leading scholars.

Tanakh: A New JPS Translation (Jewish Publication Society). A completely revised edition of the *Holy Scriptures* originally published by J.P.S. in 1917. The product of Orthodox, Conservative, and Reform collaboration.

This Is the Torah, by Alfred J. Kolatch (Jonathan David Publishers). The reasons behind the diverse laws, customs, ceremonies, and traditions that govern the writing, reading, and handling of the Torah scroll are clearly presented in a question-and-answer format.

The Torah: A Modern Commentary, edited by Gunther Plaut (Union of American Hebrew Congregations). A highly praised one-volume Pentateuch containing the Hebrew text, an English translation, profuse commentary on most verses, and an overall analysis of the subject matter.

Rituals, Customs & Ceremonies

The Code of Jewish Law, by Solomon Ganzfried. Translated by Hyman E. Goldin (Hebrew Publishing). A four-volume condensed Hebrew-English edition of the sixteenth-century *Code of Jewish Law* (*Shulchan Aruch*). All of the basic Jewish laws are presented.

How To Run a Traditional Jewish Household, by Blu Greenberg (Summit Books). Covers all aspects of Jewish home life, from observing holidays and keeping kosher to parenting and the expanding role of women in Jewish life.

The Jewish Baby Book, by Anita Diamant (Summit Books). A guide for parents-to-be that discusses the customs, ceremonies, and rituals pertaining to the new addition to the family.

The Jewish Book of Why, by Alfred J. Kolatch (Jonathan David Publishers). Hundreds of questions about all aspects of Jewish religious practice are answered in a concise, direct, easy-to-understand manner. The views of each of the denominations are presented without bias.

Jewish Literacy, by Joseph Telushkin (William Morrow). Encyclopedic in nature, this volume presents concise descriptions and analyses of the trends and concepts of Jewish history, religion, and culture.

The Jewish Mourner's Book of Why, by Alfred J. Kolatch (Jonathan David Publishers). Answers to hundreds of questions explore, explain, and analyze the reasons behind the multitude of laws, customs, and ceremonies relating to death and mourning.

The Jewish Way in Death and Mourning, by Maurice Lamm (Jonathan David Publishers). A comprehensive presentation of all the laws and customs that Jews traditionally follow when a loved one dies.

The Jewish Way in Love and Marriage, by Maurice Lamm (Jonathan David Publishers). A summary of Judaism's traditional views on marriage and its requirements, plus an explanation of the various symbols, rituals, practices, and prayers associated with the wedding ceremony.

The New Jewish Wedding, by Anita Diamant (Summit Books). Offers practical advice on planning the wedding celebration, from finding a rabbi to selecting a photographer.

The Second Jewish Book of Why, by Alfred J. Kolatch (Jonathan David Publishers). This complementary volume to *The Jewish Book of Why* probes more deeply into the reasons behind the observance of the ceremonies and rituals of Judaism. Covers many aspects of Jewish life not covered in the first volume.

To Be a Jew, by Hayim Donin (Harper Collins). A popular presentation of the laws and observances of Judaism. Covers home rituals, synagogue rites, all the holidays, and life-cycle events.

History

Auschwitz: A History in Photographs, by Teresa Świebocka (Indiana University Press). A haunting collection of photographs taken by former prisoners that records the history of Auschwitz and what it looks like today.

Jewish Folkore in America, by David Max Eichhorn (Jonathan David Publishers). Hundreds of intriguing characters and episodes form the world of contemporary Jewish folklore are vividly portrayed.

The Greatest Jewish Stories Ever Told, by David Patterson (Jonathan David Publishers). Outstanding selections from Jewish literature are introduced and retold in a poignant, meaningful way.

The Holocaust, by Martin Gilbert (Henry Holt). Using the vivid testimony of witnesses, Professor Gilbert discusses not only the suffering of those who perished during the Holocaust but also how such a tragedy could have been allowed to take place.

Light in the Shadows, Barbara Milman (Jonathan David Publishers). An unusual collection of black-and-white prints depicting the experience of five young people and their families during the Holocaust.

Secret War Against the Jews, by John Loftus and Mark Aarons (St. Martin's Press). A mesmerizing account of Israel's betrayal by Western powers.

The World Must Know, by Michael Berenbaum (Little Brown). The history of the Holocaust as told in the United States Holocaust Memorial Museum. Drawing on the museum collections of artifacts and extensive eyewitness testimony, the reader journeys from the thriving Jewish communities throughout Europe to the horrors of the Holocaust.

Why the Jews? by Dennis Prager and Joseph Telushkin (Summit Books). A persuasive analysis and explanation of anti-Semitism.

Wisdom of Heschel, edited by Ruth M. Goodhill (Farrar, Straus & Giroux). Nearly 300 selections from Abraham Joshua Heschel's famous works.

Holidays & Holy Days

The Jewish Festivals, by Hayyim Schauss (Union of American Hebrew Congregations). An interesting and informative presentation of the history, lore, and legends surrounding all the major and minor festivals in the Jewish calendar.

The Jewish Holidays, by Michael Strassfeld (Harper Collins). A comprehensive guide for those who wish to observe the holidays fully, as prescribed by Jewish tradition. The text is enriched with commentary by five scholars.

The Jewish Way: Living the Holidays, by Irving Greenberg (Simon & Schuster). A comprehensive volume that treats the major and minor holidays, focusing on their history, significance, and observance.

Jewish Prayers

The Authorized Daily Prayerbook, edited by Joseph H. Hertz (Bloch Publishing). A daily prayerbook complete with Hebrew text, English translation, and explanatory notes. The editor is Chief Rabbi of the British Commonwealth.

The Complete ArtScroll Siddur, edited by Nosson Scherman (Mesorah Publications). Contains all the weekday, Sabbath, and festival prayers along with a new translation and a commentary by the editor.

The Concise Family Seder, by Alfred J. Kolatch (Jonathan David Publishers). A condensed version of *The Family Seder*.

Daily Prayer Book, edited by Philip Birnbaum (Hebrew Publishing). A complete traditional Hebrew prayerbook with English translation and notes.

The Family Seder, by Alfred J. Kolatch (Jonathan David Publishers). A full traditional Passover service complete with Hebrew text and a modern, meaningful English rendition.

Jewish Worship, by Abraham Millgrim (Jewish Publication Society). A lucid presentation of the history, significance, and development of the Jewish prayer book.

To Pray as a Jew, by Hayim Donin (Harper Collins). A detailed discussion and description of how to conduct oneself in the synagogue, plus an explanation of the prayers.

Reference Books

The Complete Hebrew-English English-Hebrew Dictionary, by Reuben Alcalay (Massadah Publishing). A five-volume set that will satisfy the needs of all students. Includes terminology currently used in Israel.

Encyclopedia of Jewish Concepts, by Nathan Birnbaum (Hebrew Publishing). An easy-to-read guide for anyone interested in learning more about the basic values of Judaism. Information pertaining to Jewish holidays, customs, and ceremonies is also presented.

Encyclopaedia Judaica, edited by Cecil Roth (Keter). An eighteen-volume set covering virtually every aspect of Judaism. Features a very detailed index.

Great Jewish Quotations, by Alfred J. Kolatch (Jonathan David Publishers). Covering the entire span of Jewish history, this volume contains the expressions of Jews on a wide range of subjects and those of non-Jews on matters relating to Jews and Judaism.

The New Name Dictionary, by Alfred J. Kolatch (Jonathan David Publishers). Contains 10,000 Hebrew and English names together with an explanation of their meanings. Particularly helpful to prospective parents.

Voices of Wisdom, by Francine Klagsbrun (Jonathan David Publishers). A unique anthology presenting Jewish viewpoints on a wide spectrum of contemporary issues.

Cookbooks

The Book of Jewish Food, by Claudia Roden (Random House). More than 800 recipes, interwoven stories, reminiscences, and history that trace the development of Jewish cooking over the centuries. The wide range of recipes recorded in this volume represent the cooking of almost every country where Jews have lived.

Chinese Kosher Cooking, by Betty S. Goldberg (Jonathan David Publishers). Authentic Chinese recipes converted into splendid kosher dishes by the author of the much praised *International Cooking for the Kosher Home.*

Complete American-Jewish Cookbook, by Anne London and Bertha K. Bishov (Harper Collins). A comprehensive cookbook covering everything from appetizers to desserts.

The Complete Passover Cookbook, by Frances R. AvRutick (Jonathan David Publishers). An inventive and comprehensive Passover cookbook containing more than 500 easy-to-follow recipes.

The Sephardic Kitchen, by Robert Sternberg (Harper Collins). Features recipes from the Sephardic kitchens of Spain, Portugal, Italy, Greece, Morocco, and Israel. Includes a short history of Sephardic Jewry and the lifestyles of Mediterranean Jews.

Traditional Jewish Cooking, by Betty S. Goldberg (Jonathan David Publishers). An exceptionally attractive cookbook devoted to traditional Jewish recipes. Each recipe is introduced with an explanation of the origin of the dish and how and when it is customarily served.

Juveniles

The Angel's Mistake, by Francine Prose (William Morrow). Hilarious stories about the "wise" people of Chelm. Illustrated in full color. For ages three and up.

A Child's First Book of Jewish Holidays, by Alfred J. Kolatch (Jonathan David Publishers). Written in simple language and enhanced by full-color illustrations, this volume introduces the very young child to the major Jewish Holidays.

Classic Bible Stories for Jewish Children, by Alfred J. Kolatch (Jonathan David Publishers). This volume introduces young readers to the biblical heroes and heroines who are an important part of the Jewish heritage. Illustrated in full color.

The Hebrew Alphabet, by Ruth Heller (Putnam). Each page of this coloring book is devoted to one of the twenty-two letters of the Hebrew alphabet. As the child colors in each letter, he or she learns the shape, name, sound, and even numerical value of the letter.

The Jewish Child's First Book of Why, by Alfred J. Kolatch (Jonathan David Publishers). The significance of some of the fascinating traditions and customs of Judaism are explained to young readers ages five to ten.

Let's Celebrate Our Jewish Holidays!, by Alfred J. Kolatch (Jonathan David Publishers). Written in easy-to-read, intelligent prose, this volume explains to readers ages six and up how each Jewish holiday originated, how each is celebrated, and the message that each offers today.

One-Minute Bible Stories, by Shari Lewis (Bantam Books). The ventriloquist widely known as the creator of Lamb Chop, presents twenty popular stories from the Bible in condensed format.

One-Minute Jewish Stories, by Shari Lewis (Bantam Books). Retells in condensed form stories about Abraham and the idols, Hanukkah, Purim, the Wisdom of Hillel, as well as lesser-known tales.

Bibliography

Arzt, Max. *Justice and Mercy.* New York: Holt, Rinehart and Winston, 1963.

Asheri, Michael. *Living Jewish.* New York: Dodd, Mead, 1978.

The Babylonian Talmud (Hebrew). Twenty volumes. Vilna: Romm, 1922.

The Babylonian Talmud (English). Thirty-five volumes. London: Soncino Press, 1935.

Caro, Joseph. *Shulchan Aruch (Code of Jewish Law).* Eight volumes. Probably a reprint of the 1874 Vilna edition. New York: Abraham Isaac Friedman, n.d.

Cohen, A. *Everyman's Talmud.* New York: E. P. Dutton, 1949.

Danby, Herbert. *The Mishna.* Oxford, England: Clarendon Press, 1933.

Dobrinsky, Herbert C. *A Treasury of Sephardic Laws and Customs.* New York: Ktav Publishing House, 1986.

Donin, Hayim. *To Be a Jew.* New York: Basic Books, 1972.

Eisenstein, Ira, editor. *A Guide to Jewish Ritual.* New York: Reconstuctionist Press, 1962.

Eisenstein, J. D. *Otzar Dinim Uminhagim.* New York: Hebrew Publishing Co., 1938.

———. *Otzar Maamarei Chazal.* New York: Hebrew Publishing Co., 1929.

Even Shoshan, Abraham. *Milon Chadash.* Four volumes. Twelfth edition. Jerusalem: Kiryat Sepher, 1964.

———. *A New Concordance of the Bible.* Four volumes. Jerusalem: Kiryat Sepher, 1980.

Freehof, Solomon B. *Reform Responsa* and *Recent Reform Responsa*. Two volumes in one. New York: Ktav Publishing House, 1973.

————. *Reform Responsa for Our Time*. Cincinnati: Hebrew Union College Press, 1977.

————. *The Responsa Literature* and *A Treasury of Responsa*. Two volumes in one. New York: Ktav Publishing House, 1973.

Graetz, Heinrich. *History of the Jews*. Six volumes. Philadelphia: Jewish Publication Society, 1891.

Greenberg, Blu. *How to Run a Traditional Jewish Household*. New York: Summit Books, 1983.

Hertz, J.H. *The Penetateuch and Haftorahs*. London: Soncino Press, 1961.

Israel Meir Hakohayn (Chafetz Chayim). *Mishna Berura*. Six volumes. New York, n.d.

Jacobs, Louis. *Jewish Law*. New York: Behrman House, 1968.

The Jewish Encyclopedia. Twelve volumes. New York: Funk and Wagnalls, 1912.

Kinderlehrer, Jane. *Cooking Kosher: The Natural Way*. New York: Jonathan David Publishers, 1980.

Klein, Isaac. *A Guide to Jewish Religious Practice*. New York: Jewish Theological Seminary, 1979.

————. *Responsa and Halakhic Studies*. New York: Ktav Publishing House, 1975.

Knox, Israel. *Rabbi in America: The Story of Isaac M. Wise*. Boston: Little, Brown, and Company, 1957.

Kolatch, Alfred J. *The Jewish Book of Why*. New York: Jonathan David Publishers, 1981.

————. *The Jewish Mourner's Book of Why*. New York: Jonathan David Publishers, 1993.

————. *The Second Jewish Book of Why*. New York: Jonathan David Publishers, 1985.

————. *This Is the Torah*. New York: Jonathan David Publishers, 1988.

————. *The New Name Dictionary*. New York: Jonathan David Publishers, 1989.

Kumove, Shirley. *Words Like Arrows*. New York: Warner Books, 1984.

Lamm, Maurice. *The Jewish Way in Death and Mourning*. New York: Jonathan David Publishers, 1972.

————. *The Jewish Way in Love and Marriage*. New York: Jonathan David Publishers, 1980.

Maimonides, Moses. *The Guide for the Perplexed.* Two volumes. Translated by Shlomo Pines. Chicago: University of Chicago Press, 1974.

———. *The Mishneh Torah.* Five volumes. Warsaw, 1881.

Maslin, Simeon J., editor. *Gates of Mitzvah.* New York: Central Conference of American Rabbis, 1979.

Millgram, Abraham. *Jewish Worship.* Philadelphia: Jewish Publication Society, 1971.

Plaut, Gunther. *The Torah: A Modern Commentary.* New York: Union of American Hebrew Congregations, 1975.

Polish, David, editor. *Rabbis Manual.* New York: Central Conference of American Rabbis, 1988.

Roth, Cecil, editor. *Encyclopaedia Judaica.* Seventeen volumes. Jerusalem: Keter, 1972.

Siegel, Seymour, editor. *Conservative Judaism and the Law.* New York: Rabbinical Assembly, 1977.

Trachtenberg, Joshua. *Jewish Magic and Superstition.* New York: Behrman House, 1939.

Trepp, Leo. *The Complete Book of Jewish Observance.* New York: Summit Books, 1980.

Walter, Jacob, editor. *American Reform Responsa.* New York: Central Conference of American Rabbis, 1983.

Weiss-Rosmarin, Trude. *Judaism and Christianity: The Differences.* New York: Jonathan David Publishers, 1965.

Index

About the Author

ALFRED J. KOLATCH, a graduate of the Teacher's Institute of Yeshiva University and its College of Liberal Arts, was ordained by the Jewish Theological Seminary of America, which subsequently awarded him the Doctor of Divinity Degree, *honoris causa*. From 1941 to 1948 he served as rabbi of congregations in Columbia, South Carolina, and Kew Gardens, New York, and as chaplain in the United States Army. In 1948 he founded Jonathan David Publishers, of which he has since been president and editor-in-chief.

Rabbi Kolatch has authored numerous books, the most popular of which are *Great Jewish Quotations, This Is the Torah*, and the best-selling *Jewish Book of Why* and its sequel, *The Second Jewish Book of Why*. Several of the author's works deal with nomenclature, about which he is an acknowledged authority. *The New Name Dictionary* and *The Complete Dictionary of English and Hebrew First Names* are his most recent books on the subject. Other books by the author include *The Jewish Heritage Quiz Book, The Jewish Mourner's Book of Why, Who's Who in the Talmud, The Family Seder, The Jewish Child's First Book of Why, A Child's First Book of Jewish Holidays, Classic Bible Stories for Jewish Children*, and *Let's Celebrate Our Jewish Holidays!*

In addition to his scholarly work, Rabbi Kolatch is interested in the work of the military chaplaincy and has served as president of the Association of Jewish Chaplains of the Armed Forces and as vice-president of the interdenominational Military Chaplains Association of the United States.